How to Be Involved in Program Evaluation

What Every Administrator Needs to Know

Keith McNeil
Isadore Newman
Jim Steinhauser

D1226170

ScarecrowEducation
Lanham, Maryland • Toronto • Oxford
2005

Published in the United States of America
by ScarecrowEducation
An imprint of The Rowman & Littlefield Publishing Group, Inc.
4501 Forbes Boulevard, Suite 200, Lanham, Maryland 20706
www.scarecroweducation.com

PO Box 317
Oxford
OX2 9RU, UK

British Library Cataloguing in Publication Information Available

Library of Congress Cataloging-in-Publication Data

McNeil, Keith A.
 How to be involved in program evaluation : what every administrator needs
to know / Keith McNeil, Isadore Newman, Jim Steinhauser.
  p. cm.
 Includes bibliographical references and index.
 ISBN 1-57886-251-5 (pbk. : alk. paper)
 1. Educational evaluation. 2. School management and organization. I.
Newman, Isadore. II. Steinhauser, Jim, 1960– III. Title.

LB2822.75.M396 2005
379.1'58—dc22

                                                    2004030970

Contents

Preface

In order to understand the purpose, implementation procedures, and interpretation of evaluation, it is crucial to view evaluation from two vantage points. One vantage point is obviously that of the evaluator—the primary person who plans the evaluation, implements the evaluation, and writes the evaluation report.

Evaluations are undertaken at the request of one of many stakeholders. The stakeholder may be the funding agency (federal, state, or local), the local administrator in charge of the program, parents of students who are receiving services, or an advisory board that is responsible for guiding the program. There are often many other stakeholders, and these will be described in chapter 3.

In this text, we will refer to the person in charge of the program as the program director. The program director has a different vantage point on the evaluation. The program director has a reason for conducting the evaluation and must therefore understand the entire evaluation process. The program director will eventually make one or more decisions because of the evaluation (even not changing the program is a decision).

This text will discuss various steps in evaluation from the vantage points of the evaluator and program director. Hence, the text will be of value to the aspiring evaluator as well as to the administrator who may be contemplating conducting an evaluation. Those evaluators and administrators who have previously been involved with an evaluation will find the structure provided by the General Evaluation Model (GEM) to be of benefit. All acronyms are identified in appendix A. The model is useful for individual teachers in reflecting on their performance or for the evaluation of a unit that is responsible for several programs. GEM can also be used to evaluate larger units, such as departments or the entire institution. The application in this text will focus on evaluating a single program. The combined 65 years of evaluation experience of the three authors (detailed in appendix B) has yielded valuable tips for (1) avoiding pitfalls, (2) making midcourse corrections, and (3) increasing the reporting options and hence utility.

The goal of this text is to improve the direction and utility of the evaluation by the program director and the implementation of the evaluation by the evaluator. It is our contention that both of these goals can best be met by the program director understanding the evaluator's role and vice versa.

Chapter 1 provides a framework for understanding evaluation. Various definitions are provided, along with the historical context. The argument is made for the value of working within an evaluation model. After discussing several definitions of evaluation, we present the one that we use. Chapter 1 ends with the discussion of why it is important for the program director to understand the evaluation process.

Chapter 2 provides an overview of the General Evaluation Model (GEM). GEM was originally developed by Newman, Vukovich, and Newman (1978) and revised by Newman and Newman (1993) and has been implemented in various evaluations.

Each of the GEM components is discussed in detail in chapters 3 through 7. Numerous examples are provided from the many evaluations that we have conducted. We include the good examples for the reader to implement, while the bad examples are also included so that the reader will not make the same mistakes that we have made. When we first started conducting evaluations in the late 1960s, there were few guidelines, no evaluation texts, and no university courses.

Chapter 8 reviews the components of GEM from the viewpoint of the evaluator and the program director. These vantage points are included to emphasize the joint effort of the two persons.

Chapter 9 presents aspects of evaluation as a profession, including standards developed by professional organizations, desired traits of the evaluator, and advantages and disadvantages of the evaluator coming from outside the organization as compared to inside the organization.

Chapter 10 discusses the need for data collection instruments and presents various examples, along with the advantages and disadvantages of the assortment of evaluation instruments.

Chapter 11 discusses the crucial role of reporting evaluation results and contains a range of examples of both traditional and nontraditional reports that we have used.

The final chapter, chapter 12, discusses how the General Evaluation Model can be used to evaluate an entire school.

CHAPTER 1

What Is Evaluation?

This chapter begins with a discussion of the various reasons program directors conduct evaluations. Various definitions of evaluation are then given, as well as an overview of the history of evaluation in the educational world. The value of working within the framework of a model is then discussed, as well as the value of a program director and an evaluator working together on an evaluation. The chapter concludes by discussing the difference between program directors and evaluators, as well as the difference between research and evaluation. The chapter should impress upon the reader (a) what evaluation is, (b) the value of evaluation, and (c) the value of a program director and an evaluator working together to conduct an evaluation.

PURPOSE OF EVALUATION

The purpose of the evaluation should be identified before the program starts. Such an early identification facilitates planning for the collection of baseline information. Often the evaluator can assist in clarifying the needs assessment and the objectives designed to meet those needs. Such planning can allow evaluators to avoid collecting the wrong information and thus conserve the program budget. The various purposes for conducting an evaluation are presented in the next sections.

Funding Agency Requires the Evaluation

Often the initial purpose for conducting the evaluation is that the funding agency requires it. A good evaluator tries to get the program director to see the value in the evaluation effort and turn the attitude around to the notion that the program needs to be evaluated so that together they can find out both what is working and what needs to be improved. The attitude should be "we want to find out how well we are doing," rather than "we have to evaluate." The evaluations of most federally funded programs, such as Title 1 or Head Start, appear to be forced rather than elective.

Selected Stakeholders Demand the Evaluation

At times, selected stakeholders have demanded that an evaluation be conducted. Whenever this is the case, there is an agenda, and the agenda is usually to eliminate or modify (a) a component of the program, (b) a particular staff member, or (c) the entire program. The most frequent instance is when an entire group of stakeholders (such as an advisory board, not just one individual) desires to know more about the program.

Cover the Actions of the Program Director

The wise administrator obtains information to document that the program is performing as specified in the contract. The wise administrator also obtains information to document that the program is performing as it really is and act to correct if the program is not performing as specified in the contract. A program director may want to make a major change in the program or staffing. Evaluation can be used as documentation for such changes. The evaluation should be fair, in that the results are not determined at the outset or that the data is not unethically manipulated to make certain aspects of the program or certain staff look bad. Specifically, the outcome of the evaluation should not be determined at the onset.

Others Are Doing It So I Should Do It As Well

Just because others like you are conducting evaluations is no reason to do the evaluation. Nor is the fact that you conducted an evaluation for the last 3 years sufficient reason to evaluate again this year. When

Joe Hansen was the evaluator for the Portland Public Schools, he told us that his district had a policy that a program would not be evaluated until the program was considered mature—until it had been in operation for several years. Then it would be evaluated until the results indicated that a plateau had been reached and that no new results were being found. When a stable program and program evaluation had been obtained, there was no more need for an evaluation of that program.

Need to Compare Two or More Programs

Evaluations are uninformative when there is no baseline for comparison. Indeed, a completely new program or a program implemented in a new location deserves to be evaluated. Some credence can be placed on the existing evaluations of that program in other locations, but the real test of the value of a program in a location is the implementation and evaluation of the program in that location.

Assess New Components of an Existing Program

Just because a program has been found to be of value does not mean that all additions to the program will also be of value. Any slight modification in a program may change the effectiveness of the program, and hence the new program (with the slight change) should be evaluated. The notion of "value-added" fits in here. Each component of the program should be a necessary component in that it adds to the value of the program. If a component cannot be demonstrated to have "value added," then that component should be dropped.

One example of a concerted effort to assess new components was the evaluation of the A Priori program. The A Priori program in the Dallas Public Schools was very successful; indeed, it obtained the status of an exemplary program by going through the Joint Dissemination and Review Panel process. However, the developers added new components almost every year and were interested in whether the new components were, in fact, effective. Annually, the developers identified the new components, and they requested that those new components be evaluated. This was an unusual example of program directors wanting to know evaluation information and guiding the evaluators in a specific direction.

Total Assessment of a New Program

Seldom is an evaluator given the total reins of evaluating a program. Usually the program has been funded with specific objectives and a limited evaluation budget. You get what you pay for in evaluation as elsewhere. Given a complex program, many components could be evaluated. Time and finances usually dictate that fewer than all of the components be evaluated, or at least evaluated thoroughly. The stakeholders must hope that the choices are wisely made regarding the components that are evaluated and the extent to which each component is evaluated. One of the few opportunities one of us has had to conduct an encompassing evaluation was the evaluation of the Dallas Learning Centers. These schools were totally refurbished with new libraries, computer rooms, and bonuses to teachers who volunteered to move to these inner city schools that previously students had been bused from under the Dallas Independent School District (DISD) desegregation order. New programs were instituted, and comprehensive staff development was provided for teachers and staff. The evaluation team of four evaluators was given free rein as to the scope and sequence of the evaluation. Certain information had to be collected and analyzed, but it was realized that there were so many new components, and sufficient evaluation funds, that many components might be of interest (to the program director and other stakeholders). The charge was to conduct a thorough evaluation of the Dallas Learning Centers. When staff of one of the components found out that their component was being evaluated, they became resistive. However, the evaluators held to their position that the component was just as important as any other component, and therefore it was evaluated.

Small Evaluation on a Periodic Basis

Some evaluations are conducted on a periodic basis, such as end-of-year teaching evaluations in most university settings. These evaluation activities evaluate such a small and usually insignificant aspect of the total program that they are often forgotten as evaluation activities. Indeed, the activity becomes so usual that the information is often gathered more for the sake of gathering information than for any decision-making value that might emanate from the data.

Obtain Resources for the Program

Sometimes evaluations are conducted at the request of the program director to identify weaknesses in staffing, materials, or training. Decision makers may not be aware of the magnitude of these weaknesses. Evaluators eventually write reports, and the written report often carries a lot of weight. Numbers on a written report carry even more weight (sometimes too much, we would argue).

DEFINITION OF EVALUATION

Numerous definitions of evaluation exist. All definitions seem to include two aspects. The first aspect is that the evaluation process is systematic—it is planned and executed in accord with that plan. The second aspect is that there is a determination of worth of that which is evaluated. Several definitions should make the point. "Evaluation uses inquiry and judgment methods including (a) determining standards for judging quality and deciding whether those standards should be relative or absolute, (b) collecting relevant information, and (c) applying the standards to determine quality" (Worthen & Sanders, 1987, p. 22). Popham (1975, p. 7) states that "systematic . . . evaluation consists of a formal appraisal of the quality of . . . phenomenon." Gredler (1996, p. 15) defines program evaluation as a "systematic inquiry designed to provide information to decision-makers and/or groups interested in a particular program, policy, or other intervention."

HISTORY OF EVALUATION

Evaluation in the social sciences has been guided by evaluation in educational settings. Initially evaluation focused on individual students and later considered the curriculum provided to them. The initial focus on outcome measures has given way to considering the processes used to get there, as well as the context of the program and the amount of money and effort expended on the processes.

Student Evaluation

The emergence of large public schools in the United States in the 1920s generated the need to keep track of the performance of individual students. Such student-level evaluation allowed educational administrators to keep track of the performance of these students, who otherwise would have been just numbers in the vast sea of children. In the 1930s new curricula and associated innovations appeared. New evaluation approaches and new instruments were devised to assess the effects of those innovations.

Program Evaluation

The 8-Year Study, initiated in 1932, marked the beginning of program evaluation in education. New programs were developed to assist teenagers who remained in school because they could not find work. The 30 schools in the study were allowed to deviate from state rules and regulations. In return, the schools had to determine the effectiveness of the revised curricula by reporting on student learning and follow-up after graduation. Teachers were involved and were challenged to go beyond what was measured by existing tests. Teachers identified important abilities, thinking strategies, and attitudes and interests that they thought were important outcomes for students. The study pursued the students wherever they went after high school, and even evaluated extracurricular activities.

Ralph Tyler was the one individual who was credited with the change in emphasis from individual evaluation to program evaluation. In making that change, he established three broad principles. First, he separated the activity of evaluation from measurement. Second, he championed the notion that since human behavior is complex, multiple measures of outcome would be necessary. Third, he was also able to identify those aspects of the curriculum that were effective and those that were not. Such differentiation facilitated the intertwining of curriculum and evaluation. Evaluation could become a feedback loop for the curriculum developer.

The Sputnik launching in 1957 resulted in massive new investments in U.S. education. Curriculum revisions were made in most areas, particularly math and science. Curriculum focused more on student inquiry and discovery, resulting in the need for new testing devices. Though there was much focus on these developments, and many professionals were involved, the resulting evaluations did not indicate that there was much improvement over what existed previously. Thus, public education was again criticized, and the U.S. Congress responded by passing the massive Elementary and Secondary Education Act (ESEA) in 1965. This was at the time of major civil rights efforts, and so the resulting legislation focused on assisting disadvantaged children. Since tax dollars were being funneled into special programs in the ESEA legislation, the Congress wanted evidence that the money was being used appropriately and effectively.

Those who demanded more evaluation in education wanted to know whether the new programs were (a) focusing compensatory education on those students who had previously been neglected, (b) bringing about achievement gains in students being served, (c) responding to valid needs of students in both achievement and nonachievement areas, (d) being designed with consideration of sound theoretical and practical principles, (e) being operated competently and efficiently, and (f) producing new and better ways of educating students.

The ESEA was the first major piece of social legislation that mandated evaluation and program reporting. Federal funding of education continues to include an extensive evaluation requirement. Often the requirement specifies (a) what information is to be reported, (b) how the information is to be reported, and (c) how much of the budget should be allocated to the evaluation.

Input/Output Model

The dominant evaluation model in the mid-1960s was the input/output model. The inputs were focused on the money that was available to solve the problem, and the output was the solved problem. The plan was that the most successful programs would be identified and then implemented across the country. The most successful would be those that could maximize the outputs for given levels of input. The outputs considered were test scores, and other possible outcomes were ignored. The model was cloned after the production model in manufacturing, after having been implemented with varying levels of success in the military. The model is based on four rather questionable assumptions:

- Assumption 1. Individuals and organizations act to maximize some identifiable outcome.
- Assumption 2. Consensus can be obtained about the attainable outputs.
- Assumption 3. Human service programs can be described in terms of resources (monetary input).
- Assumption 4. Human services programs are similar to economic decisions in that a stable and quantifiable production function exists between inputs and outputs (House, 1980).

Assumption 1 was questionable because many in the educational arena felt that there were additional outcomes that were of importance, such as absenteeism, dropout rate, and getting a meaningful job—not just the outcome of test scores.

Assumption 2 was questioned because not all participants agreed upon the desired outcome. Some just wanted minimal training to obtain a job. Others wanted the requisite training to enter college. Others just wanted a hot meal or medical attention. Others felt that existing tests were biased against the disadvantaged.

Assumption 3 was questioned because it was clear to all involved that human service programs are more than the money used to buy staff and materials. Human service programs are also a function of the administrators and the staff that implement the program. Often an important person may be the custodian or the parent volunteer who is not even being paid. Timely hiring of staff and the training the staff received were often found to be as important or even more important than the amount of money used to pay salaries or fund training.

Assumption 4 was questioned from five directions. First, those who were in the trenches realized that the production function was a poor fit with social reality. Second, the input/output model assumed that the foundation for all of the programs across the country was based on the same set of local conditions, which was not the case. Some programs assumed that there was a deficit in the environment, while others assumed that the deficit was in the training of the teachers and their teaching strategies. Third, major stakeholders implemented the programs for different reasons. Congress wanted to equalize funding for the disadvantaged. The federal agencies that implemented the funding often had as their primary goal the enhancement of achievement. Individual sites often had somewhat different reasons for implementing the programs, such as providing higher paying jobs to those in the community. Fourth, the sole reliance on test scores ignored the other potential benefits of the input. Fifth, the input/output model was designed to provide information to decision makers at the federal level but not at the local level. Thus, there was little commitment to sound evaluation practices at the local level, resulting in at least one state sending in their report to the federal officials stating only, "We done good."

The Development of Standards for Educational Evaluation

It was becoming clear that educational evaluations were not always being conducted accurately and that evaluations were not always assisting programs in becoming better. Congress was becoming impatient with evaluators' apparent inability to determine whether multimillion-dollar programs were helping to cure educational and other social ills. Individuals producing evaluation reports, as well as those using such reports, needed a comprehensive, carefully developed, objective, and useful way of judging evaluation plans, processes, and results. A number of professional organizations agreed to the development of standards, and as a result, the Joint Committee on Standards for Educational Evaluation was formed in the fall of 1975. Members were appointed from organizations such as (a) the American Educational Research Association, (b) the American Psychological Association, and (c) the National Council for Measurement in Education. In 1980, they issued the standards for evaluation. The standards appear in appendix C, with a brief description of each. The standards are grouped according to four attributes of an evaluation. They are discussed in detail in chapter 9.

Comprehensive Evaluation Approaches

In the 1970s, two general approaches evolved from the concerns of the previous decade. First, four models were developed that all focused on the management orientation. These models all expanded the rational process of decision making to include program definition, comparisons between intents and observations, available institutional resources for implementation, and the process of schooling.

The other approaches, referred to as intuitionist/pluralist (House, 1980) viewed the primary role of evaluation as that of enlightening individuals associated with a program and others about the complex dynamics and events that compose the program. Therefore, these approaches devoted the maximum evaluation resources to obtaining information about the various interactions stimulated by a program. The purpose of such an effort is to understand a program as those affected by it do.

The 1990s

Two outgrowths of the above approaches went in very different directions. The first outgrowth was that there were many researchers arguing for the inclusion of qualitative procedures—obtaining understanding from the point of view of all of the various participants in the program. The second outgrowth was that of high-stakes tests—tests that must be passed before the student can go on to a higher level or even graduate. A high-stakes test is usually designed for a particular state. The call for more authentic tests has led to the development of two forms of so-called alternative assessments: performance tests and portfolios. A performance test requires examinees to demonstrate their capabilities by creating some product or engage in some activity. A portfolio, in contrast, is a collection of samples of student work over time.

VALUE OF WORKING FROM A MODEL

Most disciplines have one or more models that guide the conduct of that discipline. The reasons for such models are numerous.

A model can provide structure to the activity. When considering an evaluation, the model can guide the planning of the evaluation. The model can provide guidance for the sequencing of activities as well as identifying the boundaries of those activities.

A model often identifies the orientation of the practitioners to the tasks. Will the practitioner take a hands-on approach or a hands-off approach? Will the practitioner focus only on outputs, or will inputs be considered as well? Will the various stakeholders be involved, or will only selected stakeholders be involved?

A model identifies the boundaries of the task. That is, will test scores be the sole source of information, or will qualitative information be collected as well? Will the focus of the evaluation plan stay the same every year or change from one year to the next?

A model determines who will be in charge of which tasks. Some models rely solely on the technical expertise of an evaluation-trained person—the evaluator—while others try to involve the various stakeholders. Whether the evaluation is conducted in-house or is contracted out may be partially determined by the model.

Most importantly, a model provides a way of conceptualizing the task. This view may minimally include some components, exclude other components, or make other components optional. Of importance is that the various components are usually identified, and thus the evaluator is unlikely to ignore considering those components.

Finally, reliance on a model that has been tested by other professionals reduces the likelihood that mistakes or omissions will be made. The model should require the necessary components in the requisite sequence. The model does much of the planning for the evaluator. When surprises occur, the model can, and should, be consulted to see if the model provides any guidance. It can act as a support, either providing direct advice or hinting at the right answer. In summary, the advantages of relying on a model are that it

- Provides structure to the entire task
- Identifies who will be involved
- Identifies boundaries
- Identifies who is in charge of which tasks

- Provides a way of conceptualizing
- Reduces likelihood that mistakes or omissions will be made

Given all of the above positives for relying on a model, are there any negatives? The primary negative is that of blindly adhering to a model when the model may be outdated or inappropriate to the task. Too many evaluators blind themselves by always relying on one model, although another model may be better for the current evaluation. Stakeholders' needs may well dictate the model chosen. Alternatively, the number of resources available to the evaluator may dictate the evaluation model. For example, there is nothing to be gained from implementing the most expensive model for the collection of pretest information and then finding out that there are not enough funds remaining to obtain posttest information.

It seems ethical to rely on a given model and only that model for any one evaluation. Why would your thoughts or best guesses be any better than a well-thought-out model—one developed, implemented, and modified over numerous uses by numerous professionals? When the client contracts for an evaluation that is based on a model, the client receives not only the evaluator, but also the utility of the model as well. Thus, it is to the client's benefit, as well as to the evaluator's benefit, to rely on a model.

Numerous evaluation models have been developed. Each has several aspects that are unique to that model. Most evaluation activities are similar in the various models. The primary difference between models at this point in model development is the attention paid to specified objectives as contrasted to being open to all events and information obtained during the span of time the evaluation is being conducted. The GEM approach borrows from both extremes. GEM relies on the objectives being identified at the beginning of the cycle but attends to necessary program changes throughout the cycle. An end-of-cycle report identifies the progress of the completed cycle and provides suggestions for change for the subsequent cycle.

There are several good resources for reviewing other evaluation models (Madaus, Scriven, & Stufflebeam, 1983; Smith & Glass, 1987). Stufflebeam (2001) assessed 22 evaluation approaches on specific aspects of (a) advance organizers, (b) evaluation purposes, (c) evaluation questions, (d) evaluation methods, (e) strengths, and (f) weaknesses or limitations.

WORKING DEFINITION OF EVALUATION FOR THIS TEXT

The definition of program evaluation to be used in this text is:

> Program evaluation is the determination of the objectives of the program in measurable ways and then the assessment of whether the objectives were reached.

WHY A PROGRAM DIRECTOR SHOULD KNOW THE COMPONENTS OF EVALUATION

The program director should want to be informed by the evaluation as to what seems to be going right and what could be improved. Usually the decisions related to the conduct of the evaluation (at least the major decisions) are identified by the program director. Most program directors view their program as their responsibility, and they are concerned about making the program as successful as possible. A good program director does not view evaluation as unavoidable, but as another valuable administrative tool that can be used to increase the likelihood of a successful program. The program director, though, must realize that others involved with the program must become active stakeholders in the evaluation process. Unfortunately, most program directors view evaluation as an activity that will likely find fault with the program—and therefore view evaluation as an undesirable activity. Only a small percentage of the program directors in the past have taken an active role in the evaluation. It is the position of this text that exposing the program director to all the stages of the evaluation will lead the program director to assume some responsibility for many of the tasks.

The evaluator provides, as much as possible, an unbiased assessment of the program. Has the program met its goals, and if not, what are some mid-course corrections or end-of-year corrections? The evaluator brings certain traits (such as keen observation, a sense of wonderment, detective-like sleuthing, an open mind, healthy skepticism of what people say, and absolute trust in data) and knowledge of the technical aspects of evaluation (such as measurement issues, how to get baseline assessment, what measures are available, information analysis techniques, and information reporting options). The evaluator is not against the program but is on the side of objectivity. The evaluator should not have any entering bias. Given a good plan for collecting information, what does the information say about the effectiveness of the program?

Shared Responsibilities in Program Evaluation

In order to understand the purpose, implementation, and interpretation of evaluation, it is crucial to view evaluation from two perspectives. One perspective is obviously that of the evaluator—the primary person who plans the evaluation, implements the evaluation, and writes the evaluation report. However, the evaluation is not conducted for the sole purpose of keeping evaluators off the unemployment line.

Evaluations are undertaken at the request of one or more of many stakeholders. The requesting stakeholder is usually the funding agency (federal, state, or local), but the requesting stakeholder may be the local administrator—program director—in charge of the program, parents of students who are receiving services, or an advisory board that is responsible for guiding the program. The program director has a different perspective on the evaluation. The program director has an intense interest in the results of the evaluation and must therefore understand the entire evaluation process. The program director eventually will make one or more decisions based on the evaluation (even keeping the program as it exists is a decision).

The goals of this text are, first, to improve the planning and utility of the evaluation by the program director in charge and, second, to improve the implementation of the evaluation by the program director and the evaluator. It is our contention that both of these goals can best be met by the program director understanding the evaluator's role and the evaluator understanding the program director's role.

Table 1.1. Aspects of Program Evaluation by Whether the Program Director Is Forced, Willing, or Committed to the Evaluation

Aspect of Evaluation	Forced	Willing	Committed
Usual time evaluation is conducted	End of program	During program and at end	Before, during, and after program
Cost	$$$$	$$	$
Involvement of staff	Little	Some	Much
Involvement of program director	Little	Some	Much
Who conducts the evaluation	Evaluator	Primarily evaluator	Joint effort between program director and evaluator
Use of evaluation for improvement	Little	Some	Lots

Outcomes When Program Director and Evaluator Share Evaluation Roles

Table 1.1 depicts several aspects of program evaluation and the results depending on the orientation of the program director to the evaluation. With respect to when the evaluation is initiated, it is our experience that when the program director takes an active role in the evaluation, the evaluation begins well before the program starts. One of the major nightmares for an evaluator is being asked to conduct an evaluation after the program has started or after it has finished.

When the program director is highly involved in the evaluation, the cost of the evaluation can be reduced. That is because program staff can perform some of the evaluation activities, and the program director knows when and how to restrain escalating costs. Evaluation decisions can be made more frugally when the program director is informed.

Of highest importance in Table 1.1 is the last row—use of evaluation for program improvement. The reason for conducting an evaluation is to improve the program and thereby improve the effects of the program. When the program director is committed to the evaluation and shares roles and responsibilities in the evaluation, there is a higher probability of the evaluation being useful for such program improvement. The program director knows why information was collected, the constraints of the information collection process, and the meaning of the information. When the program director takes an active role in the evaluation, the program director focuses more on evaluation information than on anecdotal information.

POTENTIAL DIFFERENCES BETWEEN
PROGRAM DIRECTOR AND EVALUATOR

When the program director and the evaluator work together on evaluation, they should be aware of their different backgrounds and responsibilities. We first present four general differences between the two roles, and then specific differences.

Nielsen (1975) found four major differences between the program director and the evaluator that usually need to be ironed out. First, program directors are much more concerned with monitoring specific program elements than are the evaluators, who tend to focus on the entire program. Second, program directors are most concerned with evaluating those program components over which they can exercise some control, while evaluators focus additionally on components not under the control of the program director. Third, program directors want to evaluate only those outcomes that can be directly attributed to components of the program, whereas evaluators are interested in participant outcomes that may be a function of the program plus how the program meshes with the "regular program." Fourth, program directors are more likely to be interested in questions requiring nonquantitative procedures, whereas evaluators are more likely to focus on questions suited to both qualitative an quantitative procedures.

Program directors and evaluators often have specific traits. When a program director and an evaluator work together on an evaluation, they need to know about these traits, in general, as well as how the other professional fits on the continuum. Some of the continua may require only an acknowledgement of where the other stands (such as politically sensitive versus not sensitive to rules and political considerations). Other continua may require a change of behavior by the evaluator (provide verbal feedback as well as written if the program director insists on that approach) or by the program director (consider changing some program components if they are found to be beyond repair). The specific trait differences between a program director and an evaluator are:

Program director	**Evaluator**
1. Program survival	1. Innovation
2. Status quo	2. Change for better
3. Defend and believe in program	3. Look at program skeptically
4. Bureaucrat	4. Scientist
5. Person of immediate action	5. Person of deliberation
6. Content with short periodic reports	6. Wants comprehensive report
7. Willing to sacrifice accuracy	7. Lives for detailed accuracy
8. Politically sensitive	8. Not sensitive to political considerations
9. Pragmatic	9. Realistic
10. Values people	10. Values ideas
11. Expedient	11. Reveres truth and knowledge
12. Concerned with current program	12. Interested in replicable results
13. Interested in viewpoints from everybody	13. Focus is on participants
14. Focus on whose jobs to retain	14. Focus on what jobs to retain
15. Prefers verbal reports	15. Prefers written reports

There is often a rift between the evaluator and the program director in that the program director often has to make a decision by 5 p.m. The evaluator, on the other hand, often would rather obtain more information before making the same decision. The real world dictates are not always in the forefront of an evaluator's mind, whereas they are in the mind and hence actions of a program director.

In general, the program director and the evaluator have two different amounts of information regarding knowledge of evaluation and knowledge of the program. The evaluator and the program director both need to know some of each kind of information. The evaluator cannot be entirely ignorant of the program, nor can the program director be entirely ignorant of evaluation concepts, procedures, and standards. The evaluator and program director should work in tandem for the ultimate benefit of those receiving services.

DIFFERENCES BETWEEN EVALUATION AND RESEARCH

Several differences between evaluation and research can be identified. First, most evaluations are of programs in the local setting, with seldom any interest in how the program would fare outside the local setting. Research, though, has a goal of developing knowledge that transcends the local setting.

Evaluations are usually focused on a relatively short time frame, seldom longer than one year. The goal of research is to find relationships that should hold over a much longer period. Evaluations focus on practical problems that must be attended to in the present, while research is often unconcerned with the immediate utility of results. Evaluators often rank options for program implementation, and these options and the ultimate choices are rooted in values of the evaluator, program director, and the other stakeholders. Researchers try to be value free.

Many of the tools used in research are also used in evaluation. Evaluation is concerned with the effectiveness of programs in the "real world," as contrasted with research often occurring in a more contrived and sterile laboratory setting. Evaluation looks at the big picture, including all aspects of the program and all results of the program. As such, evaluation considers the planning, funding, implementation, and results of the program. In addition, concerns of all stakeholders are taken into account. All outcomes are considered, both intended as well as unintended, and then a value judgment is made regarding improving the program or canceling the program.

The field of evaluation provides choices and recommendations for best practice and therefore is rooted in value statements. The field of research attempts to avoid value statements by trying to establish predicted and predictable relationships.

Both fields do use statistical analysis, and both attempt to include comparison groups. Evaluation usually has fewer statistics and less comparable comparison groups. The reliance on data is stronger in research than evaluation, where the many objectives and many stakeholders must all be factored into the decisions.

Some consider evaluation inferior to research. We would prefer to consider evaluation as applied research. We realize that evaluators use principles and tools of research, but they also go beyond those principles and tools. We admit that some evaluations are not very good—they rely on inadequate designs, and little data is collected to facilitate the decisions that are made. On the other hand, the more that data is relied upon, and the better the data, the better the evaluation, and the better the decision made from that data. Chapter 9 is devoted to evaluation as a profession and includes the traits needed by a successful evaluator. A successful researcher does not need most of those traits.

The premise of this text is that evaluators and program directors should work together on an evaluation, and that is one major difference between research and evaluation. Researchers usually work in isolation, often unconcerned with whether their research can be (easily or effectively) implemented in various settings different from their sterile settings. A good researcher, applying research skills to an evaluation, will not be a good evaluator unless the requisite skills are relied on and the interests of all stakeholders are considered. The researcher must work in conjunction with the program director before the researcher can be considered an evaluator.

CHAPTER 2

Overview of GEM

HISTORY OF GEM

As indicated in the previous chapter, the authors have had extensive experience in evaluating educational and social service programs. We have implemented various evaluation models, and through the years we have found that our evolution into the General Evaluation Model (GEM) has been of utility to us. The model is of value in various content settings, as well as for both large-scale and small-scale evaluations. GEM is applicable whether the evaluator is housed within the organization or is hired as an outside employee by the organization. GEM does require an investment of time and energy by the program staff, especially the program director.

OVERVIEW OF GEM

GEM is composed of five stages that are sequenced and form a feedback loop (see Figure 2.1). The five stages must be completed in sequence, as each stage provides information or rationale for the next. The final stage can be viewed as the product for that year, as well as input for the next cycle's program and evaluation. We prefer the latter view, as we consider evaluation to be a continuous process, not a one-time endeavor.

Stage 1: Needs Assessment

Needs assessment indicates why the program is needed. A program should not be implemented without this first stage. One task

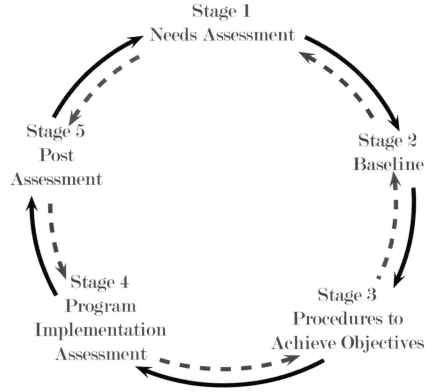

Figure 2.1. Five Stages of GEM
Note: Solid arrows indicate the primary direction of the flow of the evaluation from one stage to the next stage. Dashed arrows indicate the feedback from one stage to a previous stage—actually feedback can go to any previous stage.

is to identify stakeholders—all those who have an interest in the program.

Sometimes there are only a few stakeholders. Often there are many, some much more important than others, and some much more vocal than others. Not all of the actual stakeholders are always known before the evaluation begins, and some may appear on the scene during and after the evaluation. Examples of stakeholders are the program director, program staff, parents, community, and funding agency. Once the needs assessment has been determined and documented, it must be shared with the various stakeholders to make sure that they accept the program and the plan for the evaluation of the program.

Stage 2: Baseline

In this stage the baseline performance is determined. Program objectives are also determined and shared with the stakeholders.

Stage 3: Procedures to Achieve Objectives

Once the procedures have been developed, staff must be trained in those objectives, and some determination must be made that the training was effective.

Stage 4: Program Implementation Assessment

Program implementation assessment is the determination as to whether the procedures have been implemented as planned. Collecting information on the context of the program and the timing and amount of program funds, hiring of staff, and training of staff is crucial. How well staff was able to implement the program is another crucial aspect of an evaluation and is accomplished in this stage. Periodically informing stakeholders about the progress of the program is crucial.

Stage 5: Post Assessment

Post assessment is the evaluation activity most often solely identified with program evaluation. The post assessment, though, is only the fifth stage of GEM and is conceptualized as input for the next round of program evaluation.

SPECIAL EMPHASES OF GEM

Four special emphases in GEM are not usually found in other evaluation models. First is the importance of involving the various stakeholders. Almost every stage requires the involvement of stakeholders. Second is the cooperation of the evaluator and the program director. Most evaluation models leave most of the evaluation decisions and implementations to the evaluator. Third is the acceptance of needs. Most needs assessments are perfunctory, and the program is implemented the way it was originally thought of, irrespective of the needs assessment. Fourth is the periodic feedback of evaluation results into program planning for subsequent cycles.

Involvement of Stakeholders

Every program impacts many different stakeholders. As such, these different stakeholders should be involved in the planning of the program and in the assessment of the program's implementation. Finally, those affected by any program should be allowed to see the results of the program's objectives. We have seen too many instances of programs being developed by outside resources and then implemented by personnel who do not care to be informed by the stakeholders or who do not even know who the stakeholders are. When stakeholders are not given the opportunity to be partners in a program, they neither trust nor support that program. This may be one major reason why funding of most programs stops when outside resources are no longer available.

Most stakeholders simply want to be informed. Most do not want to run the program. Most do not take an undue amount of the evaluator's or program director's time. The more that written reports and presentations are made to large groups, the less time the program director spends with individual concerned stakeholders.

Both the program director and the evaluator should look to various stakeholders to assist them in performing various tasks. Many program and evaluation tasks can be accomplished with the assistance of stakeholders.

Sharing of Evaluation Responsibilities by the Program Director and the Evaluator

When most program directors hear the word "evaluation," they cringe and quickly think, "Do I have to do this evaluation?" When they do have to do the evaluation, they try to figure out a way to have someone else conduct the evaluation. Some evaluation models emphasize the independent functions of the program director and the evaluator. They do this under the guise of an unbiased evaluation. However, many of the evaluation tasks require little technical expertise, and the wise

Table 2.1. Management Plan for the Entire Evaluation

Task	Primary Person Responsible
Chapter 3: Needs Assessment	
1. Identify stakeholders	Program director
2. Identify program and program areas	Program staff
3. Identify sources of information	Program director
4. Develop the needs assessment instrument	Evaluator
5. Conduct the needs assessment	Evaluator
6. Write the needs assessment report	Evaluator
7. Disseminate to stakeholders	Program director
8. Make sure stakeholders buy into program	Program director
Chapter 4: Baseline	
1. Determine baseline instrument(s)	Evaluator
2. Determine baseline comparison group	Evaluator
3. Administer baseline	Evaluator
4. Analyze information	Evaluator
5. Write report	Evaluator
6. Disseminate the baseline report	Program director
7. Draft program objectives	Evaluator
8. Share program objectives with stakeholders	Program director
9. Finalize program objectives	Program director
Chapter 5: Procedures to Achieve Objectives	
1. Develop procedures	Program staff
2. Train staff	Program director
3. Determine that training was implemented well	Evaluator
Chapter 6: Program Implementation Assessment	
1. Develop program implementation assessment evaluation plan	Evaluator
2. Identify instruments	Evaluator
3. Develop instruments (if necessary)	Evaluator
4. Inform stakeholders periodically	Program director
5. Collect and analyze context information	Evaluator
6. Collect and analyze input information	Evaluator
7. Collect and analyze process information	Evaluator
8. Write reports	Evaluator
9. Relate to objectives and procedures to achieve	Program director
10. Disseminate the reports	Program director
Chapter 7: Post Assessment	
1. Develop post assessment evaluation plan	Evaluator
2. Identify instruments	Evaluator
3. Develop instruments (if necessary)	Evaluator
4. Collect post assessment information	Evaluator
5. Analyze all information	Evaluator
6. Write end-of-cycle report	Evaluator
7. Relate to objectives and procedures to achieve objectives	Program director
8. Disseminate the reports	Program director
9. Determine evaluation plan for the next cycle	Program director

program director benefits greatly from sharing many of the evaluation tasks. Table 2.1 identifies a management plan for the entire evaluation, along with the primary person responsible for each task. The tasks are discussed in detail in later chapters. The point is that the program director is involved throughout the entire program evaluation. Table 8.1 indicates that the program director is likely be involved to some extent in all but 2 of the 39 tasks discussed in this text.

Acceptance of Needs

The needs assessment stage is an important stage as it identifies the discrepancy between what should be and what currently is. The implementation of a new program, or the modification of one already in existence, should be determined from this needs assessment. Thus, it is crucial that the major stakeholders accept the findings of the needs assessment.

If the needs assessment is a perfunctory activity that has no bearing on the program, then problems will likely occur. For instance, the program may be the brainchild of the program director and hence must not be trifled with. Such was the case when a new program director began working in a particular school district. She decided to replace the existing Talented and Gifted program with one of her own design. The existing program had been well received by the parents and teachers, and the students were thriving. The only needs assessment that the new program director conducted was one of her own needs rather than those of the recipients.

When the needs assessment does indicate some crucial needs, the program should be modified to attend to those needs. That was the reason for conducting the needs assessment. However, all stakeholders should be aware of the implications of the needs assessment and agree that the proposed program modifications will attend to those needs. If stakeholders cannot see the link between the purpose of the program, the needs assessment, and the program designed to meet those needs, there will be little support by those stakeholders. They may support the program initially, but support will wane when that link is not understood.

Feedback Loop

Some evaluation models use the terms *formative* and *summative*. A formative evaluation is one conducted during the program implementation evaluation stage. Formative evaluation is referred to in the General Evaluation Model as program implementation assessment. Chapter 6 is devoted to this topic. A summative evaluation is viewed as the end-of-cycle report—the report usually written at the end of the cycle and filed away. GEM uses the information in the end-of-cycle report as information for modifying the program for the subsequent cycle. Therefore, the end-of-cycle report is summative for the cycle, but more importantly, it is considered formative for the subsequent cycle. The more important function is the feedback for the subsequent cycle. The current cycle's participants have already been served, and whatever they received cannot, at the end of the cycle, be altered. The next cycle's recipients hope that the program will be improved for their sake.

Figure 2.1 indicates, with dashed arrows, feedback from one stage to the previous stage. In this sense the evaluation model is iterative. Evaluation becomes a learning exercise. What is learned at each stage informs the previous stage so that more (or more accurate) information will be provided. What is learned at each stage also informs the next stage and improves the program being evaluated. Each arrow to the next stage is solid, implying that the information flow is ultimately in that direction.

Two feedback loops are particularly informative in the General Evaluation Model in Figure 2.1. The first particularly informative feedback loop occurs between Stages 1 and 2. The needs assessment may have been conducted on last cycle's recipients and the baseline on this current cycle. This cycle's cohort may not have the same array of needs as did the last cycle's. In this case, Stage 1 should be revisited with a modified list of needs. Even though the baseline was conducted primarily for information for Stage 3—procedures to achieve objectives—and for comparison to results at the end of the cycle—post assessment—baseline can enlighten stakeholders as to just what needs this cycle's cohort has.

The second particularly informative feedback loop occurs from Stage 4 back to Stage 3. Each program implementation assessment should be reviewed to determine if midcourse corrections are called for in the procedures to achieve objectives. Program directors who stick rigidly to their program configuration do not serve their recipients well. Program directors who change their programs flippantly or based on information from a single source that is not substantiated also do not serve their recipients well. Process information that consistently calls for program changes should be attended to and relied on to make changes in procedures to achieve objectives. Programs are not experiments. Experiments are designed in a particular way and should be faithfully implemented that way. Experiments are focused on specific outcomes, whereas evaluations are of programs that are complex and not implemented in a sterile environment. Programs can be considered "online experiments" and therefore have a responsibility to assist recipients as much as possible. Midcourse corrections in program procedures facilitate that responsibility. The hope would be that midcourse corrections would be of less magnitude each successive cycle, with corrections being almost transparent to the program recipient after about two cycles of the program.

Generality of the General Evaluation Model

The General Evaluation Model is presented in this text as a way to conceptualize and facilitate program evaluation. GEM has been used in other evaluation situations. When an individual instructor is interested in improving instruction, GEM can be quite useful because every teacher has to be an evaluator of his or her own performance. The good teacher must know where students are academically and must be able to evaluate alternative curricular programs, texts, and supporting materials. Guskey (2000), Stiggins (2001, 2002), and Block, Everson, and Guskey (1995) discuss student assessment in much the same manner as GEM.

The General Evaluation Model can also be used to evaluate entire departments or organizations. No matter what the unit of analysis, there will be objectives for that unit, various stakeholders, implementation activities that should be evaluated, and, finally, the outcomes that were identified in the initial objectives.

CHAPTER 3

Needs Assessment

After you have finished chapter 3, you will understand the six components of the needs assessment stage. You will know how to identify the various stakeholders who have an interest in the program. You will also know how to identify the aspects of the program that need to be evaluated. You will be given information on how to either identify already existing instruments or how to develop one that will better meet the current situation. Once all of these components have been considered, you will be ready to conduct the needs assessment. The various procedures and the aspects of the management plan for actually conducting the needs assessment are presented. Finally, hints for obtaining the acceptance of those needs from the various stakeholders as well as the importance of obtaining acceptance are presented.

Needs assessment is the first stage in the General Evaluation Model (GEM), as depicted in Figure 3.1. The information collected during the needs assessment drives the entire evaluation effort. Needs assessment is the process of collecting, from all stakeholders, information that indicates the nature of the program that will be implemented. The information is the discrepancy between what should be and what is. The program then is designed to eliminate the discrepancy between the two. Entire textbooks have been written on the subject of needs assessment (Altschuld & Witkin, 1999).

The discrepancy can be conceptualized as a thermometer as in Figure 3.2. Two determinations must be made on the scale. One determination is the current level (what is), and the other is the desired level (what should be). If the current level is not at the desired level, then something should be done—the program should be altered to minimize the discrepancy.

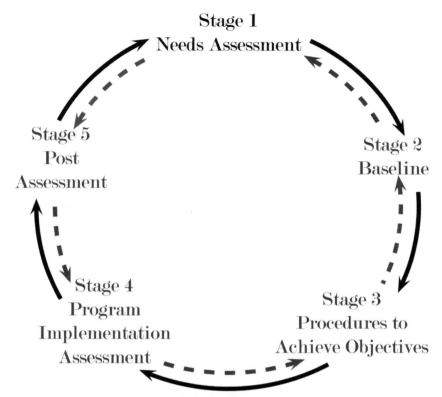

Figure 3.1.   The Needs Assessment Stage
Note: Solid arrows indicate the primary direction of the flow of the evaluation from one stage to the next stage. Dashed arrows indicate the feedback from one stage to a previous stage—actually feedback can go to any previous stage.

The values of a needs assessment are:

1. Someone (the stakeholders) must identify the current and desired levels.
2. Someone must identify specific areas of concern and focus on the desired outcomes of the contemplated program.

The problems of a needs assessment are:

1. It is not always easy for stakeholders to identify "desired" and "current" levels.

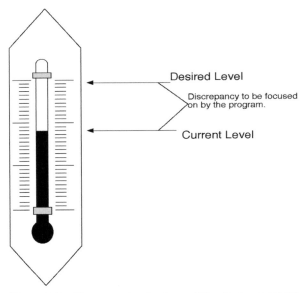

Desired Level

Discrepancy to be focused on by the program.

Current Level

Figure 3.2.   Thermometer Analogy of Needs Assessment

2. Usually many stakeholders are involved, often having different views about levels and how much discrepancy there is in any one area.
3. Usually there are many areas of concern.

The issues related to needs assessment are addressed in the remainder of this chapter by the eight tasks in the needs assessment stage:

1. Identify stakeholders
2. Identify program areas
3. Identify sources of information
4. Develop the needs assessment instrument
5. Conduct the needs assessment
6. Write the needs assessment report
7. Disseminate to stakeholders
8. Make sure stakeholders buy into the program

IDENTIFY STAKEHOLDERS

The term *stakeholder* in evaluation refers to each person or group that has an interest in the program and hence an interest in the outcome of the evaluation. Sometimes there are only a few stakeholders. Often there are many, some much more important than others, and some much more vocal than others. Though not all of the actual stakeholders are always known before the evaluation begins, and some of them may appear on the scene during and after the evaluation, categories of likely stakeholders can be identified before the program begins, including:

- Program director
- Program staff
- Advisory board
- Funding agency
- Parents
- Participants
- Influential community members
- Central office administrators
- State or local regulatory agencies

Program directors are themselves important stakeholders and are likely to consider that the program is also a major stakeholder. All of the efforts of the program director and program staff are usually geared toward providing the best possible program. Any problems identified in the evaluation should be immediately attended to. The evaluation report reinforces what the program is doing or identifies weaknesses that the program can hopefully rectify. Of course, the program cannot do anything. People fund the program, people plan the program, and people implement the program. Since people are funding, planning, and implementing, they perform these functions at various levels of proficiency. Innovative or newly implemented programs are particularly susceptible to human frailties or errors that can be identified through evaluation. The persons funding, planning, and implementing are the stakeholders that the program director is most interested in.

Program Director

The program director wants the evaluation to inform as to what seems to be going right and what could be improved. Usually the program director identifies the decisions related to the conduct of the evaluation (at least the major parameters). Most program directors view their program as their responsibility, and they are very much concerned about making the program as successful as possible. Only a small percentage of the program directors that we have worked with in the past have taken an active role in the evaluation by providing guidance and enthusiasm to the effort. A good program director does not view evaluation as unavoidable but as another valuable administrative tool that can be used to increase the likelihood of a successful program. The program director, though, must realize that others involved with the program must become active stakeholders.

Unfortunately, most program directors view evaluation as an activity that will likely find problems—and therefore an undesirable activity. From our experience, the vast majority of program directors will tolerate the evaluation or see it as unavoidable. Approximately 25% of the program directors will actively either ignore the evaluator and evaluation results or act to impede or discredit the evaluation. Our (very approximate) estimates of program directors' perceptions towards evaluation are:

- Tolerable—60%
- Ignore—20%
- See as necessary evil—10%
- Impede program activity—5%
- Provide valuable guidelines—5%

Program Staff

Process information (information obtained during the program—also called formative information) is of particular value to program staff. Once the program director makes the information available to the program staff, they can clearly identify where the problems are and attempt to remedy those problems. This is a more systematic approach to program improvement than thinking that you have a problem and then trying something else to resolve the problem, possibly not even informing all program staff. If the evaluation effort has been designed as a continuous process, process evaluation will be consistently available to the program staff. Such comprehensive and all-encompassing information will be of more value for decision makers than anecdotal information that is not substantiated by other program staff or on subsequent occasions.

Summative information (information obtained at the end of the program) is also valuable for program staff. We have found that most program staff work very hard and feel very dedicated to the program (otherwise, they would have joined the few others that have left the program). The staff deserves to know the overall impact of the program. Often they are caught up in their own roles in the program, and they lose insight of the overall impact as well as the accumulated impact over the years.

The terms *process* and *summative* are essential to the context, input, process, and product (CIPP) evaluation model (Stufflebeam, 1983, 2001), a model that is incorporated in GEM. If the product information is not used in the refinement of the program for subsequent cycles, the information is summative. GEM treats the product information as product information for the current year and process information for the next year.

Most programs are complex enough that not one outcome can be directly attributed to any one particular staff member. In other words, all outcomes are a joint effort of many individuals. Hence, the program director should not make any staffing decisions based solely on evaluation results in one area. We do recommend, though, that evaluation results be used in conjunction with all other available information to make decisions such as remedial staff development, change in assignment, or firing.

Advisory Board

The advisory board is usually composed of persons who are not program staff. Most of these persons neither know about nor care about the day-to-day specifics of the program. They may, though, have a better understanding of the history of the program—why it was implemented in the first place, and where the political support is for the continuation of the program.

Often the advisory board is composed of parents, other community members, and administrative staff from the same organization or one that is similar. These people have other responsibilities, and when they are faced with an evaluation report, they want only general information about what they consider to be the most crucial aspects of the program. They do not want detailed information, such as what happened on Day 13 in Room 131. They will not have time to digest such specific information. The advisory board will want to know (a) in general, how the program is functioning and (b) what the program director intends to do to correct any identified problems. The evaluation report crafted for the advisory board provides a framework for program improvement efforts of the program director.

The evaluator's efforts can be on the agenda of each advisory board meeting. Having the evaluator and the program director at the advisory board meetings provides the following benefits:

- Keeps the evaluator on task
- Encourages the timely completion of evaluation reports
- Keeps the advisory board focused on improving the program
- Provides one agenda item that is not the direct responsibility of the program director
- Indicates to the advisory board the commitment of the program director to evaluation
- Opens communication between the advisory board and the evaluator

Often, a separate evaluation report can be produced for the advisory board. In order for the advisory board to make informed suggestions or decisions, they need to have sufficient information. The evaluation report can provide a perspective on the program that was not previously clear.

Funding Agency

Often the initial and primary impetus for the evaluation is the requirement to evaluate what has been specified by the funding agency.

In addition, that requirement often identifies exactly what must be reported to the funding agency. The wise program director contracts with the evaluator to provide not only the required information but additional information as well. This additional information can be linked to the required data, and therefore will amplify it. Such additional expenditures can have a geometric effect on the amount of information gained. The more information that a program director has, the better the decision making. Based on our experience, it is logical to expect that the relationship between dollars and information is exponential. A few extra dollars can lead to a large amount of extra information.

The crucial aspects of reporting to the funding agency are to (a) get the information by the due date and (b) get the information in the format required by the funding agency. Most funding agencies require that an evaluation be completed for the activity to continue. Seldom, though, does a funding agency take action based solely on the evaluation report. The wise program director uses the required evaluation as one tool in program improvement.

Miscellaneous Stakeholders

Depending on the program and the setting of the program, other stakeholders may be crucial. One or more parents may be particularly influential. Perhaps an influential member of the community should be listened to or placated. Perhaps someone in the administration should be consulted. The effective program director is aware of the powerful "movers and shakers" and encourages their involvement in the needs assessment. What should not occur is obtaining the needs assessment from only one stakeholder or stakeholder group. A program usually cannot succeed when there is support from only one stakeholder. When all stakeholders have had a chance to have input, there is a greater likelihood that the program will be well designed and that it will have the support from all.

"Hard-to-Reach" Stakeholders

Many recipients of social services can be considered "hard to reach." As such, they are generally the most vulnerable and least empowered

members of society. Examples include (a) those in extreme living conditions, (b) those that have health problems, (c) those that are homeless
or move often and thus do not appear on phone lists, mailing lists, or
voting registrations, (d) those whose native language is other than the
predominant language, and (e) those that are highly skeptical of the
evaluation process in general. As a consequence, these stakeholders are
(a) difficult to recruit and retain, (b) more skeptical of the purposes of
data gathering, (c) usually more interested in protecting the confiden-
tiality of the information they provide, and (d) often unwilling to provide information. The evaluator must recognize these constraints and
concerns and respect the desires of all stakeholders.

IDENTIFY PROGRAM AREAS

The first decision in program evaluation is to decide which program or
program areas to evaluate. The choice may be arbitrary—the funding
agency may have required it, or there may be a local requirement. The
magnitude of effort is often negotiable, though federal evaluation usually runs between 5% and 7.5% of the total budget.

Even if the evaluation is funded at only 5%, there are usually enough
resources to allow those resources to be placed in certain areas. Often
the program director (sometimes in conjunction with the evaluator)
makes the decision as to which programs or program areas to evaluate.
Getting more people involved in this decision might be more productive. Involving an advisory board in this decision is one approach. Con-
vening a focus group of interested stakeholders would be another way
to get input. Perhaps requirements that are more stringent will not be
put in place until the 2nd or 3rd year of implementation. The focus of
the evaluation will likely change when the program is evaluated for 5
years.

In those instances where there is more latitude, perhaps resources
should be focused on programs that have new or questionable components. Programs that demonstrated success in previous years do not
need to be evaluated as much (or at all) as those that are new or have
equivocal results. If the program director can identify specific new
components, perhaps those should be a focus. If there is a logical chain

of events, then it would make sense to focus on each event, particularly the last in the chain.

Separate Versus Additional Areas

The first aspect to consider is whether the program is an "add-on" or is completely separate. Our experience is that most programs are "add-ons"—they operate in conjunction with the "regular program." Of course, there is a continuum of the extent to which add-on programs are conducted in conjunction with the goals and constraints of the regular program. Consider a compensatory education program that is closely linked with the regular program. Most of the curriculum would be considered the "regular" program. Only a small amount of time in a pull-out program is supported by Title I. Charter schools usually have to meet certain, but not all, requirements of the regular schools. As such, charter schools rely less on the "regular" program and provide other alternatives to children than what is typically found in an add-on Title I program. Home-based schooling allows for more latitude than the previous two cases. A home-based school curriculum may rely very little on the typical regular curriculum. That is, the child receiving home-based schooling is provided a very different curriculum than the child who is in the regular school, regular school plus Title I, or the charter school. In summary, the regular schools in some states must follow a state curriculum, at least as the curriculum relates to objectives or elements. Most compensatory education programs focus on at least a subset of those objectives. Charter schools often are allowed to deviate from some state requirements, while individuals conducting home-based schooling may not even be aware of the state curriculum.

Length of Funding

The contemplated length of funding will have an impact on the needs assessment. If the program is only going to be for 1 year, then the needs assessment will be shorter and focused on fewer areas than if the funding is for, say, 5 years. When conducting a needs assessment on a program with longer funding, there should be more effort to involve more stakeholders. A 5-year program will likely involve more dollars and become more visible than a shorter program. Finally, the longer program will more likely be incorporated into the regular funding at the end of the special funding cycle.

Single Versus Multiple Program Areas

Few programs have a single focus. Even when a program has a focus on one single area, it usually affects other areas. For example, assume that a Title I program is funded to assist low achievers with their reading. One could argue that reading is a "multiple area," but assume for now that it is a single area. On the one hand, in order to spend more time in reading, students will spend less time in other areas. On the other hand, improved reading will improve performance in many other areas. Any single area has either a direct effect or an indirect effect on many other areas. Therefore, needs assessment should consider all directly and indirectly affected areas.

Delivery of Services

One focus of the needs assessment should be on the quality of the delivery of services to recipients. One should not lose sight of the purpose of the program, but the recipients of the program should never be forgotten. If the staff is not implementing the most effective delivery strategies, then the monies spent on the project are not spent wisely.

IDENTIFY SOURCES OF INFORMATION

Once all the issues in the preceding section have been determined, the actual program or program areas that will be implemented and evaluated have been determined. The next task is to identify sources of information and determine the ones that will be tapped for this needs assessment. Some possible sources of information in an educational setting might be:

1. Testing results from:
   - Norm-referenced achievement tests
   - Criterion-referenced achievement tests

- End-of-chapter tests
- Teacher grades
2. Permanent record cards containing information such as:
   - Number of siblings
   - Home language
   - Number of parents in the home
   - Qualifying for free or reduced-price lunch
3. Attitudes or opinions on processes from:
   - Principals
   - Teachers
   - Aides
   - Students
   - Graduates
4. Direct observation of:
   - Teachers
   - Students
5. Direct observation by:
   - Teachers
   - Parents
   - Students
6. Existing records, such as:
   - Transfers
   - Attendance
   - Library usage
   - Vandalism
   - Diagnostic tests
   - Task force recommendations
   - School board minutes
   - Minutes of parent meetings

No single needs assessment would rely on all of the information in the previous list. The program director and the evaluator should consider the value of each source for the particular needs assessment under consideration. Some of the information will already be available, while other information will have to be collected. Some information will be more relevant to a particular needs assessment, while other information will be totally unrelated to that needs assessment.

Table 3.1. Planning Matrix for Sources of Information by Stakeholder for a Needs Assessment

Source of Information	Students	Parents	Teachers	Principals	Advisory Board
Tests	✓	—	—	—	—
Permanent records	—	—	✓	—	—
Attitudes	—	✓	✓	✓	—
Direct observation	—	—	✓	—	—
Existing records	—	—	—	—	✓

Every needs assessment effort must limit the amount of information obtained. Each source of information has a cost associated with it, as well as a benefit. The evaluator and the program director must decide which sources to tap and the stakeholders to involve with each source. A planning matrix to facilitate such decisions is presented in Table 3.1, which indicates that student test results will be reviewed, along with teachers' information in the students' permanent records. Attitudes of parents, teachers, and principals will be obtained, and teachers will be directly observed. Finally, the existing records of the advisory board will be reviewed. The planning matrix of some other needs assessments, even at the same educational institution, may look very different. The differences would result from the program areas under concern, availability of information, time constraints, resources available to conduct the needs assessment, and the predilections of the program director and the evaluator.

DEVELOP THE NEEDS ASSESSMENT INSTRUMENT

When it is time to develop the needs assessment instrument, several questions must be answered. First, the stakeholders who will provide the needs assessment information must be identified. Second, the person responsible for the development of the needs assessment must be identified. Third, the actual construction of the needs assessment must be accomplished. This process may lead to adoption of an existing needs assessment instrument, modification of an existing instrument, or construction of a completely new instrument. These issues are discussed in detail in the following sections.

Needs Assessment Stakeholders

The needs assessment stakeholders are representatives of identified stakeholders. Not all of the stakeholders will be involved in the needs assessment, but the needs assessment must be developed with them in mind. No stakeholder should feel left out of the needs assessment, nor should any information obtained in the needs assessment discriminate against any stakeholder. The best needs assessment occurs when all stakeholders feel that they have been given a chance to be heard.

The areas to be covered in the instrument were identified in the previous stage. All the areas should be included on the needs assessment instrument. Furthermore, these areas should be written in such a way that they are readable by stakeholders.

Who Develops the Needs Assessment?

The primary person responsible for developing the needs assessment should be the evaluator. This is because the evaluator has more experience in designing needs assessments and can identify some potential problems. The program director, though, should be an integral participant in the development. This is because the needs assessment results must be seriously considered by the program director, and the program director must then implement a program that addresses the identified needs. Finally, the program director can review the needs assessment instrument for local relevant issues and concerns.

How Should the Needs Assessment Instrument Be Developed?

The easiest way is obviously to adopt some other needs assessment instrument. The stakeholders and program areas that are of concern in one locale, though, would not necessarily be of concern in another. Therefore, a needs assessment instrument cannot always be imported into a new locale.

What often occurs is a modification of an existing needs assessment. Some items are reworded, or some program areas are added. The tendency in modifying an existing needs assessment instrument is to make very few changes. If this is the case, the needs assessment instrument may not be developed critically. The result may be a needs assessment instrument that is "almost" acceptable, but does not really do justice to the needs assessment process.

Where Do You Find Such Needs Assessment Instruments?

Program directors from nearby communities may very well have needs assessment instruments that can be readily modified. Just make sure they involve all the stakeholders that you are intending to involve.

Professionally, Division H (School Evaluation and Program Development) of the American Educational Research Association (AERA) holds an annual competition for the outstanding examples of needs assessment, evaluation plans, evaluation implementation, evaluation instruments, and evaluation reports. The finalists in each category can be contacted for examples of needs assessment instruments.

Federal and state governments contract needs assessments all the time. Various needs assessment instruments and reports can be obtained from these entities. Unfortunately, there is seldom a professional review of those instruments. In some cases, though, the needs assessment instrument was constructed by a professional working in a reputable organization, and the instrument had to undergo scrutiny from an advisory board, as well as the knowledge that the instrument would have to remain in the public domain. Furthermore, these needs assessments are usually funded at a high level, providing ample resources for a quality and thorough needs assessment. Finally, there are resources in most university libraries that provide examples of instruments that have been used.

In order to conduct a needs assessment of your program, it is best to modify the methodology of an existing instrument to respond to the constraints imposed by your stakeholders.

Suppose that you have a 5-point Likert scale that states: "The extent to which mathematics is important to high school students."

❑	❑	❑	❑	❑
Very Unimportant	Unimportant	Unsure	Important	Very Important

If you were evaluating literacy in a Head Start program, you could reword the Likert item as follows: "The extent to which literacy is important to Head Start students."

❑   ❑   ❑   ❑   ❑
Very   Very
Unimportant   Unimportant   Unsure   Important   Important

A second example is when you are evaluating an in-service program and you have available an existing instrument that had been used to evaluate an in-service program in another setting:

What need is more important for training teachers?

❑   Acquiring strategies for improving student's classroom discipline
❑   Acquiring strategies for helping students to read

The modification for the Head Start program would be:

What need is more important for training Head Start teachers?

❑   Working with parents
❑   Instilling interest in learning

Hints for Developing the Needs Assessment Instrument

If you are planning to develop your own needs assessment instrument, here are a few hints that may facilitate that development.

Try to anticipate all the relevant program areas. Otherwise, a stakeholder may feel disenfranchised or write (often nasty) comments to you that will take time to read, to respond to, and to figure out how to incorporate into the needs assessment report. "Collecting Data on Job Description, Present Functions, and Ideal Functions" in appendix D contains a needs assessment form that looked at three factors: what was supposed to be, what was, and what was the ideal.

Try to make all items as quantitative as possible. Whenever constructed responses are permitted, analysis of that information and decisions based on that analysis become more difficult. Though people often feel good that they can speak their piece, their responses are often idiosyncratic and therefore cannot be aggregated with other responses. Instead of having a voice in the needs assessment, these idiosyncratic voices are lost and hence do not contribute to the needs assessment.

Get the needs assessment finished on time. If the needs assessment is to be viewed as worthwhile, it should be well planned and implemented in a timely fashion. A hurried needs assessment gives the impression that the task is being completed perfunctorily rather than with meaning. If you want stakeholders to provide their considered opinion, you have to create the reality that you have thoroughly considered the development of the needs assessment instrument and have planned for the collection of the needs assessment information such that the information can be used in the planning of the program. Moreover, if the needs assessment is to be used in planning, it must be completed in a timely fashion.

CONDUCT THE NEEDS ASSESSMENT

Once the needs assessment instrument has been constructed, the stakeholders can complete the instrument. Four major questions need to be answered to complete the needs assessment. First, how will the information be collected? Second, from whom will the information be collected? Third, when will the information be collected? Fourth, what does the management plan look like?

How Will the Information Be Collected?

There are two major methods for collecting such information. First, the information can be collected in an interview format. Interviews can be conducted by telephone or in person. Interviews allow for clarification and probing for extension. Interviews can also identify and explain needs that were not originally considered. The two major disadvantages of interviews are the cost and the difficulty of aggregating the obtained information. See Newman and McNeil (1998) for more detail on these issues and the ones that follow.

A second and much less expensive way to collect information is with a "paper and pencil" instrument—one that is structured and can be completed with a pencil without the direct involvement of another person. Such a paper and pencil instrument can be either mailed or distributed in person to a large group. Mailing requires more time and resources and usually results in a low-percentage return. The cheapest procedure, and the one most likely to obtain information from the largest number of stakeholders, is the large-group paper and pencil procedure. Of course, it is not always possible to get all stakeholders to a large group meeting, and it is often difficult to get all the stakeholders from one group to attend any one meeting. However, if you can get some of the stakeholders to a meeting, you can usually give them all a chance to respond to the needs assessment.

Mailed Surveys

One of the most frequently used surveys is the mailed survey. It is the most widely used technique in the social sciences. Its popularity may be due to the mistaken belief that it can be easily constructed. Unfortunately, many surveys of this type have been hastily thrown together, resulting in ambiguous questions that produce negative attitudes in the respondents. These attitudes then tend to lead to (a) the responses being biased and, therefore, not representative or (b) the survey being thrown away. In either case, conclusions would be incorrect. An advantage of this type of survey is that a large sample can be reached in an economical manner.

The developer of a well-constructed mailed survey must allow for many factors. The survey should be accompanied by a brief, nontechnical cover letter clearly explaining its purpose and relevance. If this letter can be written on official stationery and signed or endorsed by a well-known figure relevant to the topic, then the return rate will be increased.

The developer of the survey should be concerned about aspects such as length, pertinence, clarity, and types of responses, since long surveys are less likely to be returned. The response time for a survey should not exceed 20 minutes. This time estimate can be adjusted depending on the audience, the purpose, and how crucial it is to obtain the results. Since the survey may give the appearance of requiring more response time than it actually takes, the survey developer may choose to include in the cover letter information concerning the expected amount of time needed to complete the survey. One way to control the length is to make sure everything asked is pertinent to the objectives underlying the study. This is a crucial aspect, as well as a difficult one.

There are two major disadvantages to using mailed surveys. The first is that the return rate is generally quite low. Heberlein and Baumgartner (1978) reported a synthesis of the literature on nonrespondents and suggested that the average return rate for the first mailing is 48%. One wonders about the validity of generalizing from this (likely biased) set of responses to the entire population. One way of improving the return rate is by sending follow-up letters, cards, and surveys. The follow-up mailing should restate the purpose of the survey in clear and nontechnical terms. It may state a reasonable deadline for the return and may again offer to share the survey findings. Floyd and Fowler (1993) reported that the first follow-up will result in 63% return rate, the second in 83% return rate, and the third in 96% return rate. One might wonder, though, if these later returns have been filled out as honestly as those that were first returned. In addition, there is increased cost with each follow-up.

The second limitation to mailed surveys is more ominous. There is generally no way for the researcher to check the accuracy of the responses. Often the responses are anonymous, and even when they are not, there is no guarantee that the responses are those of the person to whom the survey was mailed. The evaluator is totally at the mercy of the person filling out the survey.

Because of these two limitations, if it is possible, other procedures for collecting the survey information should be used. If other procedures have been ruled out, it is essential that either at least an 80% return rate is achieved or characteristics of those who have not responded are obtained. Gathering information about the people who did not respond enables the evaluator to place limitations on generalizations that will make the interpretations more accurate.

Directly Administered Surveys

It may be the case that the survey can be administered directly. An example of such a situation would be administering a survey to students in a classroom or at a meeting of the group to which the results are to be generalized.

For purposes of construction and format, the procedures for developing such surveys are identical to those suggested for mailed surveys. The major difference between the two is that poor return rate is generally not a problem with directly administered surveys. When possible and appropriate, directly administered surveys are preferred to mail surveys.

Telephone Surveys

Telephone surveys are popular because information can be obtained quickly. They are most appropriate, though, when simple and superficial information is desired, and only a few questions have to be asked.

Again, check your objectives to decide if a few simple questions are sufficient to gather the information. If these questions do not require in-depth responses, then a telephone survey may be appropriate. However, it should be recognized that people tend to be uncooperative in providing information over the telephone, and this may be a major limitation for your survey. Finally, not all phone numbers are listed, and those people who are not listed may very well have provided different answers than those whose numbers are listed.

In-Person Interviews

In-person interviews are conducted face to face, usually with one respondent at a time. Such in-person interviews require social skills and quick thinking by the interviewers. Procedures for in-person interviews can be divided into three broad categories: (a) structured, (b) partially structured, and (c) unstructured.

The structured interview is constructed using the same considerations as mailed and directly administered surveys. The structured in-person interview consists of an interviewer reading the questions and the possible answers, and then recording the answers. This type of interview is most appropriate when one is not interested in attitudes or personal feelings. The structured interview has the advantage that the interviewer can gain additional information—such as how the respondent interpreted the question and what was meant by the responses—using follow-up questions.

The partially structured interview is similar to the structured interview in that both have a core of objectives around which the questions are built. The difference is that the interviewer in the partially structured interview is interested in the reasons behind the responses and will try to explore those reasons in depth. This procedure requires extensive training to achieve a high degree of skill by the interviewer.

In the unstructured interview, there is no basic core of questions; the procedure is primarily useful when the purpose is to obtain highly personal information, such as information on sexual behavior or drug use. The effectiveness of the unstructured interview in gathering information is very dependent on the skill and training of the interviewer.

The major advantage of the in-person interview over the other survey procedures is that the interviewer can obtain insight into why the respondent answered the way he or she did. For example, suppose the following question was asked, "Do you consider present-day education important?" Ten people may have answered yes, but each may have a different reason for giving this response. The in-person interview procedure has the unique advantage of allowing the investigation of these different motives. This important additional information allows the evaluator to make valid interpretations of the data, which can yield meaningful solutions to the problem.

Some disadvantages of using in-person interviews are that they require an inordinate amount of time and expense. When using the in-person interview approach, it is crucial that the interviewer be well trained. This training is both time-consuming and expensive, but it is essential if one is to have data that are reliable and valid. To ensure reliability of the data, the researcher must train the interviewers to ask the questions in as much the same way as possible to make sure that each question is presented to the respondents with the same frame of reference. Additional expense is incurred when the researcher feels that it is necessary to check the reliability of the data. Having more than one person interview the same respondent allows the evaluator to see if the responses are consistent.

The validity of the in-person interview is generally controlled by training the interviewers to be sensitive to their own biases and by checking to make sure that the questions are not loaded with socially desirable or hidden biases. This simply means that the estimate of validity for an interview tends to be content validity, which is not the strongest type of validity estimate. It is appropriate to survey with an in-person interview when (a) one is interested in collecting data that is of a sensitive nature, (b) one is working with children, or (c) there is not a more appropriate procedure that is less expensive.

Internet Surveys

Recent technology advances have ushered in the capability of collecting survey information over the Internet. Most of the issues related to mailed surveys also relate to Internet surveys. Internet surveys, though, are likely to be completed by the person that they were sent to. When Internet surveys were first used, there was concern about anonymity, but that concern has been taken care of by the various companies that facilitate construction and collection of information on the Internet.

Some advantages of Internet surveys are that (a) the cost of follow-up mailings is low, (b) anonymity is guaranteed, (c) consent to participate is demanded by some Internet survey providers before the survey is distributed, (d) response rate can be continuously monitored, (e) there is no reliance on the U.S. Postal Service, and (f) data can easily be downloaded into a spreadsheet in the form chosen by the evaluator (Whicker, 2004).

Comparison of the Five Survey Procedures

As can be seen in Table 3.2, it is not the case that one survey method is the best in all identified considerations. The directly administered survey is the least costly (rating of 1 for inexpensive), but it requires facilities and does not allow for follow-up questions. The mailed survey eliminates biases on the part of the developer, but the validity of the responses is unknown, as there is no opportunity for follow-up questions. The telephone survey allows for such follow-up questions but results in much lower return rate—people refusing to answer over the telephone. The in-person interview requires training of the interviewers but allows

Table 3.2. Considerations in the Selection of a Survey

	Paper and Pencil		Interview	
Consideration	Mail	Direct	Telephone	In-person
Inexpensive	2	1	3	4
Facilities needed	No	Yes	No	Yes
Researchers must be trained	No	No	Yes	Yes
Long data collection time	3	1	2	4
High return rate	4	1.5	3	1.5
Group administered	No	Yes	No	Yes
Follow-up possible	No	No	Yes	Yes
Respondent bias	4	2.5	2.5	1
Researcher bias	1	2.5	2.5	4
Ease of tabulation	1.5	1.5	3	4

Note: Numbers in table indicate rank order: 1 = most positive; 4 = least positive.
Source: Adapted from Wilkinson & McNeil, 1996.

for probing when there is uncertainty in an answer or a desire to pursue a line of questions.

From Whom Will the Information Be Collected?

Needs assessment information should be collected from each of the stakeholders. Each stakeholder group will provide information on only some aspects of the program. It is important to ask for input only from those who care about the objectives and can provide input. Asking stakeholders to respond to a lengthy instrument that includes items they do not care about, or cannot possibly know about, is definitely not a good approach. Such an insensitive approach is, indeed, a bad approach.

It is often possible to cut costs by sampling from some of the stakeholder groups. It is appropriate to sample stakeholder groups that are large enough. Groups such as parents, teachers, or students often can be sampled. Sampling should be conducted under the premise of cost-effectiveness and should not be perceived as purposefully omitting some stakeholders. If such a perception cannot be easily avoided, it may be politically advisable to spend extra resources to measure all members of that stakeholder group. However, as long as the evaluator can get a representative sample, a surprisingly low number of respondents can provide an accurate indication.

One technique that can be used to obtain information is referred to as a "focus group." One or more stakeholders come together in a small group to discuss various questions posed by the leader of the focus group. This procedure includes the following advantages:

- Stakeholders learn that their concerns are shared by others.
- Some stakeholders might validate (or invalidate) concerns of other stakeholders.
- The leader can clarify questions and answers.
- Unexpected information can be obtained.

Focus groups work best when a limited number of compatible people have the opportunity to discuss their shared interests within an open and nonthreatening environment, guided by a skillful moderator who uses well-crafted questions (Morgan, 1998).

The number of instruments and the length of the instruments should also be taken into consideration. For instance, there is no need to measure 3- and 4-year-old children with four tests of achievement (McNeil & Steinhauser, 2001). There is no need to ask the same questions more than once. Concerns about reliability (accuracy of information) and validity (extent to which instruments actually measure what they purport to measure) must be parlayed against the associated costs. These cost estimates fit into the bigger picture of the relationship of evaluation to the program being evaluated.

> Evaluation research deals with people and the programs in a real-life action environment. The research is not the primary activity; the program is. When there are conflicts between requirements of research and needs of the program, priority generally goes to the program. The evaluator, whose basic function is to provide information useful to decision-makers, can hardly justify interference with optimal operation of the program, and thus may be called upon to adjust strategies (or less benevolently, compromise standards) to accord with realities of program life. (Weiss, 1972, p. 7)

Reducing costs through sampling of instruments and respondents can still provide accurate information. A plan that includes more instruments or more sources but relies on sampling of those sources may be no more costly than a plan that measures all sources on fewer instruments. The plan that uses sampling may, though, provide more information. Differences in program effectiveness indicators are a function of the instrument, the source of information, and the kind of information, but not the size of the sample. Smaller samples do not affect the value of the mean, only the confidence that the sample mean reflects the "true population" mean. These notions on sampling apply to all the information-gathering settings.

When Will the Information Be Collected?

The needs assessment information must be collected before the program is designed, because the needs assessment information should direct the design of the program. Most federal and state requests for proposals have a short time fuse. That is, there is little time between the announcement of the funding opportunity and when the proposal must be submitted. Hence, needs assessments are often done hastily or not at all. The wise program director has one or more needs assessments already completed. The proposal can then rely on this already collected information, making a stronger case for the proposal and eliminating the necessity for spending time and resources on conducting a needs assessment during the short proposal writing time.

The needs assessment should be conducted in as short a time as possible. Once one stakeholder group discovers that other stakeholders have had an opportunity to comment, they will want to provide input as well. The condensed time also communicates that the needs assessment will be used.

One overriding concern is that the stakeholders should not be inconvenienced during the collection of the information. Obtaining the information during regularly scheduled meetings is the process we would suggest. The stakeholders are attending a meeting for reasons important to them, and the (short) needs assessment is just one more item on the agenda. In general, those stakeholders who attend meetings are the most concerned and the ones who can provide the most valuable information. All attending the meeting can observe that each is getting the same opportunity to provide information. We believe that this is the least painful, most informative, and least costly way to collect needs assessment information.

What Does the Management Plan Look Like?

Developing a management plan is a crucial aspect of the needs assessment, particularly since the program director and the evaluator are going to share in the various responsibilities. The management plan in "One Possible Management Plan for a Needs Assessment" in appendix D is one that might be of value. The one person responsible for each activity should be the one who can best fulfill the activity. The program director may be the one who can best fulfill activities 1, 3, and 6. The program director, though, should be involved in all activities. Bell (1994) gives additional advice on how to manage an evaluation step by step.

WRITE THE NEEDS ASSESSMENT REPORT

The next step in this stage is to write the needs assessment report. A major requirement of the report is that the report must communicate to the various stakeholders. This can be accomplished by minimizing the technical aspects and by including an executive summary. As much of the material as possible should be presented in figures, and the report must be communicated in a timely fashion. Finally, all of the cultural, financial, legal, and educational realities should be kept in mind when writing and disseminating the report.

Report Must Communicate

No matter how technically accurate the report, if the report does not hold the attention of and communicate to the stakeholders, then the report is of no utility. In fact, if the stakeholders find the report difficult to understand, the report may be interpreted negatively. You do not want any stakeholders to think that they are having the wool pulled over their eyes. One of the major aspects of ensuring that the report communicates is to know your stakeholders. What are their interests in this program, and what are their limitations? What did they indicate as the most important needs? How can you communicate the needs assessment of the other stakeholders? Sometimes the most difficult task is to convince stakeholders of the importance of needs that other stakeholders have identified.

Minimize Technical Details

One sure way to lose your stakeholders is to use words that they are not familiar with or words that you feel they should know but do not. You are not writing this report for other evaluators but for the various stakeholders. If you also want to write a technical report, do so, but make sure that you label it as such, and do not cram it down the throats of the stakeholders who do not understand technical jargon. You should follow the publication guidelines stipulated in the APA *Publication Manual* (APA, 2001). If you feel that it is imperative that some technical matter be included in the report, tuck it away in an appendix. In that way, you can meet your own technical needs without losing the interest of your stakeholders.

Begin With Executive Summary

You need to realize that many stakeholders will not be as interested in the needs assessment as the program director and the evaluator. Some may just want to make sure that the information they provided in the needs assessment has, in fact, been attended to. Others can get the drift very quickly as to what the needs assessment has determined. Many of these potential readers can be satisfied with a brief executive summary. Such a summary should be no longer than two pages, highlighting the major findings of the needs assessment. The summary statements do not have to be supported with data in the executive summary, as that data will be included in the report or in appendixes to the report. Make sure that someone who has not been involved in the needs assessment reviews the executive summary. That will increase the likelihood that no assumptions are made and that all the crucial information is provided.

Timely Feedback

The most informative reports are those that follow closely on the heels of the data gathering. The process is fresh in the minds of the stakeholders, and there should still be interest in the findings. Timely reporting facilitates staying on the good side of the stakeholders. It also maintains momentum, especially if the needs assessment must go into a proposal. With all of this in mind, it is a good idea to have the type of analysis and tables in mind before the data is collected. For instance, will the results be primarily in tables or figures?

Try to Present as Much Information as Possible in Figures

Most stakeholders are not sophisticated consumers of data. Hence, they will appreciate seeing the results depicted as figures. The writer of a needs assessment report should take to heart the old adage that "a picture is worth a thousand words." We now present three sets of data in tables, with the same data depicted in figures. Most stakeholders would feel more enlightened with the figures. Table 3.3 illustrates how frequency data can be depicted in a table, while Figure 3.3 illustrates the same data in a stacked histogram. The stacked histogram has more than one category in each bar of the histogram, thus facilitating the understanding of the composition of the groups in each category. Table 3.4 indicates how trend data can be depicted in a table, while Figure 3.4 illustrates the same information in a line graph. The line graph has a line for each category and facilitates how that category has changed over time. Table 3.5 illustrates how a budget can be depicted in a table, while Figure 3.5 illustrates the same information in a pie chart. The pie chart facilitates understanding of the relative contribution of each part to the whole.

Table 3.3.   Number of Students Served and Waiting by Ethnicity

Ethnicity	Served	Waiting
Anglo	20	40
African American	40	80
Hispanic	40	100

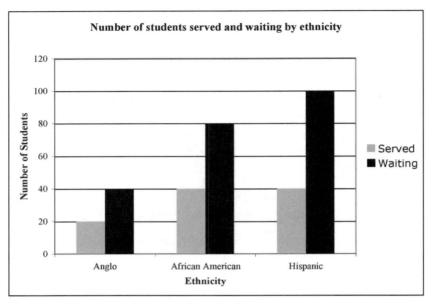

Figure 3.3.   How Frequency Data Can Be Depicted With a Stacked Histogram

Remember who your stakeholders are. This is a rehash of the first part of this section but is included here again to emphasize the point. The needs assessment report is not a report just for the program director, the evaluator, or the funding agency. It is a report that the various stakeholders must have available, be excited about reading, and be able to read. The report should be written for them, to them, and in their language. The report must reflect any constraints that any of the stakeholders might have, or any constraints surrounding the program. This is why it is particularly crucial that the program director review the needs assessment report before distribution.

Table 3.4.   Percent of Students Passing in Three Consecutive Years by Content Area

Content Area	2000	2001	2002
Nursing	80	85	90
Computer	45	55	77
English	42	45	46
Math	42	40	33

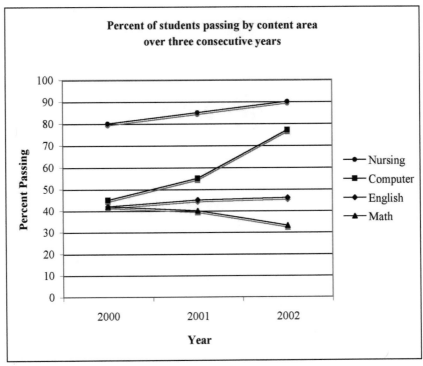

Figure 3.4.   How Trend Data Can Be Depicted With a Line Graph

DISSEMINATE TO STAKEHOLDERS

You must realize that most stakeholders are not going to go out of their way to find and read the needs assessment report. It is the responsibility of the program director to get the report in their hands and to facilitate their understanding the report. If necessary, the evaluator might have to expand on the report. Therefore, the evaluator should attend all

Table 3.5.   Sources of Program Funds

Source	Amount
Federal	$43,000
Local	$2,400
Corporate	$4,000
Student tuition	$6,500

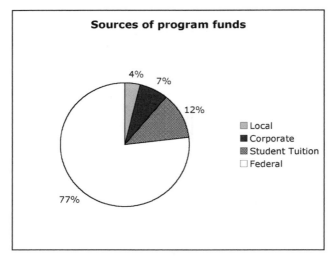

Figure 3.5.   How a Budget Can Be Depicted in a Pie Chart

of the stakeholders' meetings where the needs assessment report is presented and discussed. This provides an opportunity for each of the stakeholders to understand what is written in the report and to clarify any errors that might have been made.

MAKE SURE STAKEHOLDERS BUY INTO PROGRAM

Careful writing of the needs assessment report and efforts to assist in the understanding of that report should lead to the stakeholders' understanding the report and agreeing to its conclusions. The evaluation of any program rests on the assumption that there is a program and that all the concerned stakeholders agree to the tenets of that program. Time spent on the development, implementation, and reporting of the needs assessment contributes to each of the stakeholders agreeing to the tenets. This agreement is more crucial to the program director than the evaluator, but if there are disagreements on the tenets of the program, then there will be problems for the evaluation. What is of importance to the evaluator and the evaluation is that the stakeholders buy into the importance of the evaluation (as well as buying into the program).

Some stakeholders will be interested in knowing only the major thrust of the program, what the program is primarily going to accomplish. Other stakeholders will want to have more detailed information about the processes that will lead to accomplishing the desired outcomes. Others may be interested in details such as timelines and the specific training the staff will be receiving. It is the task of the evaluator and the program director to provide just the right amount of information to each of these stakeholder groups—and to each of the primary stakeholders within each stakeholder group. Not enough information may lead to concern about deceit, and too much may lead to boredom or the feeling that "the powers that be do not understand my concerns."

One should remember that just presenting information to a group does not guarantee that the members of that group have understood the material. Leaving a paper copy of the report is one way to encourage understanding. Another way is to ask questions of the stakeholders. Not that you will be giving a quiz, but express interest in seeing if they understand the material. Once the question is asked, you could even encourage the stakeholders to look up the answer in the report. In that way, each stakeholder in the stakeholder group will become more familiar with the organization and content of the report. You have made a good-faith effort to communicate the important points and provided them with a paper copy of the report for future reference. This also means that the program will have to go in the general direction indicated by the needs assessment. You have made the needs a matter of public record and therefore have to continue on that path—developing a program to address those needs.

Most needs assessments will identify minor changes in the planned program. In some cases program directors will try to minimize some of the identified needs that their program is not designed to meet. Our concept of needs assessment is in line with what has been called "evaluability assessment." Originally developed by Wholey and further refined by Wholey, Hatry, and Newcomer (1994), the process assesses the program to see if it has clearly defined objectives, well-defined activities or components designed to meet those objectives, and the necessary resources to meet those objectives. During the implementation stage, the process information must establish that the program has been implemented in sufficient amount and quality to bring about the change. Then the objectives must be measured in the intended way. Finally, if there is no use for the program after the evaluation cycle is over, why implement the program in the first place?

Newman, McNeil, and Frass (2004) discussed these same ideas in terms of the replicability of a program. Their argument was that if a program has a low probability of continuing, or of being implemented somewhere else, why implement the program in the first place?

CHAPTER 4

Baseline

Once the needs assessment has been conducted and communicated to all stakeholders, the current or initial status of the program and its participants must be determined. Figure 4.1 indicates the place of the baseline stage in GEM. The needs assessment has been completed and informs the baseline tasks, and the baseline tasks lead to the development of the procedures to achieve objectives. The baseline stage involves the tasks of determining instruments, identifying comparison groups, and administering the instruments. After the baseline information has been collected, that information needs to be analyzed, and the report must be disseminated to all stakeholders. Then specific objectives have to be developed and shared with all stakeholders so that the program objectives can be finalized.

DETERMINE INSTRUMENT(S)

What should be measured during the baseline stage is indicated by the needs assessment. The needs assessment identifies discrepancies between what the stakeholders want and what the current state of affairs is. The feedback sessions with the stakeholders determine those areas that will become the focus of the program. These areas will likely be fewer than those in the needs assessment. The instruments will focus on the program, program staff, and the recipients of the program.

Inclusion of widely used standardized measuring instruments is always a good idea. Although such measures often do not meet all of the specific needs of a given program, they are defensible to many stakeholders, particularly the funding stakeholders. Stakeholders feel

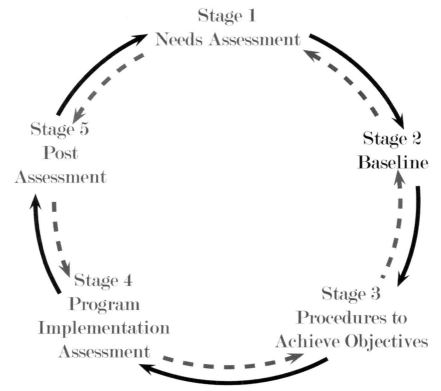

Figure 4.1.   The Baseline Stage
Note: Solid arrows indicate the primary direction of the flow of the evaluation from one stage to the next stage. Dashed arrows indicate feedback from one stage to a previous stage—actually feedback can go to any previous stage.

more comfortable with measures that have been used by others and are therefore more accepting of results from such measures. The values of standardized measures are that (a) they have had a lot of development effort put into them, (b) many practitioners and psychometricians (experts in test development) were involved in the development, (c) errors in logic and content are likely removed, (d) and the instruments are usually designed to measure the same trait over a number of years, allowing for gain to be determined.

Information to Be Collected

The constructs that will be measured in a program can be conceptualized into three areas. The first area of constructs is within-person information—those characteristics of the individual that result in individual differences. Examples are a student's motivation, a student's achievement level, and a staff member's commitment to the goals of the program. A second area of constructs is those influenced by the context surrounding the person or program. Examples are socioeconomic status (SES) and cultural upbringing. The third area of constructs is variables relevant to the task itself. One example is whether the test is multiple choice or essay. Some students prefer to take multiple-choice tests, whereas others prefer being tested with essays. Those who prefer essays probably have done better in the past on essay exams. Another example is whether the interview is done by telephone or in person. Different people agree to be interviewed in the two situations, and somewhat different results are obtained with these two methods, as discussed in chapter 3. Some components of the program can be ascertained with instruments from more than one area, whereas other areas can be ascertained with instruments from only one area. Failing to incorporate all three areas can lead to less than a full picture of the program and its effectiveness. Collecting information from many areas costs additional resources, so the cost-benefit ratio must always be kept in mind. If a large program is being evaluated, then sampling different participants for different objectives may be beneficial.

Source of Information

Another question that must be addressed is, "Who should provide the information?" The answer will be specific to each program, but it is a good idea to consider the entire spectrum of who can provide information. Several sources of information that might be of value and some examples of what they can provide are:

Recipients	Performance on standardized tests
	Attitudes
	Career choices
Staff	Attendance at in-service programs
	Attendance at special events
	Implementation of in-service topics
	Attitude about program
	Turnover rate and reasons
	Innovative implementation of program

Relatives of recipients	Attitudes of recipients
	Behavior of recipients outside of program
	Comparison of recipients to older siblings
	Perceptions of community
Community members	Attitude toward program goals
	Perceptions of success of program
	Willingness to volunteer in program
Existing records	Attendance by recipients and relatives
	Discipline referral rate
	Staff performance evaluations
	Staff turnover
	All above information in comparison locations
Unobtrusive information	Amount of litter surrounding building
	Respect for "Do not walk on grass" signs
	Appropriate noise level (low during "quite time" but high during "get noisy time")

Recipients are often the major source of information. After all, the program is designed to help them. Their baseline should be measured so that whether they have been helped can be determined. The recipients are also often the best source of information, as they can best describe their situation and how they feel.

Staff is often measured as well. Examples are how much in-service training they have received, how well they have implemented the program, and how they feel about the program. Staff is also a good source of information about the recipients, since they are in frequent contact with recipients, and staff understands the goals of the program.

Relatives of recipients are often overlooked but can be a valuable source of information, particularly if the recipients are young. In fact, some measures of preschoolers, such as the Ages and Stages Questionnaire (Bricker & Squires, 2001), rely solely on parents for the developmental achievements of their children. This category can be expanded to include friends of the recipients, such as classmates filling out a sociogram.

Community members are another potentially valuable source that is often overlooked. This group is particularly crucial if the program has enough visibility to affect how the community might vote on the next bond election. Sometimes collection of evaluation information performs a political function as well as an evaluative function.

Existing records can be a very valuable resource as little additional expenditure of time and money is usually necessary. In addition, existing records contain information that has been deemed in the past to be important—such as attendance, discipline incidents, and standardized test scores. A good evaluation plan attempts to incorporate as much existing information as possible, building upon that source, rather than reinventing the (data) wheel. Finally, relying on existing information validates the information collection scheme that has been in place.

Unobtrusive information is that which can be collected without interfering with the daily routine of whoever is providing the data. Unobtrusive information is usually not directly related to the goals of the program, but its utility can be inferred with the risks that are usually associated with such inferences. Thus, such information is called "high inference information." However, the advantage of not interfering with the daily routine makes such information appealing. Sechrest (1979) and Webb, Campbell, Schwartz, Sechrest, and Grove (1981) have written entire books on the technique. It is our contention that these kinds of measures should be used more often. We would suggest, though, that planned collection of unobtrusive information is preferred to anecdotal after-the-fact reporting of such information. One example of unobtrusive information is the amount of litter surrounding the building that houses the program. If the amount of litter is less than before the program was implemented, then one could infer that participants have a better attitude toward the program. Notice the inference that is being made and the possibility that there may be other reasons for the reduced litter.

What Information Should Be Collected From What Sources?

The answer to this question depends on the program to be evaluated. Table 4.1 provides a starting point for consideration, but the evaluator

Table 4.1.   Possible Content Areas From Sources

Source	Attitudes	Achievement	Social	Environment
Recipients	✓	✓	✓	
Staff	✓	✓	✓	✓
Relatives of recipients	✓		✓	✓
Community members	✓			✓
Existing records	✓	✓	✓	✓
Unobtrusive information	✓		✓	✓

and the program director are urged to consider all content areas and all sources. Obviously, resources are limited and thus not all sources will be used to provide information on all content areas.

Table 4.1 identifies the most likely scenario—for example, relatives of participants usually cannot provide reliable achievement measures, but they can provide information on all other content areas. Community members are capable of providing attitudinal and environmental information. Table 4.2 contains the evaluation plan that resulted from the considerations in Table 4.1 in the evaluation of the Head Start Transition Program (McNeil & Steinhauser, 1999). Students and parents were to provide information only about how the program was implemented and the outcomes of the program, while the school district (LEA) and Head Start were to provide information in all four content areas. The central Head Start office was to provide information on the setting of the program, hiring of staff and purchase of equipment and materials, and training and implementation of the program, but not any information on program outcomes. Table 4.3 illustrates the specific type of information obtained from each source.

Table 4.2.   One Evaluation Plan Regarding Sources of Information

Component	Source				
	Parent	LEA	Student	Head Start	Central
Context		✓		✓	✓
Input		✓		✓	✓
Process	✓	✓	✓	✓	✓
Product	✓	✓	✓	✓	

Table 4.3. One Example of a Plan for Obtaining Information

Component	Source				
	Parent	LEA	Student	Head Start	Central
Context		Reports		Records	Journal
Input	Surveys, attendance, interviews	Surveys, interviews		Surveys, interviews	Records, interviews, journal
Process	Surveys, attendance, interviews	Attendance, surveys, interviews	Surveys	Surveys, attendance, interviews	Journal, interviews, records
Product	Surveys	Interviews, journal	Grades, interviews	Observation, surveys	

The Kinds of Information Obtained May
Very Well Change Over Time

What is important for Year 1 of the evaluation of a 5-year program is not necessarily the same for Year 5. Therefore, the focus of the evaluation may change over time, particularly if the evaluation is designed to cover a number of years and there is a concern about the longitudinal benefits of the program after the recipients leave. What also may change are the kinds of recipients, such as their age. In a 5-year evaluation of Head Start, we had five cohorts. Cohort 1 was in their last year of Head Start when the program started in 1997–1998. In Year 5, Cohort 1 was in the 3rd grade. On the other hand, in Year 5, Cohort 5 was in their 2nd year of Head Start.

"Timeline for Evaluation Activities" in appendix E contains the 5-year plan for the Head Start Transition Program evaluation depicted in Tables 4.2 and 4.3. Notice in that appendix E there is no emphasis on achievement in Years 1 and 2. Half of the Year 1 Head Start students were still in Head Start in Year 2 of the program. It was not until Year 4 that the entire initial cohort of children had at least 2 years of public school. The program goal was to assist these children to succeed in public school on a long-term basis, not just the 1st year. Thus Year 5, the last year of the evaluation, focused almost entirely on student performance (achievement and deportment). All of the kinks of the program delivery system had been resolved in the first 2 years, and the requisite staff development had been in place for several years. Nothing new was happening in those areas. Year 5 was when the proof of the pudding was to be tested—was the Head Start program resulting in positive long-term gain?

Comparison of Information Collected
During Needs Assessment and Baseline

Since both needs assessment and baseline entail a lot of information collection, the reader may be a bit confused. Though there are many similarities in the two information collection efforts, there are substantial differences.

Obviously, the timing is different, with the needs assessment occurring before the program is planned; the needs assessment directs the development of the program. The baseline occurs as close to the beginning of the implementation as possible.

The focus of the needs assessment is on the information provided by the stakeholders. The baseline focus is on the staff and the participants. The needs assessment reports on the discrepancy between the desired goals and the existing state of affairs. The baseline reports on the state of affairs at the beginning of the program. Baseline information may be obtained from participants as well as the particular staff that will implement the program. This leads to the fourth aspect of the difference between needs assessment and baseline—the generality of the information. The needs assessment of necessity must cover the entire spectrum of possible goals. The baseline covers only the specific goals identified from the needs assessment.

The sources of information for needs assessment are usually the various stakeholders. The perceptions of stakeholders form the majority of needs assessment information. Stakeholders are relied upon because the discrepancy between what stakeholders think should be and "what is" is a perceptual issue that only the stakeholders can answer.

Involvement of stakeholders is crucial during the needs assessment but is minimized during the baseline. That is not to say that an evaluation should be immune to the effects on the stakeholders, but the program is designed primarily for the benefit of participants, not the stakeholders.

Finally, there is a big difference in the time frame of needs assessment instruments and baseline instruments. Needs assessment instruments take a snapshot of what exists at a particular time. Some of the needs may already be met, whereas the baseline time frame must consider not just the pretest but also the posttest. That is to say, instruments must be able to detect growth over a designated period, which may be a year or more. Such instruments must be readable by the respondents at their various ages, and the content must make sense to respondents of various ages, abilities, and sociocultural backgrounds. Finally, the instruments must have the capability to compare performance over time with scale scores (scores that mean the same thing over time). All of the above argues for including commercially available standardized and normed instruments as part of the baseline.

DETERMINE COMPARISON GROUP(S)

Knowing what the expected value of a program should be is a necessary component of a good evaluation. Unfortunately, often such an expected value cannot be obtained or is not obtained. This has often been the case, even in our own work. We present the most commonly used expected values, along with some rather unusual ones that can be used in the right circumstance.

Arbitrary Goal

Most of the ways to obtain an expected value are time consuming, costly, and often just not feasible. Hence, many program evaluations are based on expected values that have been arbitrarily set. Such goals are often defended because they "feel good." They make some intuitive (if not logical) sense, such as 70% mastery. Why should 70% be a feel-good value? Often such a value is widely accepted by the field and hence by the funding agency. But as everyone knows, or should know, 70% mastery on an easy test is much easier to obtain than 70% mastery on a difficult test. Clearly, 70% does not mean the same thing for these two tests.

An example of the expected gain in Title I evaluation of 3 Normal Curve Equivalents (NCEs) was an arbitrary goal that gained acceptance and obtained mythical status. Since percentiles do not constitute an interval scale, adding percentiles and obtaining a mean is not mathematically sound. An interval scale that has been developed that is similar to the percentile scale is that of Normal Curve Equivalents—NCEs. Because NCEs are an interval scale, it is appropriate to determine means, and that is why most test reporting forms contain NCEs. Why not 4 NCEs, 2 NCEs, or 3.48 NCEs? An NCE gain of 0 represents normal growth. An NCE gain of 1 or 2 sounds like not too much of a gain. An NCE gain of 3 is a little more, but in many cases it is not significantly more than a gain of 0. However, since the Title I Evaluation and Reporting System (TIERS) was designed to be implemented by the local public school evaluator, it avoided statistical analysis. Hence, a 3 NCE gain was established as a reasonable feel-good expectation that most program directors felt they could make (Tallmadge & Wood, 1976).

The arbitrary goal assumes that the program was implemented as proposed. The arbitrary goal does not take into account process information. That is, if the process information indicates the program was not implemented well, there is no guideline detailing how the arbitrary goal should be adjusted.

Comparison Group Post Assessment

If one can find a group of individuals who were in another treatment (preferably the currently accepted treatment), then they can provide at post assessment an expected value of what the program should have accomplished. Such a group is most beneficial when the treatment they received can be considered the status quo treatment. That is, the treatment they received is the accepted standard treatment. Your program is obligated to show better results than the current standard treatment.

When such a comparison group can be found, they are seldom a mirror image of the program participants. They may come from a different socioeconomic status (SES), live in another school district, or have a different level of trained professionals serving them. In addition, comparison groups are seldom funded to the same level as the treatment group and hence have little incentive to serve as guinea pigs. Furthermore, they believe that what they are currently doing is the most effective. There is little for them to gain by cooperating with the evaluation process and possibly finding out that they are wrong.

The Texas Statewide Initiative is an example of a reasonable comparison group. The Texas Educational Agency (TEA) funded programs to be implemented in selected sites within a local agency. Since there was not enough funding for the program to be implemented in all sites, comparison sites could be identified within the same agency. In the El Paso Region 19 Head Start agency, for example, comparison sites were similar in terms of region of the county, SES, training level of teachers, and percent age of Mexican-Americans.

The Comparison Group Model was identified in TIERS as Model B. Model B was seldom implemented in Title I because Title I funds went to almost all low-achieving students in low SES Schools. Since the lowest achieving students in the lowest SES schools received Title I funds, there were no students available to constitute a comparison group.

Since Title I was a compensatory, add-on program, another assumption was that the regular programs in the treatment and comparison sites were equally effective. Model B was not able to verify that assumption. Hence, that assumption remained as a competing explainer to the evaluation results.

Notice our choice of the term "comparison" when referring to non-treatment sites. You may be familiar with the term "control." We feel that seldom is there any semblance of "control" in the social sciences and that it is better to acknowledge this with the term "comparison." The design does, after all, compare the two groups—groups that received not only different treatments but were likely different in many other ways. In reporting on their evaluation of the Chicago Child-Parent Centers, Conyers, Reynolds, and Ou (2003) indicated that the comparison students indeed had many of the same preschool experiences as did the treatment children. They pointed out that the value added would likely be underestimated because of those experiences. However, that is exactly what is needed to argue for the Chicago procedure over other procedures.

Matched Groups

One way to improve on the comparison group design is to match individuals on one or more relevant characteristics. Unfortunately, there are often no good matches for many individuals. Furthermore, usually many relevant variables must be matched. When additional matching variables are considered, the number of successful matches dwindles drastically.

Baseline to Post Assessment Gain

When one has baseline and post assessment information on the same individuals, one is essentially matching each individual with herself or himself. No assumptions or approximations are necessary. Person A at baseline is an exact match for Person A at post assessment. While the matching concern is settled with this design, the assumption that the baseline status is what we would expect at post assessment time is not likely a valid assumption.

You would expect to see some growth over time, especially with young children. Thus, maturation is a competing explainer in this model. Furthermore, we do not know if the observed gain is any greater than would be obtained from other treatments. What if a less costly treatment can generate an equal gain or an even larger gain?

Previous Year's Cohort

One way to solve the above problem is to use the performance of last year's participants as the expected value of the new treatment. The performance with the old treatment was at a particular level, and the new treatment is expected to yield better results than the old treatment.

There are two major advantages of this model. The first advantage is that the expectation is based on the same kinds of participants. For instance, the SES of the baseline year's participants can be assumed to be similar to those of subsequent years. The second advantage is that if the appropriate information has already been obtained by the organization, it is available at no charge and no hassle. The main disadvantage is that often the appropriate information has not been collected in previous years, or only a small subset of the desired information has been previously obtained.

National Norms

Whenever a nationally normed test is used, the national norms become the obvious expectation. If the goal of the program were to be better than the national norms, then performance above the 50th percentile would be desired.

Two assumptions are made when using national norms. First, you are assuming that your students are like those in the norming group. Second, you are assuming that the programs that the norming group received are similar to yours (e.g., if your program is funded at $5000 per student and the norming group average funding level was $4000 per student, the norming group is not a good comparison). It is unlikely that either of these two assumptions is entirely valid. The extent to which the assumptions are not valid is difficult, if not impossible, to determine.

The performance of the program participants may already be above that of the national norm at baseline. In this case, improvement over previous performance would be a more reasonable goal. What should be the exact amount of expected improvement was discussed in the section "Arbitrary Goal."

The major advantage of the national norms model is that stakeholders recognize that a lot of effort has gone into the development of the norm-referenced test (NRT). Secondly, teachers and curriculum experts have contributed to the development, and revisions in the test are made periodically. Finally, scores are available on various subscales so that the results can lead to specific student and program refinements.

One disadvantage of the national norms model is the cost in obtaining NRT data. Costs include (a) obtaining the tests, (b) training test administrators, (c) administering the tests, (d) scoring the tests (or, more likely, paying to have them scored by the publisher), and (e) interpreting test performance for all the stakeholders.

NRTs are often criticized for being too narrow in focus and for measuring only the lower levels of student knowledge. NRTs usually use multiple-choice and single correct response format. NRTs do not measure what the student can produce but what the student can regurgitate.

The national norms model gained prominence when TIERS was implemented in Title I evaluation (Tallmadge & Wood, 1976). The national norms model was designated as Model A and was the most widely implemented model. Two reasons that Model A was implemented more often were that it (a) required less testing than the comparison group model, designated as Model B, which required testing a comparison group, and (b) required less technical knowledge than the regression discontinuity model, designated as Model C, to be discussed below. Probably the primary reason most evaluators used it was that it was very similar to what they had been using before the TIERS system was mandated. There is always a lot of comfort in continuing to do what one has been doing in the past.

State Norms

The trend in the 1980s and 1990s was to use state-level criterion-referenced tests (CRTs). These tests measure specific skills considered appropriate for the students in that state. Since all of the students (at specific grade levels) take the CRT, state-level norms can be developed.

Major decisions are often made based on state-level CRTs. Student advancement can be precluded if the student does not reach a certain level. Schools are often placed on probation or rewarded when certain levels are reached. Realtors use such information to encourage the sale of homes in high-performing areas. These major decisions have led to the term "high-stakes testing." Many educators, evaluators, and psychometricians decry the use of one test—one slice of a student's or school's performance—in making such major decisions.

Many schools spend an inordinate amount of time preparing students for these high-stakes tests (NRTs as well as CRTs). Parties are often held when schools perform well, and wakes are held when schools do not meet the expected (albeit arbitrarily imposed) level of performance.

Regression Discontinuity Model

In Model C, all students in the LEA are tested at baseline on a selection test. Those who are at or above the cutoff on the selection test receive just the regular program, while those scoring below the cutoff receive both the regular program and the compensatory program. Once all students take the posttest and the relationship between the selection test and the posttest is determined for the noncompensatory students, one can use that prediction equation for the compensatory students. This prediction indicates how the compensatory students would have scored on the posttest had they participated only in the regular program. This no-project expectation is then subtracted from the compensatory students' actual posttest scores to yield the measure of project impact.

Model C has many advantages over the other models. First, Model C reduces the amount of testing by using the selection test in the analysis. Model A requires a separate selection and pretest, as well as the posttest. Model C does not require the assumption of an average curriculum, as both groups receive the regular curriculum of the LEA. Finally, Model B requires a comparison group similar to the compensatory group of students, whereas Model C uses students in the same LEA who are different (on the selection test). In Model C, the major assumption of concern to evaluators is that the relationship between selection test and posttest is assumed to be the same in the comparison group and the compensatory group. Additional information on Model C and how to analyze the data from Model C can be found in McNeil, Newman, and Kelly (1996).

ADMINISTER BASELINE

Most information collection activities can be broken down into the following six steps:

- Reread purpose in program plan and evaluation plan
- Obtain instrument
- Arrange for testers
- Pilot instrument administration
- Plan for instrument administration
- Collect information

The evaluator and the program director should be developing a plan for the entire information collection process. They both must understand all the necessary steps required to obtain the desired information. Time and resources involved will become clearer when the entire plan is developed. Because of the sequential nature of most of the steps, the plan must be initiated in a timely fashion, or the program will be over before the baseline can be accomplished.

Reread Purpose in Program Plan and Evaluation Plan

The program plan and evaluation plan should be reread to make sure that the purpose of the information-gathering activity is clear. It is not financially sound to test all participants when only a sample is needed. Not all stakeholders need to be surveyed if the evaluation plan called for only community leaders to be surveyed.

Obtain Instruments

It may sound obvious, but the instrument must be available before testing can be initiated. You must know who the publisher is and make sure that the test is still in print and the requisite copies are available.

If the instrument is to be locally developed, time and human resources must be allocated to develop the instrument.

Most information collections include a demographic sheet—collecting information such as sex, age, and racial-ethnic background. There should be a reason and a plan for the requested information; otherwise, it is not ethical to obtain the information. Furthermore, the information should be obtained in the fashion that it will be analyzed. For instance, do not ask for actual annual salary if you intend to break the sample down by over $50,000 and $50,000 and under. If that is your intent, then ask the question that way—it is easier for the respondent to answer, and it requires less work on your part.

Arrange for Testers

The person or persons administering the instrument need to be identified or hired. Often multiple testers are needed who have expertise (or are trainable) in administering the instrument. Since you are hiring them only for a short period, you need to make sure they are available and committed to collecting the information. You need to make sure the testers are aware of any special requirements, such as transportation or facility with the language of the respondent.

Pilot Instrument Administration

The instrument must be piloted. If the instrument is a commercial one, the test administrators need to become familiar with the standardized testing conditions. If the instrument is locally developed, the instrument must be administered to a small group of respondents to see if they can respond to the instrument, and if the test administrators can administer the instrument. During the pilot effort, questions about individual items should be asked to determine if any items should be reworded or omitted. Once the revised instrument has been successfully piloted, you are ready to plan for the collection of data.

Plan for Instrument Administration

The instrument must be distributed to the respondents, or testers must be given instruction as to where to go to and when to go. Respondents (and those in charge) should be notified of the impending information collection activity. Protocol regarding access to respondents must be obtained, internalized, and followed.

Collect Information

Collection of information is now possible. In all instances, and at all times, the test administrators are in the house of someone else and must act as a guest. The test administrator's activity, while important, is not the major activity of the program. That is why it is so important to understand and follow local protocol. It is also important to make sure the data-gathering instrument is meaningful to the respondents. It should be neither intrusive, objectionable, nor unrelated to program objectives.

Check for valid information when it is returned to a central location. This is particularly crucial when the information gathering process spans a number of days. Misunderstandings of the testers can be clarified so that all test administrations subsequently are obtaining the information in the same way. A short meeting to discuss unexpected happenings at the end of the first few days, or at the end of each week, can be fruitful.

Examples of Information Collection Plans

We present in appendix E three plans illustrating these steps in different situations. "Plan for Administering Baseline: Survey of Staff" outlines a short survey conducted during a staff meeting. An outline of classroom observations conducted by several observers on an instrument that was locally developed can be seen in "Administering Pretest: Classroom Observation Form." "Administering Pretest: Administering Achievement Tests Individually" outlines a large information collection effort that required 10 testers, some of whom had to be able to administer norm-referenced achievement tests in Spanish and English.

ANALYZE INFORMATION

One can envision four discrete steps in the analysis of data. First, the information must be entered into a computer file. Second, the information must be cleaned, that is, checked for errors. Third, summaries of the entire sample on each variable should be produced. Fourth, specific group comparisons can be produced. Each of these steps is discussed in detail in the following sections.

Entering Information Into a Computer File

First, it must be determined what information will be entered. Usually all of the information collected should be entered—that is the ethical route to take. However, there may be additional information, such as identification number for site, baseline (vs. post assessment), tester, language used in testing, and teacher. None of these variables might have been on the protocols, yet they may be of value or even necessary. Baseline will certainly be a necessary piece of information, for the baseline scores will be analyzed in comparison to the post assessment scores. The language that the child was tested in will be an important piece of information, for the norms tables are often different (or non-existent) for languages other than English.

Second, the categories for each variable must be determined. Usually the ethical route to take is to ask respondents to respond to the categories in the same way you intend to analyze the data. That is, if you intend to have only two categories of age (e.g., 3 years old and 4 years old) then the age question on the protocol would have only those two categories. There is no need to ask for the birthday or the birth month, unless you need that information for other purposes, say for the transformation of the raw scores to scale scores.

Third, each piece of information must be placed in its own column. The easiest way to accomplish this task is to develop an information-coding sheet as in Table 4.4.

It takes only a short amount of time to develop an information-coding sheet, but its value will be evident on many subsequent occasions. Notice that the full name of the variable is indicated in row 1. The evaluator may not need the full name, at least at the moment of entering the data. However, the evaluator, and the program director, in a month or two, will benefit from having recorded the full name. Of benefit is indicating the specific value for the categorical variables, as done in the bottom rows of Table 4.4. This saves much head scratching a

Table 4.4. Information in an Excel File

Student ID	Time	School	Teacher	Racial Ethnic	Sex	Treatment
1001111	1	2	1	1	0	0
1001112	0	3	2	4	1	1
	0 = Baseline 1 = Post	1 = Lincoln 2 = Garfield 3 = Zaragosa	1 = Teacher 1 2 = Teacher 2 3 = Teacher 3	1 = Mexican-Am 2 = African-Am 3 = Asian-Am 4 = Anglo 5 = Native-Am 6 = Other	0 = Male 1 = Female	0 = Comparison 1 = Treatment

Student ID	IQ Non V 1	IQ Verbal 1	IQ Non V 2	IQ V 2	Tester
1001111	99	112	100	115	1
1001112	110	98	113	100	2
					1 = Jose 2 = Alex

year (or day) later when trying to remember if sex was arbitrarily coded as a 1 = male or as 1 = female. In most cases, it makes a difference in interpretation.

We code dichotomous variables with 1s and 0s—the so-called dummy coding because it really does not matter what two scores are used. Why then do we prefer 1,0? The mean of a 1,0 variable will be the proportion of people who have a 1 on that variable. Therefore, if the mean of the Sex variable (assuming 1 = female and 0 = male) is .46, then 46% of the sample is female. More importantly, if one is going to use the General Linear Model (and we would since we wrote a text on the extremely versatile technique: McNeil et al., 1996), representing a dichotomous variable as 1,0 makes a lot of things a lot simpler and easier to interpret—so much so that what others call "dummy variables" we call "smart variables."

The Excel file in Table 4.4 can be analyzed within the Excel program, or necessary fields can be copied and pasted into computer programs such as SPSS, SAS, or Web-based sites such as http://faculty.vassar.edu/lowry/VassarStats.html. Be sure to save the Excel file before you use the data.

Information Cleaning and Labeling

It is extremely important to clean your data—check for incorrect information entries or invalid responses. Too many evaluators enter their information hurriedly and skip to the analysis, assuming that their information is correctly entered. As you should know by now, computers only analyze what they are given in the way that they are instructed. Therefore, it is a good idea to know the legitimate range of all your variables and to check if any information falls outside the legitimate range. Another data quality check is to see if two tests measuring the same construct deviate more than, say, 20 NCE points. Since such a discrepancy is not very likely, although possible, there is likely an error. Best to check.

Since missing information is a major problem for analysis, one should take several precautions. First, the importance of responding to all items on a survey, or of testers obtaining all tests on each child, must be emphasized. Second, checks should be in place to prevent missing data. Pilot studies can identify potential missing information problems. Usually scanning completed surveys before respondents leave the room can ensure that you do not have missing data. Third, if there is missing data in the computer file, it would be fruitful to check to make sure the data really is missing and that there has not been an omission from raw data to data entry.

There is no good approach to resolving the missing data problem. There is no problem if data is missing at random. However, most often certain kinds of people have missing data. Usually the evaluator does not know what kinds of people failed to return surveys or did not completely answer the survey. If one knows, say, the proportion of females that were sent the survey, then one could compare the percentage of females responding to that proportion in the total population.

Almost all published evaluations and research reports have missing data. Missing information becomes a problem when those entities who have missing information are different from those who do not have missing data. Fortunately, there are statistical procedures available to discover these differences and to partially take care of the problem (McNeil et al., 1996).

Basic Descriptive Information

Most stakeholders are interested in knowing basic descriptive information about the program and its participants. In program evaluation in school settings, results reported by such variables as ethnicity, schools, grade levels, and sex are usually of interest.

Initial Group Differences

It is a good idea to explore differences between groups at baseline. There should be no differences between groups at baseline—you want the groups to be as similar as possible. However, since evaluations are conducted in the real world, often with little control over the nature of the comparison group, there are often large differences between treatment and comparison groups. Knowing this as soon as possible may facilitate doing something about the problem, such as (a) finding another comparison group, (b) eliminating some sites or classrooms from either the comparison group or the treatment group, or (c) identifying variables that can be used to level the playing field. You want to have as representative a distribution as possible of all the relevant variables.

WRITE REPORT

While many aspects of the report on baseline are the same as the one for needs assessment, there are some differences. First, the purpose of the report is to document the specific needs that have been identified. Second, the report must be completed quickly as the specific needs must be addressed in the revision of the program. Third, the audience for the baseline report is primarily those who will be developing and implementing the program. Fourth, the results must be clearly identified for those stakeholders.

Purpose of the Report

The purpose of the baseline report is to document the specific needs of the intended recipients. The purpose of the needs assessment report, on the other hand, is to identify general areas of need based on past performance of program recipients. The baseline thus provides the opportunity to identify the particular weaknesses of those who will be receiving the new (or revised) program.

The Baseline Report Must Be Timely

The report provides direction to (a) the one responsible for the management of the program—the program director, (b) those developing the program, and (c) those implementing the program. Thus, the sooner the report is available, the sooner the program can be tailored to the specific needs of those who are the intended beneficiaries. Development of the program should be an ongoing effort, with the needs assessment providing the general directions and the baseline report providing the information for final small adjustments. The timeline below provides one scenario for this fine-tuning (with development steps of the program in regular type, and implementation steps of the program in italics).

May 95	Needs assessment on 4th graders
June 95	Initial development of the new program
Aug 95	Baseline of new cohort of 4th graders
Aug 95	*Initial program implemented with new cohort*
Sept 95	Baseline report fine-tuning based on NA
Oct 95	*Revised program implemented*

Note that the new cohort of 4th graders in this timeline has had several weeks of the initial program before the baseline report was completed and the program planners had a chance to revise the initial program. That is why it is so crucial for the needs assessment to clarify as much as possible the specific needs and for the baseline to be collected, analyzed, and reported as quickly as possible.

Audience for the Baseline Report

The audience for the baseline report is primarily the program director, the program design person(s), and the implementer(s) of the program. All other stakeholders have provided needs assessment information and have received the needs assessment report—providing them with the big picture. The baseline report provides the information for minor modifications in the development of the program. The program director should be involved, as that person is ultimately responsible for the program. First, that person should be knowledgeable about how the program fits in with all other programs in the organization and all other programs relevant to the participants. The program director knows what funds are available for what functions and thus is in a position to facilitate the development of the program. The implementers should be involved in the development, as they have insight into the day-to-day realities and constraints. Since they are the ones who will be providing the program to the participants, they need to be convinced that the program is the best available (given all the resource constraints) and can be implemented by those who have that responsibility. A program that makes unrealistic demands on its implementers is doomed from the beginning.

Results Clearly Communicated

Although the report must be completed quickly, it must communicate results clearly and forcefully to those who are charged with developing the program. The developers do not have much time or, in many cases, the expertise to digest a lot of information. The report must accomplish those tasks for them. Therefore, the report should clearly indicate the specific needs of those who will initially be in the program. It is our experience that most program planners appreciate summarized information presented as figures. Figures facilitate quick (a) understanding of the data, (b) comparison between potential needs, and (c) decisions as to the necessary components of the revised program. In many instances, the baseline information confirms the results of the needs assessment. In some instances, the baseline information requires minor modifications of the initial draft of the program. Finally, the baseline information may identify entirely new components that should be added into the program. These new components may be a result of (a) the instruments used for the baseline not being the same as those used for needs assessment, (b) the difference between those who provided needs assessment information and those who provided the baseline information, or (c) reviewing the draft program and realizing that some changes should be made that are not specifically indicated by the baseline report.

DISSEMINATE THE BASELINE REPORT

As indicated in the previous section, the baseline report must be completed and disseminated to the necessary audiences as quickly as possible. The report should be written so that the program developers can easily incorporate the baseline information. The program director and the evaluator should present the baseline report to the program developers. Either the program director or the evaluator, depending on the nature of the question, can answer clarification questions. Since the baseline information must be used to refine the program, all program developers must clearly understand both the baseline results and the implications of those results.

We recommend that the program development team (program director, program designers, and program implementers) be called together and that the evaluator guide the team through the baseline results. Copies of the needs assessment report should be available. How the baseline results compare with the needs assessment results should be part of the baseline report. Since we recommend that the program director take an active role in writing the baseline report, the program director can assist in guiding the team through the baseline report. When the program director takes such an active role, the rest of the program development team will have more respect for the information in the report.

The baseline report should be available to other stakeholders, although it does not seem to us to be necessary to make copies for all stakeholders. This baseline report is more detailed than the needs assessment report and focuses on just the recipients and how the program should be fine-tuned to serve them.

DRAFT PROGRAM OBJECTIVES

The new, revised program should have clearly identified objectives. Having these objectives written down facilitates the development of the program. Program planners sometimes lose sight of the forest (the objectives) by focusing on the each of the trees (activities, sometimes supported by only one developer). These objectives identify constructs, operational measures of those constructs, and the minimum level of proficiency on the measures. For example, the construct of attendance could be measured by attendance at in-service training with a minimal level of teachers attending five out of six meetings. The construct of implementation of in-service training could be measured by whether or not the teachers incorporate strategies in their lesson plan, with a minimal level of four out of five strategies required. The construct of student performance could be measured by the ABC Test, with a minimal level of 90% of the students scoring above 40%. The construct of parent participation could be measured by involvement in workshops, with a minimal level of 90% of the parents involved. The construct of attitude could be measured by the Attitude Test, with a minimal level of a mean gain greater than 2.00. The construct of teacher involvement could be measured by whether they volunteer to present on some topic, with a minimal level of at least 75% of the teachers volunteering to present at one of the six in-service programs or at a countywide conference. The construct of implementation could be measured by classroom observation, with a minimal level of 90% of the teachers implementing three of the four techniques presented at the previous in-service program.

The program development team develops these program objectives. The team may want to consult with selected stakeholders who (a) may have expertise related to certain objectives, (b) may be perceived to possibly disagree with a program objective, or (c) may be able to make a contribution to the development of program objectives.

Some of the development of program objectives will occur after the needs assessment report is disseminated, while refinements will occur after the baseline report is disseminated. If the baseline report does not indicate major program objective changes, then stakeholders may not need to be consulted.

SHARE PROGRAM OBJECTIVES WITH STAKEHOLDERS

Regardless of whether or not the baseline report modifies the program objectives, the program objectives should be shared with each of the stakeholder groups. Some stakeholders may not initially be interested in the details, but the stakeholders have been informed and may rely on that information sometime later. The program objectives provide a rationale for what is to occur in the program, as well as for all the evaluation activities. The program objectives also indicate, by omission, what the program will not be responsible for.

If the baseline results in modified program objectives, we suggest that those modified objectives be clearly identified. Then a paper copy should be distributed to all stakeholders and one copy kept in the program director's office.

FINALIZE PROGRAM OBJECTIVES

Only after the baseline report has been digested by the program development team and stakeholders have been informed (and have responded to substantial program objective changes) should the objectives be considered finalized. The actual process of developing the program objectives might be as identified in the following example. The process begins with seven objectives (1–7). The needs assessment conducted on parents only attends to a subset of those objectives (1–5). The entire needs assessment might result in new objectives or omission of some (5 omitted). The baseline assessment also may result in either new (8 and 9), omitted (7), or revised objectives. Upon sharing the baseline information with stakeholders, new, omitted, or revised objectives (9) may result. One possible outcome might be:

Initial objectives: 1   2   3   4   5   6   7
Needs assessment of:
    Parents on objectives 1   2   3   4   5

Students on objectives 1   2   3   4   5   6
Program director on objectives 1   2   3   4   5   6   7
Program developer(s) on objectives 1   2   3   4   5   6   7
Program implementer(s) on objectives 1   2   3   4   5   6   7
Results in objectives: 1   2   3   4   6   7, with #5 omitted
Baseline of students:
Results in objectives: 1   2   3   4   6   8   9, with #7 omitted
Sharing program objectives with stakeholders:
Results in final program objectives: 1   2   3   4   6   8 and revised 9

During needs assessment, all stakeholders should have input into what the objectives should be. The only nonprogram stakeholder listed above is parents. They might have information and particular concerns about objectives 1–5. Students provide information on objectives 1–6. The program director, program developer(s), and the program implementer(s) might each have information on objectives 1–7.

The timeline above indicates that, because of the needs assessment, objective 5 is no longer of any concern. Thus, objectives 1–4 and 6 and 7 would be the focus of the baseline of students. Because of the baseline information, objective 7 was dropped because the new cohort of students had already reached minimum mastery on that objective. The baseline, though, identified two additional objectives on which this new cohort was deficient. The program development team agreed that these two areas were crucial and that they could be (and should be) added to the program. Therefore, objectives 8 and 9 were added to the program. Review of the objectives (1, 2, 3, 4, 6, new 8, and new 9) with stakeholders resulted in acceptance of all objectives, after revision of objective 9.

CHAPTER 5

Procedures to Achieve Objectives

The previous chapter brought us to a finalized list of objectives. In order to accomplish those objectives, a program must be planned and integrated into the existing environment. See Figure 5.1 for procedures to achieve objectives in the GEM. This existing environment may well include the previous program and staff dedicated to the previous program. All staff members must be somewhat involved in the development of the new program. A good program cannot succeed with even a small proportion of the staff either unfamiliar with the program or uncommitted to the program.

All of the comments in the previous paragraph are relevant to other types of evaluations. The reader should always keep in mind that the GEM is applicable to not only program evaluation but to all other levels of evaluation, from individual lesson plans and personnel evaluation to departmental evaluations and the evaluation of an entire institution.

Developing procedures to achieve objectives includes (a) development of the procedures conceptually and on paper, (b) training of staff, and (c) determination that the training was implemented well. The evaluator must be involved, to some extent, in these tasks—particularly in determining that the training was implemented well.

DEVELOP PROCEDURES

Procedures to achieve objectives must be determined by one or more people. We suggest that a small planning committee be formed and one

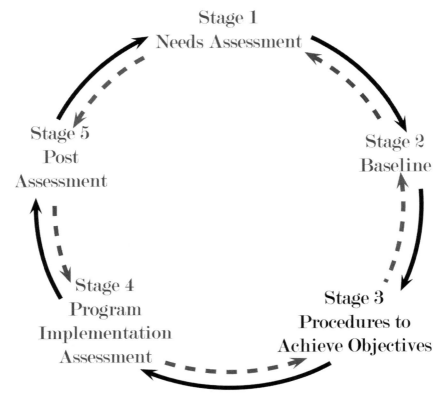

Figure 5.1.   The Procedures to Acheive Objectives Stage
Note: Solid arrows indicate the primary direction of the flow of the evaluation from one stage to the next stage. Dashed arrows indicate the feedback from one stage to a previous stage—actually feedback can go to any previous stage.

person be put in charge. That person is then responsible for bringing the team together, providing the relevant needs assessment information, and keeping the team on target. The team should review those final objectives determined by the needs assessment and then decide on the scope of the program. Their decision may result in adopting an existing program or developing a new program.

Identify the Program Planning Team

The team should be composed of representatives from each of the affected units. For example, if the new program is an after-school program, the curriculum staff, activities staff, and food service staff probably need to be involved. All of these people should be invited to participate and should be informed of the expectations and time commitments of being on the planning team.

The planning team should be brought together for reviewing the final objectives. During this meeting, the program director should make sure that the planning team understands the objectives and that they agree with the objectives. Bribing the planning team with financial and gastronomical incentives is suggested in order to get them to attend to the task that they might otherwise think is an extra task.

Have Planning Team Review the Final Objectives

The first activity of the planning team is to review the final objectives. This is suggested to make sure that each team member understands the objectives and that the program will be based on those objectives. Once it is clear that each understands the objectives, a commitment to those objectives must be obtained. Do not assume that understanding and commitment are automatic. Do not assume that understanding implies commitment.

Decide on the Scope of the New Program

The next activity is to decide on the scope of the new program. Will it be a relatively easy modification to the existing program, or will it be an addition to the existing program? Will the new program be a complete revamping of the existing program or a totally new program?

Decide How to Obtain the New Program

The planning team are the ones to develop the curriculum if the choice is other than a new program. If they decide on a totally new program, then they have to evaluate their options. Are there commercial programs that will accomplish the objectives? If so, how have these programs fared in similar institutions? It is best not to make the same mistake that your colleagues in other institutions have already made. For sure, do not rely on the assurances of the company representatives.

Two other options exist, neither of which are good options. First, the writing of the new program could be contracted out. This is not a good option because if it is taken, staff will not have as much personal stake in the program. The second option, having the planning team develop the program, is a better option. This requires a modicum of program planning expertise and time, commodities that the planning team may not have.

Keep the Planning Team on Target

The program director must keep the planning team focused on the objectives. Professionals often have their own pet methods or content, and if these are not in line with the objectives, they must not be included. Periodic review of the objectives should keep the planning team on task.

TRAIN STAFF

Training staff on the objectives and the implementation of the program is crucial and requires a well-thought-out plan. The plan should have three components: (a) how the training will be delivered, (b) a process for ensuring that trainers understand the entire program and training component, and (c) a process for determining that the training was implemented well. The first two components will be described in the next section, and the last component will be described in the subsequent section.

The plan for the delivery of training should have three elements: (a) identification of needed training, (b) systematic devising of that training, and (c) appropriate delivery of training. The question of what training is needed is answered through another needs assessment. The program director can do an introspective needs assessment. It is better to get more heads involved by asking the planning team to determine what training the staff should receive. Some members of the planning team understand what staff already knows and what they can already do. You do not want to provide training that is irrelevant or redundant. Your training budget is likely limited, as is the time available for the training.

The second component is that the training must be devised in a systematic fashion. The training for the entire cycle should be planned and reviewed by the planning team. The need for training must be balanced with the requirement of delivering the program. That is, program staff is being trained while implementing the program. Therefore, at the beginning of the program, the "new program" is really an amalgamation of the old program and the new program. Only after the last staff training and the time necessary for staff to transfer that training to their delivery of the program is the "new program" really being implemented. This is one reason why some evaluators do not focus on the products of the new program in the 1st year of, say, a 5-year program. They focus instead on the processes that are supposed to be implemented in the 1st year or so.

The third component is that the training be systematically delivered, so that the staff is not overwhelmed. These people have to turn the training (often conceptual) into practical, everyday practice. It may be difficult to "get inside the head and heart of the staff being trained," but making that attempt may identify training practices that are effective and some that were not so effective. Why do you think hands-on activities and "make and take" sessions are so popular?

The program director should continuously check on the assumptions that are usually made. There are five assumptions regarding training that we have often seen made. Usually these assumptions are not valid.

The first assumption is that staff is actually attending staff development. In a small program, this is usually not a problem and easy to determine if it is. However, in a large program, staff may choose not to come to staff development or to leave early.

The second assumption is that the participants understand what was provided in the staff development. Seldom do staff developers or program directors check for actual understanding. Most evaluations measure only the affective aspects of the staff development. Hence, it is usual to have 90% of the respondents report, "This was the best workshop that I have ever attended." When the evaluation of staff development contains only attitudinal items, evaluations will likely be positive but seldom of any substance.

A third assumption is that staff understands the parts of the old program that will be retained and how the new parts are to be integrated with the old parts. Even the program planners may understand the relationship only conceptually. It may require a major effort to actually integrate the new program with the old program.

A fourth assumption is that the trainer knows how to train adults. This is a particular problem when the staff development occurs in an educational setting with a teacher or former teacher. These teachers are probably very good at teaching children or young adults but may not understand the training needs of adults (e.g., frequent breaks, examples relevant to the job, nondemeaning activities).

A fifth assumption is that the training was integrated with previous training and that it focused only on the program. The program director should be aware of the previous training received by each staff member and the kinds of training needed by each. Perhaps only one third needs a certain kind of training, while all need other training. The program director has the responsibility to identify who needs what training. In addition, the program director should direct those providing the training as to what the desired outcomes of the training are. The program director or a designer should attend all staff development sessions in order to continuously monitor these assumptions. The next two paragraphs describe an experience that one of us had where some of these assumptions were not met.

Keith McNeil was in charge of evaluating a school district's Chapter 1 program. Staff development was held one Friday a month. The topic for several months was the bilingual component of the program. Trainers were hired from the outside. As reported by the participants on the end-of-day evaluations, the sessions were boring and provided no "hands-on" materials for the participants. Examples for the classroom came from teaching French-speaking children in English-speaking schools in Canada and the indigenous Maori in New Zealand. None of the examples were about teaching recent immigrants from Mexico, who represented approximately 90% of the students in the school district. Participants signed in when they arrived in the morning, but many of the 300 left at noon to go back to their classes (instead of returning for the afternoon continuation).

These problems were identified by the evaluator and communicated to the program director, along with recommendations to (a) make the sessions more interesting, (b) provide examples relevant to the students from Mexico, and (c) develop a mechanism for keeping attendance in the afternoon. The program director was upset with the recommendations to the extent that the evaluation team was told not to return for the remaining staff development sessions. However, one of the evaluators was new to the district, and therefore unknown to the program director, participants, and trainers. She was asked by the evaluator in charge to return to the next staff development and to keep a low profile among the 300 participants. After doing so, she reported that (a) attendance was taken at both morning and afternoon sessions, (b) door prizes were given based on afternoon attendance, and (c) most importantly, the only examples mentioned were related to the students from Mexico. The evaluation of staff development, particularly checking on assumptions, had a positive impact on this staff development. (The program director never did make amends and never did share with the evaluation team that these changes were made. We often learn about the negative effects of our actions, but seldom do we learn about the positive effects.)

DETERMINE THAT TRAINING WAS IMPLEMENTED WELL

Since a substantial portion of the budget of the program goes to training, and since a substantial portion of staff time is consumed by training, it should be evaluated. There are several times when staff can be checked for their understanding of the training or their ability to implement the training. Evaluation tools then need to be identified or developed to assess the training. Once the information is collected and analyzed, it then should be reported to the program director, trainers, and the staff who received the training.

Check to See If Staff Understands the Training

It is imperative to check to make sure that staff understands the training. This check can be accomplished by (a) interviewing the trainer, (b) having staff indicate how they feel about the training, (c) having staff indicate what content or skills they have learned, or (d) having staff indicate how well they are able to implement the training. All of the above information can be informative, but the value of that information is a function of when it is collected and what the source of information is. As indicated in Table 5.1, the value of the training is increased when the information is collected several weeks after the training is conducted. In addition, we place more value on information from observing staff implement the training than from the trainer's comments or staff feelings or staff knowledge.

Trainers (and participants) are often on a high at the end of a training session. They feel good about what has transpired during the training. In addition, there is often a tendency to provide socially desirable responses. That is, staff know that training costs a lot, and therefore they feel that they should have benefited from it and appreciate it. That is why we value very little the perceptions at the end of each session. Has the staff learned anything new? More importantly, are they willing and able to implement these new ideas or procedures? It is well known that what one says one is going to do is not necessarily what one will actually do. Hence, a good evaluation of staff training incorporates an assessment of staff attitudes, knowledge, and commitment to implementing later, say, at the next training session. However, the real "proof in the pudding" is the extent to which the staff can implement the program on a consistent basis. The ideal (and hence the highest ratings in Table 5.1) is for the staff to routinely implement the program, not just when the evaluator comes to observe the "dog and pony" show.

Table 5.1.   Value of the Training Information by Source of Information and When Collected

Source of Information	Time		
	End of Session	Week Later	Month Later
Trainer's comments	1		
Staff feelings	1	2	
Staff knowledge	3	4	
Staff willingness to implement	4	6	
Staff implementing (when evaluator makes planned visit)		7	8
Staff implementing routinely (observed during surprise visit)		9	10

Note: 1 = little, 10 = most.

Guskey (2000) considers five levels of professional development evaluation, focusing on four questions. The four questions are: (a) What questions are asked? (b) How will information be gathered? (c) What is measured or assessed? and (d) How will information be used? Some reasonable answers to these questions provided by Guskey are in Table 5.2.

Develop Evaluation Tools to Match Training Objectives

We recommend that priority be given to assessing what staff can implement in their delivery of service. This assessment should incorporate the focus of all the training sessions. This makes sense since each training session should be directed toward some part of service delivery. Since the training and the implementation are both supposed to be coherent packages, the evaluation should also be a coherent package.

Each staff trainer should be required to provide the objectives that will be met by the end of the training session. These objectives can be turned into items on the end-of-training instrument. "Development of End-of-Training Instrument" in appendix D contains one such example. The staff development topic and training objectives should be negotiated between the trainer and the program director. It is not appropriate for a trainer to contract for a topic without such objectives. The program director has the right and responsibility to pin the trainer down to specific objectives. When this is done, the program director may discover that the trainer was planning to cover objectives irrelevant to the program. The evaluator and the program director should transfer those objectives into items, which should then be reviewed with the trainer. When this process is completed, the trainer will (a) realize what the program director wants the staff to learn, and (b) be willing to implement what is needed.

Once the training objectives have been determined, the evaluator can construct the final training evaluation form. This form may contain demographic information, such as program site, title of participant, and years in the organization. Some of this information may not be of value for a particular evaluation, while there may be other relevant information. If you want to keep the evaluation anonymous (and we suggest that is the best practice), then you must consider whether filling out the

Table 5.2. Guskey's Five Levels of Professional Development Evaluation

Evaluation Level	What Questions Are Addressed?	How Will Information Be Gathered?	What Is Measured or Assessed?	How Will Information Be Used?
Participants' reactions	Did they like it? Was their time well spent? Did the materials make sense? Will it be useful? Was the leader knowledgeable and helpful? Were the refreshments fresh and tasty? Was the room at the right temperature? Were the chairs comfortable?	Questionnaires administered at the end of the session Focus groups Interviews Personal learning logs	Initial satisfaction with the experience	To improve program design and delivery
Participants' learning	Did participants acquire the intended knowledge and skills?	Paper and pencil instruments Simulations and demos Participant reflections (oral and/or written) Participant portfolios Case study analyses	New knowledge and skill of participants	To improve program content, format, and organization

Organization support	What was the impact on the organization? Did it affect organizational climate and procedures? Was implementation advocated, facilitated, and supported? Was the support public and overt? Were problems addressed quickly and efficiently? Were sufficient resources made available? Were successes recognized and shared?	District school records Minutes from follow-up meetings Questionnaires Focus groups Structured interviews Participant portfolios	The organization's advocacy, support, accommodation, facilitation, and recognition	To document support and prove organizational support To inform future change agents
Participants' use of new knowledge and skills	Did participants effectively apply the new knowledge and skills?	Questionnaires Structured interviews with participants and their supervisors Participant reflections Participant portfolios Direct observations Video or audio tapes	Degree and quality of implementation	To document and improve the implementation of program content

(continued)

Table 5.2. Guskey's Five Levels of Professional Development Evaluation (*continued*)

Evaluation Level	What Questions Are Addressed?	How Will Information Be Gathered?	What Is Measured or Assessed?	How Will Information Be Used?
Student learning	What was the impact on students? Did it affect student performance or achievement? Did it influence students' physical or emotional well-being? Are students more confident as learners? Is student attendance improving? Are dropouts decreasing?	Student records Questionnaires Structured interviews with students, parents, teachers, administrators Participant portfolios	Student learning outcomes: cognitive (performance and achievement); affective (attitudes and dispositions); psychomotor (skills and behaviors)	To focus and improve all aspects of program design, implementation, and follow-up To demonstrate the overall impact of professional development

Source: Guskey, 2000.

demographic information destroys the anonymity. You really break trust if you tell staff that the information is anonymous while the type of information you ask for clearly communicates that it is not anonymous. "Training Evaluation Form" in appendix D contains the completed evaluation form arising from the information in "Development of End-of-Training Instrument."

You could ask what the three most valuable topics were, as well as the three least valuable topics. You probably should ask the participants how important those least three valuable topics were. If they are perceived as crucial, then the training session was not as successful as it should have been.

Plan and Collect the Information

The evaluator should construct the plan for the collection of the in-service evaluation. The plan should then be presented to the program director to make sure that (a) all local protocols have been met, (b) the evaluation effort does not interfere with required program implementation requirements, and (c) the total financial and personnel commitment is within the program budget.

All instruments should be ordered or constructed well in advance of their administration. Last-minute construction or substitutions often result in less than desirable evaluation tools. Once the evaluator drafts the instrument, as many people as possible should review it—including the advisory board, staff implementing the program, and especially the program director.

We recommend that the evaluator collect as much of the information as possible. If the evaluator cannot collect the information, the evaluator must take an active role in training those who do collect the information. The evaluator should review procedures at the beginning of information collection to ensure that all information is being collected in the desired manner.

There are several additional benefits when the evaluator is intimately involved in the information collection. First, the program staff sees the evaluator, which emphasizes the importance of the information collection effort. Second, additional information can be obtained, providing context for some of the evaluation findings in reports. Third, the evaluation team approach underlying this text is emphasized. The team, not just the program director, is collecting data.

Analyze the Information

The analysis consists primarily of frequency distributions. No other sophisticated data analysis is called for. Means could be calculated on responses that are on a Likert scale. (A Likert scale provides several options, usually between 4 and 7.) Often the ends of the continuum are defined with words such as "strongly agree" or "strongly disagree."

One may want to combine some of the Likert responses. For example, say that the program director, in conjunction with the trainer, determines that responses of "agree" and "strongly agree" would be considered positive. All other responses ("neutral," "disagree," and "strongly disagree") would be considered problematic and would need to be dealt with at the next staff development meeting.

If there are sufficient participants to warrant analysis by subgroups (e.g., site or primary course assignment) then such analyses may be informative. Perhaps all of the problematic responses discussed in the previous paragraph were from the same site. The program director would not need to wait for the next staff development to deal with the issue. A telephone interview with site staff or a visit to the site might clear up the matter.

Report to Trainer, Program Director, and Participants

A succinct report, completed in a timely manner, is called for. The trainer needs to know what objectives were not successful, particularly if that same trainer will be providing more training. The program director needs to know which objectives were not met so that modifications can be made in the training schedule. Participants need to see the results of the evaluation for two reasons. First, they need to see that the time they spent filling out the evaluation was worthwhile. Second, each participant needs to see how the others viewed the staff development and their willingness to implement the program. Most participants of staff development have a small cadre of friends or acquaintances with whom they discuss the staff development. The report may broaden their perspective of staff development as well as that of the program. "Example of a Staff Development Evaluation Report" in appendix F contains a report derived from the "Development of End-of-Training Instrument" and "Training Evaluation Form" in appendix D.

Some staff development evaluation forms contain questions that call for lengthy answers. We recommend avoiding such questions, although many respondents enjoy telling you their life history. First, not all respondents have the same inclination to provide a wordy response. Some might be less verbose, feel that such responses do not carry as much weight as the fixed response, or may have a time constraint and forego spending time responding to an open-ended question. Thus, the respondents who respond to open-ended questions are not a representative sample of all the respondents. Second, the responses need to be categorized, and that may be problematic. Finally, our experience is that idiosyncratic responses (those given by only one respondent, reflecting their unique biases) are given either an inordinate amount of weight or no weight at all. In the latter case, if the response is in line with the desires of the program director, then the program director accepts the response. If the response is not in line with the desires of the program director, the response is ignored. The wise program director does not use such items, but if they are used, the responses are incorporated into the evaluation form at the next staff development to discover how all the workshop attendees feel.

CHAPTER 6

Program Implementation Assessment

This chapter discusses how to conduct Stage 4 of the General Evaluation Model—program implementation assessment. (See Figure 6.1.) Each of the 10 tasks in Stage 4 are discussed, often with accompanying instruments, plans, and examples of reporting formats.

Program implementation assessment occurs during the implementation of the objectives. The primary question being answered in program implementation assessment is, "Is the program being implemented as it was planned?" If the program is being implemented, then the planned results should occur. However, if the program is not being implemented or is not being implemented well, then we should not be surprised if the product results do not meet expectations.

The program implementation assessment cannot be haphazard. A plan needs to be developed for the program implementation assessment of program director, staff development, staff implementation, and advisory board—if there is one. This plan will include (a) identifying instruments that have to be purchased or developed, (b) keeping stakeholders informed periodically, (c) collecting and analyzing the context information, (d) collecting and analyzing the input information, (e) collecting and analyzing the process information, (f) writing the reports of each of these analyses, (g) relating the various results to the objectives and procedures to achieve objectives, and (h) disseminating the reports. All of these tasks are described in detail in the following sections.

The program implementation assessment evaluation in GEM incorporates three components of the often-used context, input, process, and product (CIPP) model. The CIPP evaluation model was developed by Stufflebeam (1983, 2001). The last component of CIPP—product

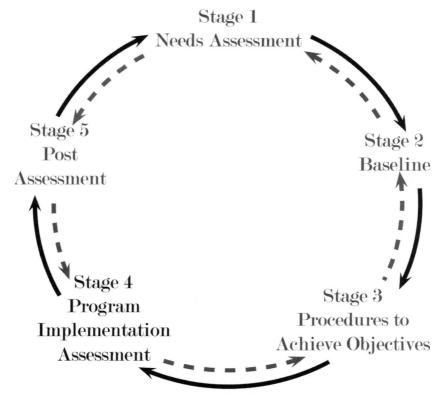

Figure 6.1. The Program Implementation Assesment Stage
Note: Solid arrows indicate the primary direction of the flow of the evaluation from one stage to the next stage. Dashed arrows indicate the feedback from one stage to a previous stage—actually feedback can go to any previous stage.

testing—is discussed in the next chapter. The first three components of the CIPP model are all included under program implementation assessment. The CIPP components correspond to GEM Stages 4 and 5. The first three stages of GEM are not considered as part of the evaluation process by the CIPP model. A description of each of the context, financial, and other resource inputs, as well as implementation processes, is included in this chapter.

DEVELOP PROGRAM IMPLEMENTATION ASSESSMENT PLAN

The program implementation assessment plan includes context and input information, as well as process information. The plan should be written as soon as the program is funded and should be as comprehensive as possible. The three primary sources of information will be the program director, the staff development trainer, and the staff implementing the program.

We have found that asking the program director to keep a journal of each day's major events is a good way to keep track of the pulse of the program. Entries would include delay of available funds, timeliness of staff development, timeliness of ordering of supplies and evaluation instruments, next steps, and decisions made—and their rationale—that changed the course of the program (see "Diary of a Program Director" in appendix F for one example). Entering information into the diary on a daily basis preserves a record of the time of events and the factors surrounding the events. This is a much better way to collect information than to ask the program director to retrospectively remember events, order of events, and why some decisions were made.

The program implementation assessment plan should contain (a) the dates the events will occur, (b) the events that will be evaluated, (c) who is responsible for the collection of information, (d) what evaluation instrument will be used, (e) the number of evaluation instruments needed, and (f) whether or not sampling is to occur. The program director and evaluator should jointly develop the list of context, input, and process activities that will be evaluated (see "Program Implementation Plan" in appendix E).

The person ultimately responsible for the evaluation is the evaluator, but others may be responsible for collecting the information. Usually the best instrument costs the most, and therefore a compromise must be made. Because program objectives may be unique, existing evaluation instruments may not be available. The evaluator should develop the instrument with some involvement from the program director and the program staff for three reasons. First, the program director and the program staff likely have a different perspective of the program than does the evaluator. Second, by involving program staff, they will likely take more ownership in the evaluation and the results of the evaluation. Third, the evaluator may not be aware of all the nuances and constraints of the program, the institution, and the community.

IDENTIFY INSTRUMENTS

The evaluator should take primary responsibility for deciding on the evaluation instruments, but the program director should be aware of the decision and the financial impact on the program. The choices are to purchase already existing instruments (including response protocols and scoring) or to develop your own custom-made instrument. Custom-made instruments appear to cost much less because development time is easy to overlook. The value of existing instruments is that their psychometric properties (reliability and validity) may already have been investigated. In addition, they may have national norms and hence scores that have a built-in baseline.

If the choice is to use an already existing instrument, one could use four sources. Probably the easiest approach is to use information collection procedures that are already in place in the organization. Examples of routinely collected information include attendance, performance on state criterion-referenced tests, and remission rates. Given that this information is already being collected, the information has been identified as important to the organization. No new procedures need to be instituted to get the desired information. Minimal disturbance to the system is always appreciated.

If existing information is used to evaluate the program, there is less likelihood that stakeholders will view the program as being at odds with the goals and objectives of the program it replaced or modified. In addition, the evaluation will cost less if existing information can be used.

One problem with using existing information is that the evaluator and the program director may have little control over the collection of the information. Therefore, the intricacies of the information collection process may not be known, the information may not be available when the evaluator needs it, and changes may be made without a warning to the evaluator. If the evaluator understands and can handle these issues, using existing information is usually beneficial.

Colleagues in Neighboring Programs

Often there are similar programs in neighboring areas. There are schools in almost every town in the United States, there are Head Start programs in almost every town, there are community colleges in every region of the state, and so on. If you are evaluating your program, your colleagues are likely evaluating theirs also. They may have solved some of the evaluation (and program) challenges with which you are struggling. Often there are regional and state associations, and these are good places to network to discover solutions to your challenges.

Similarly Funded Programs

If the program being evaluated is funded by a state agency or the federal government, there are usually other such funded programs. These programs have the same kinds of evaluation requirements and in many cases have similar objectives, if not exactly the same objectives. Discussing your challenges with these other program directors may solve your challenges. Hiring an evaluator who has experience with similarly funded programs is also advantageous, although not a necessary requirement. As GEM indicates, the evaluation tasks are the same no matter what kind of program is evaluated. Knowledge of funding agency requirements and instruments used in the past simply give your evaluator a "leg up" on the evaluation.

Library and Internet Resources

There are many printed resources in libraries and on the Internet. Most resources catalog the available instruments by content area and provide a brief description of each. In some resources, additional studies on those instruments are reported. "Sources for Instruments" in appendix G lists several sources for instruments. The Internet has become a major resource for information about instruments. "Internet Sites That Focus on Instruments" in appendix G lists several Internet sites that focus on instruments.

DEVELOP INSTRUMENTS (IF NECESSARY)

The development of custom-made instruments can require many resources and therefore should be undertaken with caution and only after the investigation of available resources has not identified a useful instrument. That is why the first two parts of this section focus on reviewing the need for, and purpose of, developing a new instrument. The third part encourages the modification of existing instruments, and the last emphasizes the need to obtain comments from the program director and program staff.

Make Sure That Objectives Call for the Custom-Made Instrument

Because developing a new instrument is a costly endeavor, the decision should not be made without exploring all options. All of the avenues discussed in the earlier section "Identify Instruments" should be explored before you decide on developing a new instrument. The cost of developing this new instrument should be estimated; this estimate might lead to the adoption of a less than desirable existing instrument.

More importantly, you need to review the objectives to make sure the instrument that you plan to develop is actually called for. Some evaluators thrive on developing new instruments, whether the objectives of the program call for the instrument or not. Others include their favorite questions or techniques. If the objectives do not require such an instrument, then the resources that go into the development of that instrument have been wasted. Though the evaluator's ego or research agenda might have been satisfied, the assessment of program objectives certainly has not been satisfied.

Information May Only Indirectly Bear on Objectives

If an available instrument produces information that only indirectly bears on the objectives, the instrument should not be used. Each evaluation instrument should measure as exactly as possible whatever program objectives it is identified to measure. Usually custom-made instruments are assumed to measure the objectives perfectly, because that was the intent of the developer. Because the developer is not an expert in test construction, some of the custom-made instruments are not as good as existing instruments. It is probably better to use an existing instrument to partially measure your objectives than to spend the resources on developing a custom-made instrument that, in the final analysis, does not do any better and may do worse.

Modify Existing Instruments

When the program's objectives are somewhat different from those measured by an existing instrument, a reasonable alternative is to modify the existing instrument. Perhaps only some of the subscales need to be used. On the other hand, perhaps items need to be translated into the native language of the respondents. Perhaps one additional subscale needs to be locally developed. In all these cases, the existing instrument is only minimally modified, and therefore the psychometric properties of the instrument are still somewhat applicable.

Get Comments From Program Director and Program Staff

No matter what decision has been made, the program director and the program staff should review the instrument chosen for the evaluation. They may identify substantial problems with the proposed instrument. They might be able to recommend changes that will make the instrument a better measure of the objectives for the participants. Of greatest importance, the evaluator does not want any surprises surrounding the evaluation. Giving the program director and program staff a chance to review the instrument minimizes the likelihood that program staff will claim that they had no part in identifying the evaluation instrument.

INFORM STAKEHOLDERS PERIODICALLY

A good evaluator does not wait until the end of the fiscal year to report on the program. Short reports should be completed after every major event. These reports can then easily be combined into the final report. Stakeholders want to know that the program is continually being implemented, in only a general sort of way. Furthermore, staff that have provided information want to know how others feel and how the information looks when it is aggregated with the information from other respondents.

Stakeholders Want to Know in General What Is Going On

Most stakeholders want to keep abreast of the program, but only in a superficial manner. They do not need details, only that the major components are occurring and that the program is generally on track. Making the "executive summary" available to stakeholders keeps them informed of the program at the general level that most desire.

Staff Who Provide Information Want to Know Specifically What Is Going On

Program staff want to know specifically what has been occurring and what other staff think about staff development, implementation of the program, dissemination of the program, and so on. These reports should be completed and shared with program staff as soon as the activities have occurred. The quicker the turnaround, the more positive the program staff feels about the program and the evaluation of the program. When program staff see evaluation reports of the information they provided, they realize that "someone out there really does care," which leads to a more positive attitude about the evaluation.

CONTEXT INFORMATION COLLECTED AND ANALYZED

The context information describes the existing state of affairs of the community, organization, sites where program services are delivered, the staff at those sites, the "old program," and the participants. There are three purposes for the context information. The first purpose is to describe the setting in which the program was implemented for those unfamiliar with the setting. Others considering implementing the same new program might gain some insight from such information.

The second purpose is the comparison of the various sites (or classrooms). Such a comparison can assist the program director in understanding the potential challenges. This information might assist in taking care of problems before they actually materialize. For example, the program director might schedule more time at some sites than at others.

The third purpose is to provide the "big picture" of the current program before implementation of the new program. Such information is often of more interest to some stakeholders than is the change in specific outcomes because of the new program. Information such as "there are now nine degree programs at the community college when there were only seven before" is of interest to some stakeholders, irrespective of the productivity of the two new degree programs.

What Kind of Context Information?

There is a lot of context information that could be collected, and we are not recommending that all of it be collected. Much of the information may already exist, and the remaining should be relatively easy to collect. Perhaps asking the funding agency how important the information is to them might guide your decisions. On the other hand, your judgment of how "different" as compared to how "important" your context is from that of others may help make the decision. If you think your context is very different, and it is important for at least some stakeholders to know that, then describe the context. The next sections discuss potential kinds of context information.

Community Information

Community information such as socioeconomic status (SES), population density, number of languages spoken, and mobility are just a few of the variables that could describe the community. Information about previous efforts by the community to have a program like the new one might also be valuable. The amount of support (or nonsupport) of the new program would certainly be valuable information.

Central Office Staff Information

Central office staff information, such as organizational charts showing lines of authority, are often quite valuable. Who the program director reports to can often be valuable information to the evaluator and ultimately to the success of the program. The amount and kinds of central office support for those delivering the services are also usually very critical. Hatry (1994) and Nightengale and Rossman (1994) provide additional suggestions for collecting data from agency records.

Site Demographics

Site demographics may be different from one site to another. Even the physical arrangement, including number of classrooms and proximity of the site administrator to each staff member at the site may have an impact on the productivity at that site.

Site Staff Information

Site staff information, such as their previous training, experience in the program (or similar programs), "team spirit," and involvement in the development of the program can all be of value to the program director. These variables may also help explain why the program achieved different results at different sites.

The Overall Existing Program

The overall existing program should be described, and then site deviations can be documented. The program director can then either tolerate these deviations or work to sell the new program (either without deviations or with fewer deviations) to the sites. It is important not to assume that the existing program was (and the new program will be) implemented in exactly the same way at each site.

The Overall Picture of Participants

The overall picture of participants can be painted with such information as number of participants, their SES, language spoken at home, and mobility rate. However, participants also may be different from one site to the next. Moreover, since these participant differences may affect the success level of the program at that site, they should be documented.

When to Document Context Information

The context information should ideally be documented before the new program is implemented. Often the new program is the impetus (in terms of person power, financial resources, and need to know) for the collection of some of the context information. In these cases, the context information is collected as part of the evaluation of the new program and should be collected as soon as the program is funded. If the information is not collected immediately, it may be difficult to accurately obtain what is now historical information. The information may be nonexistent, difficult to obtain, or fuzzy in the minds of the information providers because of recent changes. Human beings often have less capacity for accurate recall than for selective recall, faulty recall, or no recall at all.

Who Collects the Context Information?

The program staff and the program director can provide much of the context information. They may already know much of the information, and they will benefit from knowing the remaining information. The program director and the evaluator should decide on the remaining information that needs to be collected. The information can be collected through structured interviews, as in "A Structured Interview" in appendix D. A structured interview contains all the questions that the interviewer asks and is used when no further questions or follow-up clarifications are desired. When you want to obtain the same information from each site, such a structured interview is desired. If the information is straightforward and does not really require an interviewer, a short survey can be distributed to the sites. Site administrators can fill out the survey at their convenience, saving some information collection time. (See "A Survey for Collecting Context Information" in appendix D for an example of a survey used to collect context information.)

How to Analyze Context Information

The analysis of context information is usually simple frequencies and percentages, along with some prose. If there are several sites, the analysis should provide the same information for each site. The report should be as brief as possible.

INPUT INFORMATION COLLECTED AND ANALYZED

The input information identifies what resources were involved in the program and when they were made available. Existing programs, as well as new programs, need financial, physical, and personnel resources to operate. These resources need to be at least at a minimum level for the program to operate. Moreover, they need to be in place in a reasonable time frame in order to facilitate the program. There are three purposes for obtaining input information. The first purpose is to document the amount of resources in the program. The amount of resources includes not only the actual dollar allocation, but also the in-kind contribution of the organization. Examples of in-kind contribution include these: (a) The program may be housed in an existing building provided by the organization; (b) the program may be supported by central office staff who provide such support as accounting documentation, employee benefits, and community liaisons; and (c) the support may be in terms of transportation of participants or publicizing the program.

The second purpose is to document when these resources become available to the program. Just because an organization was awarded a $5 million grant does not mean that all that money was available on day 1 of the program. If all the red tape has not yet been completed, it is highly possible that none of the money is available, and the organization may have to support the program until all the red tape has been completed. If some of the materials have not yet arrived or have not been made available to staff, the program should not be held accountable. The following paragraph contains an example of tests not being available at baseline.

Having tests available at baseline can be problematic, as funding may have only recently been approved and made available to the program director. Region 19 Head Start ordered tests that the funding agency required them to use in evaluating their State Literacy Initiative. In several cases, only one vendor—the company that developed the test in the first place—sold a particular test. The Region 19 central office required each of the vendors to sign a letter indicating that they were the only one selling that particular test. One of the vendors was a little lax in signing the letter, and hence the tests were late in arriving. Instead of waiting for all four tests to arrive, the baseline was initiated with two of the tests. When the final test did arrive, testers were trained on the test and returned to the sites to test the children on the remaining two tests. As sometimes happens, what was initially a problem turned into a positive solution. The length of the testing session for all four tests had been estimated to be just 75 minutes. Actually, the first two tests took about 80 minutes. If the 3-year-olds and 4-year-olds had been tested on all four tests at one time, the testing session would have been over 2 hours long; many would have become restless, and the testing situation would have deteriorated.

The third purpose is to document the use of the resources. Funded budgets are often amended to reflect program needs that were not originally envisioned. For instance, if the assistant program director is not hired until 4 months into the program, the salary that is not used for the assistant program director can be used elsewhere. Additional organizational resources may be made available (or needed, and not made available). The program director may determine that additional staff development should occur or that a more costly curriculum should be implemented.

What Kind of Input Information?

The input information represents the infrastructure of the program—the finances that were available and used to buy the infrastructure. If the infrastructure does not exist, then the program cannot have its intended effect. If the infrastructure is not completed on time, the program may be substantially hindered. Experienced program planners incorporate the expectation that a new program cannot be implemented as soon as funding is made available. Some organizations even wait an entire year before conducting post assessment of a new program. "One Way to Document Input Information" in appendix F provides one example of how input information can be documented.

When to Document Input Information

The procedure for documenting input information should be designed at the beginning of the program. Documenting when resources are brought into the picture should be an ongoing process. If you wait until the end of the year, the actual dates may be forgotten or become fuzzy in your memory. The more systematic the record-keeping, the easier in the long run to document and to assess the impact of the various inputs. We recommend updating the input information at the end of each week.

Who Collects the Input Information?

The program director is the best person to record the input information. That person is the most knowledgeable about the proposed budget and the actual expenditures, presuming the program director signs off on the purchase orders and the staffing. The program director's supervisor and assistants may also be involved in identifying input information, particularly in-kind inputs from the organization. The staff might more accurately know the actual dates that some inputs are received. Discussing input information during regular staff meetings may help to avoid problems, or at least to identify problems. The evaluator is involved only to the extent of setting up the process and ensuring that the input information is being collected in a timely fashion.

How to Analyze Input Information

The analysis consists of two parts. First, the facts can be presented, and second, the effect of those facts on the program can be discussed. The facts can be presented in tabular form, as in "One Way to Document Input Information" in appendix F. The exact timing of the various inputs is not up for interpretation (whether they occurred before schedule, on schedule, or behind schedule). What is up for interpretation is the effect of those inputs. One of the many responsibilities of the program director is to make the best of inputs that do not occur as scheduled. Not being able to fill personnel positions in a timely manner, for whatever reason, may have a short-term positive impact on the budget, but a long-lasting negative impact on the program.

An analysis of the impact of delayed resources is the second part of the analysis of input information. Because the program director is the primary author of the input report, the slant could become self-serving. For instance, a report that says "the program was a failure because the funding was late and the organization refused to allow me to hire staff until the 3rd month of the program" could be a result of the program director not understanding how to get things accomplished in the organization, rather than funds not being available. The evaluator must critically review the draft input report to separate the real problems from the imaginary ones.

PROGRAM IMPLEMENTATION INFORMATION COLLECTED AND ANALYZED

Process information is information collected on what is usually thought of as "the program." Process information includes the training of staff and how the staff provides services to the participants. The focus is on the direct services, not on the effects of those services. Most of the process information would be collected at the beginning of the program so that changes in the delivery of the program can be made as a function of the process information results. If the processes are not being implemented well, they need to be modified. This modification should occur as soon as possible so that the product results can occur at the expected level.

What Kind of Process Information?

As indicated above, process information falls into two major categories: staff development and direct services. The two categories are interrelated, as the scope and quality of staff development has an impact on the quality of direct services.

Staff Development

Staff development should be identified in the initial needs assessment. These topics should be sequenced and the timing of the various staff development sessions planned so that (a) the material is presented as soon as possible, (b) the sessions are spaced so that staff have an opportunity to try to implement what was learned in the staff development, (c) there is monitoring of staff to determine if they are integrating the staff development in their delivery of the program, and (d) there is continuous and available central office support for those providing direct services.

In our experience, staff development is often not well planned and is usually seen as unavoidable by staff. Staff often are overloaded with ideas but provided few practical techniques that can be used without modification. Often there is no connection between one staff development session and the next. Most staff developers are unaware of what staff development has already occurred. In other instances, material presented duplicates material presented in recent staff development sessions. Part of the responsibility of the program director is to plan the staff development to avoid these problems. Desimone, Porter, Garet, Yoon, and Birman (2002) identified six key features from the literature. These included three structural features: (a) the activity organized as a reform type in contrast to a traditional workshop, course, or conference, (b) the duration of the staff development, and (c) the collective participation of groups of teachers from the same unit. They identified three core features: (a) active learning, (b) coherence in each teacher's professional development, and (c) the degree to which the activity has a content focus. Their national evaluation found that most district-supported professional development did not have the six characteristics.

The planning should be based on the initial needs assessment, as well as information gained throughout the life of the program. Staff should be asked at the end of each staff development session about the quality of the material presented. In addition, they should be asked if they would be able to implement the presented ideas and material. Staff should be asked to identify additional topics they think should be included in future staff development sessions—in reality a continuous needs assessment. Finally, staff should be observed when they are providing services to determine if the desired goals of the staff development are indeed being achieved.

"Example of a Staff Development Evaluation" in appendix D contains a staff development evaluation form that addresses all of the above topics, with the exception of the final aspect of observation, which is discussed later. Section A contains the list of all the staff development topics and identifies the one being evaluated. This puts the present topic in focus for the staff and for the staff developer. Section B obtains demographic information, without identifying the specific person. Such anonymous evaluations are usually the most honest and the most valuable. Section C focuses on how well the topics were covered, using a Likert response scale. Section D requests an assessment of how likely the participant is to implement techniques, and Section E asks the participant to identify two specific techniques that will be implemented in the next 2 weeks. Asking participants to identify two specific techniques focuses them on the staff development session, and it can provide the evaluator guidance in subsequent observation. Section F is the continuous needs assessment. Answers in this section should be read carefully before action is taken. If the identified topics are the same as those supposedly already covered in previous staff development sessions, then those previous staff development sessions either did not present the topics or did not present them well. If the identified topics are new ones, and a substantial number of staff indicates the topic, then that topic should be covered in a future staff development session.

Staff development presenters should be made aware of the evaluation form. They can be involved in the development of sections C and D and should definitely be provided the results. Involving them in the evaluation makes them accountable.

We have seen too many staff development presenters appear on the scene from more than 50 miles away (which automatically makes them an expert), perform their "dog and pony show," and leave. These presenters did not know or care about (a) why they were there, (b) who the audience really was, (c) what specific needs the audience had, (d) what previous staff development occurred, (e) what the topics for future staff development were, or (f) what the staff's evaluation of their staff development was. These staff development presenters are usually paid enough to care about these issues. It is the responsibility of the program director and the evaluator to make sure they do care. Making staff developers aware of the evaluation form before they have traveled their 50 miles is one step in that direction.

Delivery of Direct Services

Delivery of direct services is the second category of process information that should be evaluated. Just because there is a written plan for
the delivery of services and there is staff development does not mean
that staff will want to, or can, implement the program well. If the program is not implemented well, then the proposed products of the program will likely not occur (or if the proposed products do occur, they
are not a result of the planned program). Most staff in the helping professions are dedicated to quality service, want to help participants, and
have the basic skills and knowledge to provide quality service. Not all,
though, may be as committed to following "the program." In addition,
not all may be as capable of providing the necessary program services.
Wanting to provide good services and having the basic knowledge and
skills are necessary but not sufficient ingredients. Following the prescribed program is another necessary ingredient. Wanting to provide
good services and following the program should lead to successful
products. However, before products are looked at, successful implementation of the program should be assured.

For the purposes of delivering a program, staff skills and knowledge
can be thought of as an iceberg. Approximately 90% of the iceberg is
below water. You cannot see the part of the iceberg below the water, but
it is there, supporting the tip. What is below water is analogous to the
basic skills and knowledge of staff—aspects that are crucial to delivery
of services, but often not a part of "the program." The program is usually an addition to the basic knowledge and skills. Programs presume
that staff have the basics and build on those basics. The various tips of
the iceberg can be thought of as topics crucial to the implementation of
the program and hence topics presented at the staff development sessions. Note that neither is the entire program presented in staff development nor may all the tips be covered in staff development. When an
evaluator observes in the field, what is seen is the whole iceberg, and
any inadequacies in any part of the iceberg may have a negative impact
on ability to implement the program. The focus of observations is "the
program" and, specifically, the topics covered in staff development.

Process information should be collected on a regular basis from each
of the persons providing direct service. Such observations should be

presented to staff as evaluations of the program in general and staff development in particular. Since the evaluator is usually not the supervisor of staff, the information obtained in observations should not be used for individual staff performance evaluations. Staff, though, would be well advised to listen to what the evaluator might say.

One frequent source of process information is observation of classroom teachers. One example of classroom observation is in "Another Example of a Classroom Evaluation Form" in appendix D, used in an evaluation of the State Literacy Initiative in Head Start. These items identify specific teacher strategies that were supposed to be part of the literacy initiative. The items were identified as soon as the program was funded in multiple sites in Texas. Each site was funded to provide staff development in the areas needed. Much effort was spent to get programs in various agencies to be uniform in terms of their implementation.

Supervisors of staff can also provide process information. Specifically, principals in schools where the program is implemented need to be aware of the program and supportive of the program. When evaluators observe teachers in a school, they should arrange to discuss their observations with the principal. Evaluators should always respect the fact that when they are in a building such as a school, they are guests in someone's home. They need to respect the rules of that home, and keep the "homeowners" informed of what they see going on in the home. During such discussions with principals, questions can be asked of the principals to identify their knowledge of, and commitment to, the program. "Interview of Principals" in appendix D contains one such interview protocol. See "Example of a Chart Essay" in appendix F for a summary of the results obtained with this protocol.

Sometimes part of the planned process evaluation is to meet with parents. Parents should be aware of the program and should be supportive of the program. If either of these two goals is not being met early in the life of the program, the program director must do something about that, or the life of the program may not be very long.

The form "Parent Meeting Evaluation" in appendix D follows several guidelines. First, the form is short. Second, the form does not ask for the name of the parent or child, and the demographic information cannot identify any particular parent. Third, the questions ask for perceptions, not knowledge. Parents should feel good about what the school is doing for their child, and they should have a general idea of the program. Detailed knowledge of the program is the responsibility of those delivering the program. Fourth, a valuable item that should be included is to ask if parents have learned new activities that can help their child. Parents that come to parent meetings are usually the ones that are interested in helping their child. Moreover, the program should build on this desire by incorporating such topics into the parent meeting.

A final process activity evaluation form that we would like to discuss is one of parents visiting schools, specifically Head Start parents visiting the public school that their child will be going to next year. The form "Evaluation of Parents Visiting Schools" in appendix D was part of the Head Start Transition evaluation. Parents and their children were bussed from the Head Start site to the next year's public school. The school staff knew that they were going to visit, and usually had planned for the visit. The program director wanted to know (a) how many parents took part in the visit, (b) how the principal treated them, and (c) how the parents felt about the visit. Notice the use of faces in "Evaluation of Parents Visiting Schools" in appendix D.

When to Report Process Information

The process information should be documented as soon as each activity has been completed. Any confusion or expressed additional needs should be incorporated as soon as possible. Feedback to the program director, staff developers, and staff should be completed as soon as possible. Staff should see the summary of the process evaluations to establish that their evaluations are looked at. Evidence that the program director incorporates or acts on their evaluations is even more crucial. Why would anyone want to continually provide their views when they do not have any evidence that anyone is listening?

Observations should begin to occur early in the program implementation and should continue to occur periodically throughout the year. The more often the evaluator observes direct services, the less threatening the evaluator's presence is. The increased rapport between evaluator and staff usually leads to more and better quality information. More importantly, the more rapport, the more likely the staff is to divulge difficulties with program implementation. Admitting that you have a problem and seeking out a solution are the first two steps to improvement.

Who Collects the Process Information?

The evaluator is ultimately responsible for the collection of process information. In practice, the program director likely attends all of the staff development sessions, staff meetings, and planning sessions, and therefore is in a position to economically collect the information from those process activities. We strongly urge that the evaluator be responsible for setting up the information collection process, particularly for the staff development. The staff development sessions are critical to the success of a new program. Not only is the content of staff development critical, but also critical is the attitude of the program director and the staff developer to the delivery of staff development.

How to Analyze Process Information

Frequencies and percentages are usually sufficient analyses of process information. If the objective was to conduct six staff development sessions, then it is sufficient to list those (minimally six) sessions. If the objective was to get at least 80% of the participants to agree that the staff development focused on a need relevant to the program, then the percentage of participants agreeing is sufficient information. The documentation of process information is the number of participants responding in a certain way and the level of their response. Additional ideas on collecting and analyzing process information can be found in Scheirer (1994).

WRITE REPORTS

Some evaluations consist of only one report at the end of the year (usually several months after the end of the year). A report at this time does not provide information for decisions throughout the year, nor is it likely to be disseminated in time for program modification for the subsequent year. One of the basic tenets of GEM is to provide evaluation information continuously to relevant stakeholders. Therefore, we emphasize brief evaluation reports following each major activity. All of these interim reports can then be easily integrated into a final report at the end of the year.

Context Report

Usually the program director and program staff are aware of the relevant context information, so the context report is often not a crucial one. Rather than assuming it may not be crucial, it is better to finish the context report early in the life of the program. That way the program director, program staff, and staff developers can become informed regarding the entire context in which the program is implemented.

The information in the context report is of varying value to the various stakeholders. All the stakeholders know some of the information. Other information may be new to some and already known to others. Finally, some information is new to all stakeholders. Information that is already known is still of value, because stakeholders often feel validated when, for instance, information about their site has been shared with others. You may already know, for instance, that the huge proportion of children on free and reduced meals particularly challenges your school. Knowing that your colleagues in the more affluent schools also now have that same information can be comforting. Knowing how affluent those schools are may not be as comforting but may lead to further understanding.

The tables of contents of two context reports are in appendix F. "Table of Contents of a Context Report" is for a context report that followed the format of previous years and context reports from other programs in that same school district. Therefore, the information is probably not as valuable for the stakeholders of that particular program. "Table of Contents for a Context Report for a Stand-Alone Educational Program," on the other hand, is for a context report that was written specifically for that program. There were no outside constraints as to what information had to be collected. In fact, the kinds of information to be collected were discussed and cleared with the program director.

Once the context report is shared with stakeholders, additional context information might be identified, resulting in the need for additional context reports. In general, you cannot have too much information, as long as that information is presented clearly and is of use to decision makers.

The context report should be distilled into the end-of-cycle report. Because the context report can be referenced and will have been available for interested stakeholders to read, only the most important context information should be in the final report.

Input Report(s)

We suggest that an input report be completed soon after the program is begun—say 1 month after planned start-up. Those new programs that are implemented in large organizations may not receive the attention that is necessary to begin in a timely fashion. An evaluation report documenting that problem may assist the program director in getting the program implemented. (See "Example of a Table of Contents of an Input Report" in appendix F for an example.)

Additional reports should be planned on a periodic basis until all problems have been resolved. When major problems surface, additional input evaluation reports are called for. These reports should be relatively short, should focus on the current situation, and should minimize the expected problems caused by late implementation. The highlights of the input reports should then be folded into the end-of-cycle report. No new input information should appear in the final report. New assessments of the value and damage of early or late input, though, can and should be included.

Process Report(s)

A process report should be written at the conclusion of each major program activity. The more timely the reports, the more convinced all stakeholders become that evaluation is an important part of the program. Frequent process reports keep the program director and program staff informed and accountable for their efforts. Figure 6.2 contains an example of a process report figure. The figure indicates the technical

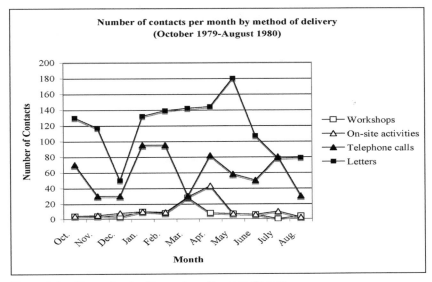

Figure 6.2.   Example of a Figure for a Process Report

assistance activities of a technical assistance center serving six states. Breaking the data down by month and method of delivery can identify weak areas and annual trends.

These process reports will also be condensed into the final report. The final report will need to tie each of these reports together and assess their combined impact. However, the majority of the evaluator's work will have been completed with these frequent process reports.

Keeping the Stakeholders Informed

We suggest that the program director formalize the roles of the various stakeholders into an advisory board. These advisory board members would be considered representatives of the various stakeholders and can act as the communication link between the program and the stakeholders. As such, they need to be kept informed not only of the program, but also of the evaluation. Therefore, the evaluator should have a regular slot on the agenda of the advisory board meetings. These meetings then become part of the program and as such should be evaluated. One informal way of evaluating advisory board meetings appears in appendix D. Notice that the evaluation form is completed anonymously. The form begins with requesting nonthreatening information. The first constructed response item focuses on the positive advisory board activities ("the best thing"), while the second focuses on negative advisory board activities ("would have been better"). The last item invites the advisory board members to identify additional items for the next meeting's agenda—a needs assessment for the next advisory board meeting.

RELATE TO OBJECTIVES AND PROCEDURES TO ACHIEVE OBJECTIVES

The numerous process activities and the reports of those activities should remain focused on the objectives. Reflecting on the link of the activities to the objectives is a valuable exercise. The old adage "Don't lose sight of the forest for all the trees" applies here. Evaluating each staff development program and observing delivery of services can be challenging and exciting. However, just because the staff development is occurring and some services are being provided does not mean that the program staff are focused on the objectives. Figure 6.3 indicates the desired (and often assumed) state of affairs—the program is totally connected to the objectives. Ideally, there is an isomorphic relationship between the program and the objectives. The program focuses on all the objectives and nothing more. While this is an ideal situation, it rarely occurs. There can be a mismatch between the program staff, the program, and the objectives in numerous ways.

Figure 6.3B illustrates the more likely state of affairs—the program is only partially overlapping with the objectives. Some of what the program is and does is unrelated to the objectives—while some of the program is in fact responsive to the objectives. Obviously, the overlap is much greater in some programs than in others.

Figure 6.3C is the extreme case of no overlap between program and objectives; though unlikely to occur, it can and has. In such situations, no matter what occurs in the program, logically there will be no concomitant change in the objectives.

Figure 6.3D depicts the situation wherein the program is focused on only some of the objectives. The program has been implemented

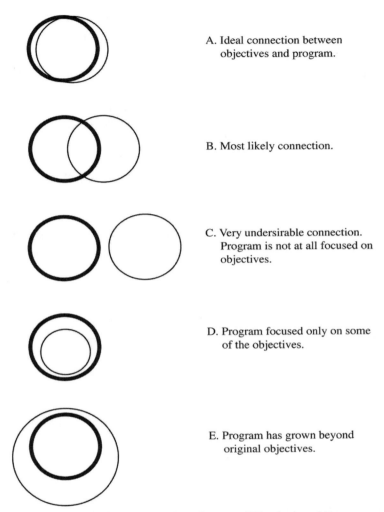

A. Ideal connection between objectives and program.

B. Most likely connection.

C. Very undersirable connection. Program is not at all focused on objectives.

D. Program focused only on some of the objectives.

E. Program has grown beyond original objectives.

Figure 6.3.   Possible Relationships Between Objectives and Program

more microscopically than had been planned. In this case, the program may have an effect on some of the objectives, but not all of the objectives. The evaluator documents that some of the objectives were not met, when in fact the program did not attend to those objectives.

Figure 6.3E illustrates an overly ambitious program—one that focuses on more than it was funded to focus on. For some reason, the program has mushroomed into more than was originally envisioned. When this happens, the program may become too diffuse and not meet some or all of the objectives.

The program director should be keeping abreast of the evaluation reports. The current situation is hopefully an overlap, as in Figure 6.3B. The responsibility of the program director is to make the overlap more like Figure 6.3A and to prevent it from being like Figure 6.3C, 6.3D, or 6.3E. If there is no overlap, as in Figure 6.3C, then the program must be redirected. If the program has become too focused, then it needs to be redirected to attend to all of the stated objectives. Finally, if the program has mushroomed, the program director needs to rein it in, to refocus it on the objectives.

A summary table, like the one presented in "Summary Table of Percent of Objectives Met" in appendix F, can facilitate the above decisions. This table has several interesting aspects. First, the information is presented as a report card. Stakeholders in an early childhood education program would understand the purpose of a report card. Second, the objectives are stated in general terms, and are grouped by roles in the program. Third, the percent met is reported for each year of operation, so the reader can see how the program is functioning over time. Fourth, some areas were not to be evaluated until the program had matured (in some cases not until the first cohort finished 1st grade).

DISSEMINATE THE REPORTS

Sharing implementation information with all stakeholders is important. Those providing direct services are usually more interested in the implementation results than are other stakeholders. As indicated in a previous section, reports on individual staff development sessions should be disseminated as soon as possible. Staff developers, staff attending staff development, and the program director should all carefully read the implementation reports to make sure that (a) the material that was planned to be covered in the staff development was in fact covered, (b) the staff learned the material, (c) the staff was able to implement the material, and (d) the staff incorporates the material in a routine fashion in their delivery of services.

Evaluation of each activity may be of less interest to some stakeholders such as the advisory board. They will likely be more interested in a summary table, such as the report card depicted in "Summary Table of Percent of Objectives Met" in appendix F.

CHAPTER 7

Post Assessment

Most programs are either funded or implemented on an annual basis. Therefore, it is usually the case that the evaluation is conducted on an annual basis. That is, all of the GEM stages occur every cycle. See Figure 7.1 for the placement of the post assessment stage in GEM. For programs that are funded for longer than one cycle, the focus in the evaluation plan may be different from cycle to cycle. For instance, the focus on product information may increase over the life of the program.

The post assessment information is primarily product information. The context, input, and process information was collected, analyzed, and disseminated during the program implementation assessment stage. The effectiveness objectives are the ones that will be focused on in this stage. The question being answered, in general, is, "How much effect has the program had?"

DEVELOP POST ASSESSMENT EVALUATION PLAN

The first task in this stage is the same as the first task in the previous stage—develop the evaluation plan. This plan is different in that it focuses on the effectiveness of objectives. The plan dovetails into Stage 2—baseline—in the sense that much of the information collected at that time is baseline assessment that is compared with performance at post assessment. Some effectiveness objectives do not require a baseline assessment, though having a baseline is advantageous. Without baseline information, how, for instance, would you know that 70% passing is a good passing rate? The first question that someone is likely

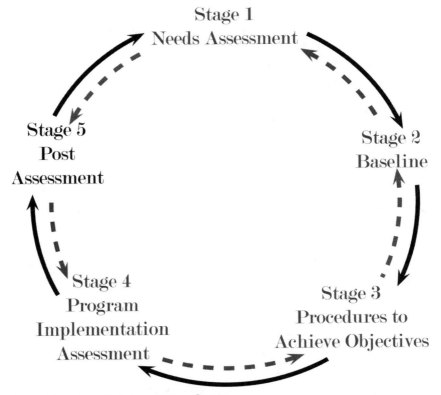

Figure 7.1.   The Post Assessment Stage
Note: Solid arrows indicate the primary direction of the flow of the evaluation from one stage to the next stage. Dashed arrows indicate the feedback from one stage to a previous stage—actually feedback can go to any previous stage.

to ask is, "How high was the passing rate before the program was implemented?"

The post assessment evaluation plan should be written early in the life of the evaluation. The plan provides a rationale for the various baseline assessments. The plan identifies the kinds of measures that must be ordered or developed and the number of those instruments that must be available. In addition, the plan should indicate how much time will be devoted to testing and how much person power will be required to collect and analyze the information, document the results, and disseminate the report.

The post assessment evaluation plan should be developed by the evaluator but discussed and approved by the program director. The evaluator has the technical skills to develop the plan and should have the experience to identify problems and shortcuts. The program director can assist in such matters as (a) the number of instruments needed, (b) anticipated staff turnover, and (c) possible problems in information collection such as holidays, site personnel who cannot be depended upon to collect information, and variations in how information is currently being collected across sites.

One possible post assessment evaluation plan is:

August	Develop program implementation assessment plan
	Collect baseline information
September	Develop post assessment evaluation plan
November	Identify post assessment instruments
December	Develop post assessment instruments
	Order post assessment instruments
May	Collect post assessment information
	Analyze post assessment information
June	Write up report
	Disseminate report
July	Determine evaluation for next cycle

We have included the development of the program implementation assessment plan and the collection of the baseline information because these two tasks are integral to the post assessment evaluation plan. In addition, since these occur at the beginning of the program cycle, we scheduled the development of the post assessment evaluation plan after the hectic first month. Much of the baseline information will be part of the post assessment evaluation plan, but additional information might need to be collected at the end of the program cycle. Hence, those additional measures should be identified early enough so they can be developed or identified and ordered. These two tasks are scheduled in November and December, early enough to have the measures available for post assessment in May. The post assessment should occur as close to the end of the program cycle as possible to allow the program to have its maximum effect yet provide time for analysis, writing up the report, and disseminating the report. These three tasks are all planned for May and June in order to allow time for the incorporation of these results into the planning of the program and the planning of the evaluation for the subsequent cycle. If this were the last cycle of the program, the analysis, write-up, and dissemination should be spread over a longer period to allow for reflection on the evaluation of the entire life of the program.

Heck and Crislip (2001) discussed the use of performance-based writing measures as a part of large-scale student testing and school accountability programs. They highlight the dilemma of using multiple measures in any evaluation.

> The increased economic costs of developing, administering, and scoring writing performance assessments must be balanced against the social and political costs of continued over reliance on standardized multiple-choice tests that may be less useful in monitoring what students can do as a result of their educations and may also be biased in known and unknown ways for some groups of students. (p. 32)

IDENTIFY INSTRUMENTS

As indicated above, many of the instruments used at post assessment are the same as those used at baseline. Some objectives may not require a baseline assessment, so the measurement of those objectives do not occur at baseline, only at post assessment.

Some instruments have more than one form—supposedly parallel forms. Parallel forms are two or more forms of a test that are equivalent in terms of the content. They have been developed to respond to the concern that some people may remember items on the baseline and thus do better on the post assessment because of remembering those items rather than as a function of the program. Our position is that for this to be a problem the following must occur:

1. The person must remember specific items.
2. If the person thinks that he or she missed the item, he or she must somehow make an effort to find out the right answer.
3. The person must recognize the item at post assessment.
4. The person must recollect the right answer.

In programs that cover 8 months or more, steps 3 and 4 above are highly unlikely to occur. Investment in parallel forms is not, in our opinion, worth the effort and expense. The following paragraph provides a personal experience that one of us had that supports our contention.

When Keith McNeil moved to North Carolina, he had already passed the driver's license test in four other states and had driven for some 14 years. He did not study the North Carolina driving laws manual. What a mistake, since the entire test was on the specific laws of North Carolina. (One example: What is the maximum speed of school buses on interstates in North Carolina? Answer—35.) Why, you might ask? High school seniors were allowed to drive school buses (at least in 1972) in North Carolina, and therefore each bus was equipped with a governor restricting the speed. After studying the manual, he went back 2 weeks later and took the test again. However, whether any of the items on the second administration were on the first administration was a mystery. He knew, in general, that all of the items on both administrations were on North Carolina–specific laws, but he could not remember whether any specific items were on both administrations.

DEVELOP INSTRUMENTS (IF NECESSARY)

Instruments administered at baseline are already available and therefore do not need to be developed. Possibly a few instruments will be administered only at post assessment, and some of those may need to be developed. These should be developed during the less hectic time of evaluation, during the middle of the program cycle. Developing these instruments early in the program cycle allows the program director to review the instrument and may provide some direction to the program director or the program staff. It is always comforting to know how you will be evaluated. One likely type of instrument that needs to be developed is that of a survey. We want to emphasize that you do not just "throw together" a survey. We say this because we have seen many that were obviously constructed that way. There should be a plan for the development of the survey; the plan must consider many issues. Here is a list of 23 questions that we think must be answered in the development of a survey (Newman & McNeil, 1998):

1. What are the basic questions I want my survey to answer?
2. How do I plan to use the information?

3. Whom do I plan to survey to obtain those answers?
4. What assistance do I need in surveying people?
5. What types of analyses are required?
6. Are computer programs available?
7. What is the population to which I am interested in generalizing?
8. What are the characteristics of the population to which I am interested in generalizing?
9. How does the accessible population differ from the population to which I want to generalize?
10. How has volunteering affected my results?
11. Where can I look for information?
12. What are the key terms for my literature search?
13. What are the best sources of information?
14. What survey procedures should I use?
15. Should I use an existing survey or develop my own?
16. Who should administer the survey?
17. What are the item format considerations?
18. What are the psychometric considerations?
19. What are the piloting considerations?
20. What are the training considerations?
21. How should I sample?
22. What analyses should I perform?
23. How should I write my report?

COLLECT POST ASSESSMENT INFORMATION

All of the considerations for collecting information discussed in chapter 4 that were relevant at baseline are also relevant at post assessment. Those considerations were discussed in chapter 4 and are repeated here.

1. Reread purpose in program plan and evaluation plan
2. Obtain instruments
3. Arrange for testers
4. Pilot instrument administration
5. Plan for instrument administration
6. Collect information

Several other considerations arise at post assessment. First, information should be collected under the same conditions at post assessment as at baseline. Second, as far as possible, the same sample should be tested on both occasions. Third, staff should be reminded that inflation of post assessment scores does negatively affect the evaluation for the subsequent cycle. These considerations are discussed in the following sections.

Collect Information Under the Same Conditions at Post Assessment as at Baseline

In order for a valid comparison to be made between the two testing times, the conditions should be as similar as possible. It is advantageous to have the same testers collecting the information. If replacement testers are needed, they should be trained to the same extent as those trained at baseline.

If information was collected in an individual setting at baseline, then it should not be collected in a group setting at post assessment. If the evaluation form was completed as an integral part of the first staff development meeting, then it should not be distributed at the end of the meeting for staff to fill out as they are packing up and leaving for the day.

We realize that evaluation in the real world is confronted with change and that all conditions at post assessment cannot be the same as those that existed at baseline. Even when using the same testers, they will be different—they will know that post assessment information collection occurs at a later point in time than the baseline. They may have increased expectations of what program staff and participants should be accomplishing. The more consistent the information collection conditions, the fewer the competing explainers about the results. Competing explainers are those extraneous aspects that might have been the cause of the results, rather than the program that was implemented being the cause of the results.

In order to use the norms tables from a standardized instrument, the standardized instrument should be administered under exactly the same conditions as specified in the administration manual. For instance, if standardized instruments were administered in the afternoon at baseline, they should not be administered in the morning at post assessment. If children were administered two of the instruments in one setting and the other two instruments in a later setting at baseline, that should be the administration procedure at post assessment.

If Sample Participants, Assess the Same Participants at Post Assessment

The rationale behind assessing the same participants is that many competing explainers can be eliminated when you use each participant as his or her own match. By assessing the same individual on two occasions, you avoid differences in the two samples. Repeated measures statistical procedures, discussed in a later section, take advantage of the fact that you have assessed the same person. Assessing the same individuals leads to more precise estimates of program effects, and therefore is more likely to find those program effects.

Consider Some of the Post Assessment Information as Baseline Information for the Subsequent Cycle

One reason for this suggestion is to reduce the burden of information collection. The burden is in terms of financial costs of collecting the information as well as time taken away from delivery of services to participants. We would like evaluations to be as nondisruptive and transparent as possible, but a large amount of time and resources must be devoted to evaluation, particularly if the evaluation is a thorough one. Using one information collection for post assessment for one cycle and baseline for the subsequent cycle is one way of reducing cost and disruption.

A second reason for considering the post assessment as a baseline for the subsequent cycle is that some (not all, not even many) staff may try to inflate post assessment measures so that they look good. These inflation efforts are particularly likely if program staff, rather than evaluators, administer the post assessments. You avoid that potential problem by having someone other than program staff do the testing. The ideal situation is the least biased estimate of participants and program performance possible—normal testing yielding "truth." Inflation of performance usually is detected and is misleading, if not harmful to participants, program, or funding agency. Inflated scores at post assessment are also harmful if the post assessment is used as the baseline measure for the next year.

ANALYZE ALL INFORMATION

Most of the analysis procedures used at baseline are employed again at post assessment. Some additional objectives, though, require assessing whether minimum requirements have been met at post assessment. In addition, procedures are employed to compare the performance at post assessment to that at baseline.

Same Analysis Procedures at Post Assessment as at Baseline

Whenever possible, the same analysis procedures should be used at the end of the cycle as at the beginning because stakeholders are often uncomfortable with analysis of information, and the more consistent you can be, the better you can communicate. Often an evaluator uses a less powerful statistical technique than would a statistician or lives with possibly questionable statistical assumptions just to conduct a "more understandable" analysis. In addition, if you change the analysis at post assessment time, you may raise the question in the minds of some stakeholders, "Why wasn't that analysis conducted on the baseline information?" In some cases, the participants do not stay very long, or they come and go at various times. Such programs are particularly difficult to evaluate.

The evaluation of Neglected and Delinquent Programs is compromised by the various entrance and exit dates of the recipients. As usual, the best approach is to collect data on as many participants as possible. The report should contain caveats, as below:

> Some difficulties in the collection and interpretation are presented because: (a) many students leave the institution before the staff is able to obtain posttest data, (b) the short stay of most of the students does not justify a regular testing schedule to circumvent the problem, and (c) the calculated gain score over such a short period of time is less reliable than

when collected over a longer period of time. . . . The GEU (grade equivalent unit) was calculated for only those students who were available for both pretesting and posttesting. Thus, one is cautioned that generalizations from the results described in this report may not be appropriate for those students who exit from the institution before a posttest can be obtained. (McNeil, 1976, pp. 5, 8)

Descriptive Analyses

Descriptive analyses are those that describe the sample and the sample only. These analyses do not lead to inferences to the larger population or to the future—such work is reserved for inferential analyses, discussed in the next section.

Descriptive analyses consist of central tendency measures including mean, median, and mode. These indexes all indicate "where the scores tend to bunch." For instance, the evaluator might report the median income of families being served or the modal number of children in the family. The specific definition of each measure and when it would be most appropriately used are contained in "Descriptive Statistics and When Most Appropriately Used" in appendix G.

Inferential Analyses

Inferential analyses are used when there is the desire to infer to the entire population from which the sample was obtained. The more likely situation is when the evaluator wants to convey some assurance that the results are stable, that they did not occur as a result of random data, and that they would occur again (during the next cycle) when the same program is implemented. In fact, our contention is that seldom are participants sampled from the population of interest; the only interesting population is the one that will occur in the next cycle and the cycles thereafter. Obtaining a random sample from those populations is impossible. What is desired is that the sample be as representative as possible of the desired population.

While most statistical procedures, including the Pearson product moment correlation, report the linear fit to the data, many relationships are not linear. Fuller and Strath (2001) reported that some studies have revealed that the lowest availability of center-based programs (for young children) may be in middle-income communities. Specifically, Gordon and Chase-Landsdale (1999) found that typical zip codes in both low- and high-income areas have 25 to 55 pre-school-age children for each operating center, compared to 75 to 85 children per center in middle-income zip codes. Fuller and Liang (1997) made the same curvilinear finding.

The objectives can best be evaluated by eliminating competing explainers. A good way of eliminating these competing explainers is by matching each baseline score with the same participant's post assessment score. The most thorough way is to use analysis of covariance to statistically adjust the post assessment means by taking into consideration the baseline performance—thereby leveling the playing field. This procedure is particularly valuable in evaluation because seldom does an evaluator or a program director have the opportunity to randomly assign participants to the "new treatment" program and the "comparison" program. There are likely to be initial differences between these groups as well as initial differences among participants within each group. To the extent that these differences are relevant to the program, they should be "leveled." The statistical technique used to accomplish this task is the analysis of covariance. All of these various statistical tools are identified in "Possible Objectives and Statistical Tools Appropriate to Test Those Objectives" in appendix G.

Teitelbaum (2003) used the analysis of covariance technique to "control for various student and background characteristics that previous research indicates are associated with student course-taking patterns and achievement" (p. 33). The control variables include student gender, race, socioeconomic status, and 8th grade math and science test scores as a proxy for student academic performance before entering high school. In addition, school average socioeconomic status was included in the regression models. In the same journal issue, Goddard (2003) also used analysis of covariance to control for prior student achievement and student demographic characteristics.

Statistical significance simply means that what was found (for instance the difference between the new program and the old program) could not have occurred by chance more often than the chosen alpha level of significance. Alpha is usually set at .05 or .01 in the social sciences. Of additional interest is the effect size (for instance between the new program and the old program). Large sample sizes can yield statistical significance with only a very small effect size. That small increase in effect may not be worth all the changes necessary in going from the old program to the new program. Teitelbaum (2003) also discusses effect size in his evaluation.

Disaggregate Information

Stakeholders in large programs are usually interested primarily in how certain subgroups have performed because of the program. That is, knowing that the program overall has been successful is not enough — they want to know if a particular subgroup has benefited. The program director and other stakeholders can inform the evaluator as to the disaggregation(s) that would be of interest. The subgrouping variables that are of interest should be determined before information is collected, so that the subgroup information can also be collected. Some subgroups that are often of interest are site, cohort, grade level, ethnicity, and gender. Reporting results by subgroup can identify particular subgroups that are not being served well, indicating that the program should be modified to meet the needs of that subgroup. We strongly encourage, though, that subgroup information should be reported only if there are significant differences, or if the differences exceed a value identified before data collection. Often readers focus on "apparent differences" rather than "practical differences." "Example of Reporting Only Major Differences Between Groups" in appendix F provides one such example where disaggregated information is reported only when there was a significant difference between groups.

WRITE END-OF-CYCLE REPORT

The report following collection and analysis of post assessment information is usually referred to as the "final report," or "end-of-cycle report" if the program will be in operation the following cycle. We refer to this report as the "end-of-cycle report" in keeping with the GEM notion of continuous feedback and in keeping with the trend of funding programs for multiple cycles. The purpose of this report is to summarize the activities and results of the entire cycle. The report should begin with an executive summary, identifying the most important results. These results consist of previously reported context, input, and process results, as well as the recently completed analysis of post assessment results. If deemed appropriate, executive summaries may be written for various stakeholders, focusing on the results that are of particular interest to each of the stakeholder groups.

As with previous reports, the end-of-cycle report should (a) clearly communicate, (b) be timely, (c) contain numerous figures, and (d) focus on the highlights. The highlights should also take into account the crucial nature of the various objectives. Finally, the report should contain a section that summarizes all of the results.

Purpose of the Report

The purpose of the end-of-cycle report is to document the activities of the program, progress of the program, and status of the objectives. The report should contain recommendations for the program for the following cycle. The report provides an opportunity for the program director, program staff, and all other stakeholders to review (a) what they wanted the program to accomplish, (b) what obstructions occurred during the cycle, and (c) what the status is. The end-of-cycle report provides an opportunity to make midcourse corrections in the implementation or expectations of the program. In the GEM perspective, the end-of-cycle report is a working document rather than a final nail in the coffin or monument.

Begin With Executive Summary

As in all good reporting, the executive summary provides an advanced organizer for the reader. Some readers may not read beyond the executive summary, so it needs to be clear, concise, and focused on the crucial results. If there are stakeholders who are interested only in certain aspects of the program, additional focused executive summaries may be in order. These additional executive summaries allow the evaluator to use the language understandable by those stakeholders and to discuss only those objectives of interest to those stakeholders. Appendix F contains an example of an executive summary.

Content of End-of-Cycle Report

The end-of-cycle report is the primary report referred to when decisions are made for the subsequent cycle and may be the only report referred to in the following cycles. Therefore, all of the cycle's activities must be included. The information in the interim reports should be synthesized and summarized. All of the major context, input, and process activities should be documented, as well as the results from post assessment.

We usually provide an overview of the program—including who is involved and what the general purpose was. The overview might also contain the philosophical orientation of the program. Next, the general goals of the program are presented. These goals are more general than the specific objectives. These goals should be understandable by stakeholders who are not steeped in the jargon of the professional. Goals would be of interest also to the news media; the funding agencies and professionals would want the more specific objectives, which are discussed later.

The next part of the end-of-cycle report is a listing of the planned major activities. Such a list provides an overview of what program staff was funded to do, in the chronological order activities occurred.

Another major component of the end-of-cycle report is the listing of the major components. There is an overlap of these components (such as staff development) with the planned list of activities, for example, staff development on "Use of new strategies" on August 22, staff development on "Record keeping'" on September 22, and staff development on "Sequencing" on October 13. These major components provide a table of contents for the summaries of each component.

Another critical section is the one documenting the results of each objective. Often tables and figures are incorporated to communicate the findings. One format that we have used often to summarize the results by component is the chart essay. We have found chart essays to be a valuable tool as they are brief, to the point, and contain all the relevant information—usually on just one page. Appendix F contains an example of a chart essay.

Note that this chart essay contains sections entitled (a) Purpose, (b) Evaluation effort, (c) Summary of the evaluation effort, and (d) Recommendations. "Example of a Chart Essay With Tabled Information" in appendix F is a chart essay that was used when a team of evaluators evaluated a bilingual educational program. Thus, we included the names of the three evaluators, of the team of five, who participated in that aspect of the evaluation. Including their names was a way of both acknowledging their contribution and holding them accountable for that piece of the total evaluation. Note that the conclusion in this section of appendix F summarizes in four sentences the extensive data presented.

The final section of the end-of-cycle report should summarize the results. The authors of this text have found that repeating the objectives—either as a list as in "Status of the Evaluation Questions" in appendix F or grouped in some fashion, for example by stakeholder as was presented previously in "Summary Table of Percent of Objectives Met" in appendix F—facilitates the writing of the report as well as the reading of the report.

"Status of the Evaluation Questions" in appendix F has an added artifact of reporting "an estimate of the percentage that is believed to be known about the answers to that question." The first estimate was provided in the first end-of-cycle report, and the second was added in the second end-of-cycle report. Given that the program was to be evaluated over a 5-year span, one would not be too concerned that 100% was not known on each question after 2 years.

Communicate With Intended Audience

The report content should be clearly communicated to whichever stakeholder it is addressed to. If you feel that some parents cannot read parts of the report, then modify the report, or write another report that can be read by those parents. The funding agency may be interested only in, say, achievement gains, and that requires a different report.

The end-of-cycle report, being a compilation of the cycle's implementation of the program, necessarily reports the highlights. The interim reports (needs assessment report and program implementation assessment report) have focused on (a) understanding the program's setting (context), (b) the support for beginning the program (input), and (c) how the program was implemented (process). Therefore, the end-of-cycle report focuses on the new information, the information gained from the post assessment. Most of the post assessment information is product information, or outcome information. Examples of product information include teacher attitudes toward the program, student achievement gains, and amount of community support.

One of the best ways to communicate information is to use figures. For many readers, a figure is indeed "worth a thousand words." While figures usually display information with less precision, they often leave the reader with a better understanding of the results. The high-precision information will be forgotten soon, but the figure and its general implications can be retained for a long time. "Example of a Table of Information" in appendix F contains data in tabular form, and "Information Turned Into a Figure," which follows in the appendix, contains the bar chart representing the same information that was used in an evaluation report.

However evaluation results are reported, it is usually the case that each objective is treated equally. In fact, it is usually the case that some objectives are very crucial, while others are not at all crucial. A valuable activity for the program director at needs assessment time is to take 100 pennies and distribute them among the objectives, based on how crucial the objectives are. Getting the various stakeholders to complete this activity might open the eyes of the program director and provide guidance to the evaluator. The activity could assist in modifying or deleting objectives that received few pennies. In addition, the allotment would identify those objectives that need to be discussed for each stakeholder group. Finally, a program that is successful on the *three most* crucial objectives should be considered a more successful program than is one that is successful only on the *three least* crucial objectives.

RELATE TO OBJECTIVES AND PROCEDURES TO ACHIEVE OBJECTIVES

The evaluation results should not be read and then filed away. As already indicated in previous sections, the results should be used to improve the program. Certain objectives may not be being met, or certain subgroups may not be achieving as much as others. The purpose of the evaluation is not to place blame but to modify the program (in whatever area is necessary—context, input, or process) so that the desired results are obtained. Understanding the evaluation results, and making correct changes because of those results, is a major effort and hence should not be taken lightly. A large amount of time should be spent on understanding the evaluation and making changes. The evaluator cannot make the program or evaluation change decisions in isolation—those decisions must be made by the program director in consultation with relevant stakeholders, such as an advisory board or the program staff. This is why it is crucial for the program director to be familiar with, and to have made a commitment to, the evaluation. All changes should be supported by ample evidence that a change needed to be made, and that the new component has some likelihood of being more effective than the original. The program director must make sure that the evidence is stable (not based on error) before giving up on the original implementation.

Think of the evaluation as a "question" and the evaluation results as the "answer"; now the program director has to respond to the answer— the question cannot be ignored or changed. One should be careful, though, not to overreact to results. If only 1 out of 15 sites has had trouble implementing part of the program, the program implementation probably does not have to be modified throughout the entire program. Processes within that one site may need to be modified. There may be a reason why the program director would not expect the same implementation problems in that one site in subsequent cycles. In the latter case, of course, no changes would be necessary.

When an evaluation is planned to be conducted on an annual basis, the 1st year's evaluation may be conducted with the sole purpose of putting the evaluation machinery in place. Perhaps no major changes would be indicated in the 1st year, as in the 1st year evaluation of Michigan's Neglected and Delinquent program: "One should not make program changes based on this data as this is the first year of intensive evaluation at the state level and the data are still not of a sufficient quality to warrant such a conclusion" (McNeil, 1976, p. 8).

DISSEMINATE THE REPORTS

A thorough review of the end-of-cycle report by the program director with the evaluator should occur before the report is disseminated to other stakeholders. If there is an advisory board, one might want to consider the report provided to them as a "draft report" until they have been briefed and had a chance to read and react to it. If the advisory board functions as a group providing direction, then they may want to see additional (or fewer) results in the report. The various executive summaries and interim reports should be all kept in one place, available to all stakeholders for future reference. Finally, the end-of-cycle report should be completed in time for it to be used as a tool for improving the program and for determining any changes in the evaluation plan for the subsequent cycle. One should have a plan for dissemination and keep track of the dissemination, as in the example below.

Dissemination of Employer Perceptions Report

- 7/90 College of Education dean
- 7/90 Executive vice president
- 8/90 NCATE committee
- 8/90 Reform committee
- 8/90 Curriculum and Instruction Department head
- 8/90 Assistant vice president for minority affairs
- 8/90 College of Education dean's advisory council
- 8/90 Interviewers
- 8/90 Recruiters who had requested report
- 8/90 College of Education advisement personnel for use in freshman orientation
- 8/90 Educational Management and Development undergraduate class studying employment opportunities and educational trends
- 8/90 Counseling and Educational Psychology class studying evaluation

DETERMINE EVALUATION PLAN FOR THE NEXT CYCLE

The evaluator and the program director should review together the end-of-cycle report and decide upon changes in the evaluation plan for the next cycle. Perhaps there needs to be more focus on delivery of services. Alternatively, perhaps evaluation resources should be transferred to following graduates to see if the program has long-lasting effects. Perhaps the results indicate that fewer participants need to be tested, or that two tests will provide as much information as the four tests that were used in the past cycle.

The crucial aspect of this step is to get the program director and the evaluator to sit down together to digest the results, objective by objective, site by site, and subgroup by subgroup. People in these two roles have different understandings of the program and the evaluation of the program. With their two perspectives, not only will a better evaluation result, but also, more importantly, a better program will result. The two perspectives and the collaborative evaluation effort by the program director and the evaluator are the topics of the next chapter.

CHAPTER 8

Review of GEM From the Viewpoint of the Evaluator and the Program Director

One major tenet of this text is that the program director and the evaluator should both be involved in the evaluation process. To clarify and emphasize this point, the following sections discuss each task within the five stages and suggest the approximate proportion of effort for each task by the program director and the evaluator. These approximate proportions are simply educated guesses on our part, based on over 70 years of combined experience in evaluating programs, and represent our ideal expectations. These estimates can vary depending upon (a) the nature of the program being evaluated, (b) the evaluation experience of both the program director and the evaluator, (c) the number of years the program is funded, and (d) the working relationship of the program director and the evaluator. The approximate involvement of the program director and evaluator in each of the 39 tasks is summarized in Table 8.1. The message in Table 8.1 is that the program director should be involved in nearly every evaluation task.

STAGE 1: NEEDS ASSESSMENT

The project director has at least 50% involvement in five of the eight tasks in this stage. In fact, the project director is estimated to be responsible for over 80% in four of the tasks.

Task 1: Identify Stakeholders

It would be foolhardy to presume that the evaluator would be in a better position than the program director to identify the stakeholders.

Table 8.1. Approximate Involvements of Program Director and Evaluator in Each of the 39 Tasks of the General Evaluation Model

| | Percent of Time on Task | |
Task	Program Director	Evaluator
1. Identify stakeholders	90	10
2. Identify program areas	90	10
3. Identify sources of information	20	80
4. Develop the needs assessment instrument	20	80
5. Conduct the needs assessment	50	50
6. Write the needs assessment report	20	80
7. Disseminate to stakeholders	80	20
8. Make sure stakeholders buy into program	90	10
9. Determine baseline instrument(s)	10	90
10. Determine comparison group(s)	10	90
11. Administer baseline	20	80
12. Analyze information	00	100
13. Write report	20	80
14. Disseminate the baseline report	30	70
15. Draft program objectives	70	30
16. Share program objectives with stakeholders	70	30
17. Finalize program objectives	50	50
18. Develop procedures	90	10
19. Train staff	90	10
20. Determine that training was implemented well	20	80
21. Develop program implementation evaluation plan	20	80
22. Identify instruments	20	80
23. Develop instruments (if necessary)	20	80
24. Inform stakeholders periodically	60	40
25. Collect and analyze context information	20	80
26. Collect and analyze input information	40	60
27. Collect and analyze program implementation information	30	70
28. Write reports	20	80
29. Relate to objectives and procedures to achieve objectives	40	60
30. Disseminate the reports	80	20
31. Develop post assessment plan	10	90
32. Identify instruments	10	90
33. Develop instruments (if necessary)	10	90
34. Collect post assessment information	05	95
35. Analyze all information	00	100
36. Write end-of-cycle report	20	80
37. Relate to objectives and procedures to achieve objectives	20	80
38. Disseminate the report(s)	60	40
39. Determine evaluation for next cycle	20	80

The evaluator's contribution in Task 1 would be to suggest other possible categories of stakeholders from previous evaluations or knowledge of the evaluation literature. The program director should especially be prodded for any additional stakeholders that might be included in the needs assessment. The estimate for Task 1 is 90% for the program director.

Task 2: Identify Program Areas

It would also be foolhardy to presume that the evaluator would be in a better position than the program director to identify the program areas that need to be evaluated. The evaluation is best served by the evaluator not being involved in the construction of the program and the identification of the areas that will be evaluated. When the evaluator identifies the program areas, the evaluation becomes the sole province of the evaluator rather than of the program director and the rest of the stakeholders. The only contribution by the evaluator in this task is to suggest other areas that might be evaluated. The estimate for Task 2 is 90% for the program director.

Task 3: Identify Sources of Information

The evaluator should have experience in collecting information from various sources. The program director's contribution would be in identifying the specific sources for this program—those people who would be willing to provide valuable information. The program director's effort in this area would be approximately 20%.

Task 4: Develop the Needs Assessment Instrument

Once Tasks 1, 2, and 3 have been completed, the evaluator should take primary responsibility for developing the needs assessment instrument. The program director, though, should be consulted on readability, clarity, appropriate terminology, and any potential red flags. Final editing by the program director would be a valuable activity, resulting in 20% effort on Task 4 by the program director.

Task 5: Conduct the Needs Assessment

The actual collection of the needs assessment data should be an evenly divided effort. The program director should be the one to (a) set up the data gathering sessions, (b) make sure that the stakeholders attend and complete the needs assessment, and (c) clearly communicate that the needs assessment is important. If the program director has taken an active role in the first three tasks, then the program director is likely to appear to be involved with, and to care about, the actual collection of the needs assessment data. Our estimate is that the program director will be equally responsible with the evaluator for this task, resulting in a 50% involvement.

Task 6: Write the Needs Assessment Report

The program director should take an active role in three areas of Task 6. The program director can (a) assist in constructing the outline of the report, (b) provide suggestions for multiple reports for the various stakeholders, and (c) review the draft of the report. The evaluator should be responsible for writing the report and turning the analyzed data into comprehensible sentences and paragraphs. The program director's effort would be about 20% in this task.

Task 7: Disseminate to Stakeholders

Dissemination of the report to stakeholders should be the primary responsibility of the program director. This task occurs early in the evaluation, and hence the stakeholders may not be familiar with the evaluator and likely have had little time to develop rapport with the evaluator. The evaluator should attend these dissemination meetings to provide technical support to the program director, thus communicating the picture that the evaluation is a management tool willingly used by the program director, rather than a necessary evil imposed by someone from outside the program. The program director's effort would be about 80% in this task.

Task 8: Make Sure Stakeholders Buy Into Program

The program director is the major person responsible for making sure that stakeholders buy into the program. The evaluator is an outside person—the program needs to be what the stakeholders and the program director want, not what is imposed from outside. Therefore, the program director would complete about 90% of this task.

STAGE 2: BASELINE

In Stage 2, the evaluator begins to take more responsibility for each task, while the program director continues to take a role in each task, as discussed below.

Task 9: Determine Baseline Instrument(s)

Though the evaluator is the primary person responsible for Task 9, the program director should be consulted. The program director may be aware of similar programs and can thus facilitate discovering if any instruments exist that may be used by those programs. The program director should review all instruments to make sure they are applicable to the stakeholders that will be completing those instruments. Our estimate for the involvement of the program director in Task 9 is 10%.

Task 10: Determine Comparison Group(s)

The program director should be consulted regarding the availability of baseline comparison groups. Data may be available from previous years of the program or from similar programs. The evaluator and the program director should discuss the actual choice of a baseline comparison group. The program director should understand why that particular group was chosen and feel comfortable that no other group is a better choice. Our estimate for the involvement of the program director in Task 10 is 10%.

Task 11: Administer Baseline

The program director's contribution in Task 11 would include (a) making sure that there is enough money budgeted for all the tests, test administration, and test scoring, (b) ordering the tests on time, and (c) alerting staff about the importance of testing and when testing will occur. Our estimate for the involvement of the program director in Task 11 is 20%.

Task 12: Analyze Information

Analyzing information is one of the few tasks that would be left entirely up to the evaluator. This task falls under the expertise of the evaluator, and therefore, the program director need not be involved.

Task 13: Write Report

As discussed in Task 6 above, the program director can be involved in (a) developing the outline, (b) deciding whether some stakeholders should have a different report, and (c) reviewing the draft report. The program director should be instrumental in deciding how many different reports are needed and the nature of the report to each stakeholder group. The program director is in the best position to know what aspects each stakeholder group would be interested in. Furthermore, the program director can assist the evaluator in making sure that all funding agency requirements have been met. Our estimate for the involvement of the program director in Task 13 is 20%.

Task 14: Disseminate the Baseline Report

The program director can facilitate decisions as to when and how the report will be disseminated. Perhaps the written report is sufficient for most stakeholders. Just the executive summary may be sufficient for other stakeholder groups. One or more stakeholders may best be served by an oral report by both the program director and the evaluator. Task 14 should involve the program director at approximately 30%.

Task 15: Draft Program Objectives

Not only does the program director know more about the program than does the evaluator, but the program director must buy into the program. In addition, the program objectives need to be written at the level understood by the program director and the program staff implementing those objectives. Therefore, this task should be led by the program director at approximately 70% involvement.

Task 16: Share Program Objectives With Stakeholders

This task also needs to be led by the program director. The evaluator needs to be there as a technical advisor, but the program director must (a) appear knowledgeable of the program objectives, (b) be committed to the program objectives, and (c) be committed to the program evaluation. Therefore, this task should also be led by the program director at approximately 70% involvement.

Task 17: Finalize Program Objectives

The evaluator and the program director should meet after sharing the program objectives with all the stakeholders to finalize the objectives. If there are changes, both the program director and the evaluator should understand and agree to those changes. The program director and evaluator should share equally in this task at 50% involvement.

STAGE 3: PROCEDURES TO ACHIEVE OBJECTIVES

Each of the three tasks in this stage requires a major contribution by the program director.

Task 18: Develop Procedures

The evaluator is unlikely to be an expert in the programmatic issues, and thus can only review the procedures with an eye toward the evaluability of those procedures. The wise program director does not allow the evaluator to assume a major role in this task. The program director must take primary responsibility for this task with 90% involvement.

Task 19: Train Staff

This task is conducted almost entirely by the program director or a representative, such as the organization's staff development personnel or an outside contracted staff developer. Some training time should be devoted to informing the staff about the evaluation activities, when they will occur, and what requirements will be placed on the staff. This would best be accomplished by the evaluator, who should attend the staff development, resulting in 10% involvement by the evaluator.

Task 20: Determine That Training Was Implemented Well

Workshop evaluation by the evaluator is only the initial aspect of this task. The program director should ensure that the training is being implemented as expected. Additional support personnel may need to be hired to facilitate the desired implementation. Any training weaknesses identified by trainees or program observation should be communicated to the program director, and the program director should immediately prepare to remedy any weaknesses. The program director would be involved with approximately 20% of this task.

STAGE 4: PROGRAM IMPLEMENTATION ASSESSMENT

The evaluator is the primary person responsible for the tasks in this stage. However, the program director has at least 20% involvement in each task.

Task 21: Develop Program Implementation Assessment Plan

The program director must read and accept the program implementation assessment plan. Evaluators who develop a program implementation assessment plan, and then begin to execute it without obtaining program director buy-in, often find themselves in deep difficulty. Likewise, if the program director does not attend to the development of the program implementation assessment plan, the plan may commit fiscal and personnel resources in a way that strains implementation of the program. The evaluation should not interfere with the implementation of the program, and the program director is the primary person responsible for seeing that that does not happen. The program director would be involved with approximately 20% of this task.

Task 22: Identify Instruments

The evaluator should take the lead on this task but should ask if the program director knows of any instruments. The evaluator must remain cognizant of the cost of the instruments (including administration, scoring, and analyzing) and keep the program director informed of the costs. The program director would be involved with approximately 20% of this task.

Task 23: Develop Instruments (If Necessary)

The evaluator obviously should take the lead in this task but should rely on the content expertise of the program director. The program director would also be involved in reviewing the instruments to determine that they are appropriate for the program. Time spent by the program director in Task 23 is approximately 20%.

Task 24: Inform Stakeholders Periodically

Again, this is a task for the program director, with the evaluator acting as the technical backup. The evaluator should resist being assigned as the only person to inform, as the stakeholders will begin to view the program director as not involved in (and possibly uncommitted to) the evaluation. The program director should be involved approximately 60% and the evaluator 40% to provide the public appearance of teamwork.

Task 25: Collect and Analyze Context Information

The program director, of necessity, provides much of the context information. Though the evaluator is responsible for writing the report, the program director should review the report, resulting in approximately 20% involvement of the program director in this task.

Task 26: Collect and Analyze Input Information

The program director provides much of the input data to the evaluator, and the program director must review the report for accuracy, resulting in approximately 40% involvement of the program director in this task.

Task 27: Collect and Analyze Program Implementation Information

The program director and the evaluator need to meet on a regular basis to collect and analyze the program implementation information. Hence, the program director is estimated to be involved in about 30% of this task.

Task 28: Write Reports

As with the other reports, the program director should be involved in the outline, writing of certain sections, and review, resulting in 20% involvement in this task.

Task 29: Relate to Objectives and Procedures to Achieve Objectives

This task reviews the process data discrepancy between what was proposed and what is currently occurring. The program director needs to look at these discrepancies and make a judgment as to whether current program activities will eliminate those discrepancies. If not, then midcourse corrections need to be made. Those corrections must be made by the program director. The evaluator should be consulted to determine when the program implementation assessment plan must be modified. It is estimated that a substantial amount of time would be required of the program director in this task (approximately 40%).

Task 30: Disseminate the Reports

As in previously discussed dissemination tasks, the program director should take the primary role (approximately 80%).

STAGE 5: POST ASSESSMENT

With the exception of the dissemination task, the evaluator should have primary responsibility for each of the tasks in this final stage. The program director should be kept informed of the status of each task in Stage 5.

Task 31: Develop Post Assessment Evaluation Plan

The evaluator should take primary responsibility for developing the evaluation plan for post assessment. The plan should be cleared with the program director, resulting in approximately 10% involvement by the program director.

Task 32: Identify Instruments

The evaluator should take the lead on this task but should ask if the program director knows of any instruments. The evaluator must remain cognizant of the cost of the instruments (including administration, scoring, and analyzing). The program director would be involved with approximately 10% of this task.

Task 33: Develop Instruments (If Necessary)

The evaluator obviously should take the lead in this task, but should rely on the content expertise of the program director. The program director would be involved with approximately 10% of this task.

Task 34: Collect Post Assessment Information

With the possible exception of alerting staff that post assessment will be occurring, the program director does not have a role in collection of post assessment information. Thus, the program director has minimal involvement with this task (approximately 5%).

Task 35: Analyze All Information

This is the second of two tasks that are reserved solely for the evaluator. The program director should not be bothered with any analyses of data.

Task 36: Write End-of-Cycle Report

The relative responsibilities for this report are viewed as the same as for previous reports—approximately 20% for the program director.

Task 37: Relate to Objectives and Procedures to Achieve Objectives

The evaluator should write the first draft but should rely on the program director's insight into the proposed program and the implemented program. The program director should critically read the draft report, making sure that inaccurate statements are not made. In addition, the program director should look for omissions. These activities constitute approximately 20% of this task.

Task 38: Disseminate the Reports

The program director must again be involved in the dissemination. The program director may need to answer questions and should communicate to all stakeholders that the evaluation remains a useful management tool. If the reports are written in the language of the stakeholders, few technical questions should arise. The program director's role in this dissemination task would be approximately 60%.

Task 39: Determine Evaluation Plan for the Next Cycle

Ideally, the evaluation focus for each cycle was in the initial evaluation plan. This focus must be revisited in light of the past cycle's evaluation. The program director and the evaluator should negotiate the evaluation of the next cycle, resulting in approximately 20% involvement by the program director.

SUMMARY OF PROGRAM DIRECTOR AND EVALUATOR RESPONSIBILITIES RELATED TO EVALUATION

An evaluator should be knowledgeable about statistics, research design, and evaluation models. Having the ability to communicate, as well as being sensitive to the needs of the people being evaluated and the community in which the evaluation is taking place, is also important. The evaluator should be able to explain what he or she is doing in a clear, nonthreatening way to everyone involved. An evaluator should be able to help the program director answer the following nine questions and decide on the most defensible approach.

1. What are the purposes of conducting the evaluation?
2. Can these purposes be measured?
3. How long will information collection take?
4. Are the time and information appropriate for the types of decisions that must be made?
5. What potential effect will the evaluation have on the project?
6. Which other stakeholders will be interested in the evaluation reports?
7. Which stakeholders will be reading the evaluation reports?
8. Are the evaluation reports written so that all stakeholders will understand them?
9. Do the evaluation reports reflect the concerns and interests of all the stakeholders associated with the project? (Newman & Deitchman, 1983)

These questions should be asked before the evaluation is initiated, and they should be used as guidelines for developing the evaluation plan. These concerns will tend to produce evaluation credibility.

It is important to realize that for an evaluation to be effective, the staff has to be involved in the evaluation and become part of its implementation. Therefore, it is important for the evaluator to suggest methods for evaluating the staff in a nonthreatening manner. The suggestions should be considered in terms of their practicality and usefulness. Choosing an evaluator is perhaps the most important aspect of a successful evaluation.

One of the most important things to remember is that it is a sign of sophistication, intelligence, and concern to ask for further explanation when something is not clear. Program directors should never say they understand if they do not (Newman, Sugarman, & Newman, 1981).

CHAPTER 9

Evaluation as a Profession

This chapter is divided into four major sections. First, we discuss the standards that exist in the evaluation profession. Second, we discuss what we consider the necessary traits of an evaluator. Third, we discuss the positive and negative aspects of the evaluator's being a staff employee (inside hire) as compared to an evaluator's being hired from outside the organization (outside hire). We finish the chapter with a discussion of the impact of multicultural aspects on evaluation.

STANDARDS

Any profession has explicit, or at least implicit, standards for the conduct of the profession. The Joint Committee on Standards for Educational Evaluation (1981) has codified the standards for evaluation. This committee was composed of members from various organizations, including the American Educational Research Association, the American Psychological Association, and the National Council on Measurement. The 30 standards appear in appendix C, with a brief description of each. The standards are grouped according to four attributes of an evaluation.

The first set of standards relates to the utility of the evaluation. The utility standards reflect the concern that program evaluations be responsive to the needs of the stakeholders. In general, the utility standards require evaluators to acquaint themselves with the various stakeholders, to ascertain their information needs, and to report the relevant information to these stakeholders clearly, concisely, and on time.

The second set of standards relates to feasibility and focuses on the realization that evaluations must be cost-effective and workable. The feasibility standards require that the evaluation plan be operable for the setting and be as careful with valuable resources as possible. Overall, the feasibility standards require evaluations to be realistic, prudent, diplomatic, politically viable, and frugal.

The third set of standards relates to propriety and reflects the fact that evaluations can affect many people in many different ways. The propriety standards require that evaluations be conducted legally, ethically, and with due regard for the welfare of those involved in the evaluation as well as those affected by the results. Newman and Brown (1996) discussed ethical decision-making as it relates to evaluation. Their abbreviated decision-making model is in "Newman and Brown's Ethical Decision-Making Process" in appendix G. They have operationalized the ethical issues discussed in the Joint Committee on Standards for Educational Evaluation (appendix C) as well as those from the Evaluation Research Society and the American Evaluation Association.

The final group of standards relates to accuracy. These standards require that the information obtained is technically adequate and that conclusions are linked logically to the data.

WHAT ARE THE TRAITS OF AN EVALUATOR?

Once an evaluator has obtained evaluation experience in one content area, evaluating a program in a related area becomes much easier. All the traits discussed in this section are necessary in all evaluations and can easily be transferred from one content area to another.

Good Observation Skills

An evaluator has to like to observe and must be alert to the people, context, and actions of the various program staff and other stakeholders. The observations must be recorded with as little rephrasing by the evaluator as possible. That is, raw observations should be recorded, not subjective interpretation through the biases and preconceptions of the evaluator.

Observation skills include knowing what to look for, where to find it, and when to look. Having knowledge of the kind of program or organization that is being evaluated certainly assists in this endeavor. Understanding the relationship of the program to the organization, the functions of the different units, and the "typical" organization can facilitate a quicker understanding of the organization and allow the evaluator to avoid asking questions to get that information. One should not, though, assume that the organization under study is exactly like other organizations in that same field. Each organization has its own idiosyncrasies, and often those idiosyncrasies are crucial to the conduct of that evaluation.

Evaluators accomplish observation by watching for what should be happening, as well as watching for what is not happening. Information can be obtained through visual observation as well as by listening. For instance, the order in which people are introduced at a meeting, who introduces them, what is said about them, and how it is said can all be valuable pieces of information. Where individuals are seated, what they are doing, and how they interact with participants is valuable information.

A memorable movie scene in *Being There* depicts the value of observation. Shirley MacLaine was on a bear rug attempting to get the attention of Peter Sellers. He was a gardener by profession (indeed, he led a very sheltered life and had a low IQ—aren't all evaluators like that?) and had spent all his free time watching TV. She asked him what he liked (meaning in the way of sex). His response was, "I like to watch [TV]." If gardening had not been his early calling, he would have made an excellent evaluator because an evaluator has to "like to watch."

Wondering

When you have observed something, then you have to wonder about it. Yes, you saw it or heard it, but what does that observation really mean? Like a good counselor not accepting the first complaint of a client, a good evaluator has to put the information into context. Would the same event have occurred if you were not present? Did everyone else observe the same event? What meaning does it have for them? Pondering is a trait that all good evaluators have. Information must be accepted and recorded at face value. However, the wonderment of that information is a process that goes beyond the data. Carefully thinking about the observation is one way to accomplish that wondering.

Sleuthing

We chose to use the term *sleuthing* when meaning "carefully thinking." One needs to keep in mind the organization, the program, staff, and goals of the program when thinking about new information. Humans are inclined to try to fit new data, even when discordant, into the already established mindset (Gilovich, 1991). Evaluators need to carefully analyze each new piece of information on its own merit before plugging it into the previous information mix. In reality, information is more valuable if it is not in line with our previous convictions, assuming that the information is valid. Redundant information is nice, but it is not as valuable as new information.

Sometimes the sleuthing is a little on the shady side. Verifying information with other sources could be viewed as not trusting the original source. You should view it as making sure the information was correct. For instance, casual discussions with secretaries can provide invaluable information. One of us worked on a program that required staff to travel by air on a weekly basis. A relatively meek secretary made the airline reservations, which were always in order, except for those of the boss. The boss treated her poorly, and the travel mix-ups were her way of getting back. Only a sleuth would posit and verify that relationship.

Logical

Sleuthing cannot be unrestrained. An evaluator has neither enough time nor enough money to pursue every wonder. Some "wonders" have to remain as just wonderments. Others can be logically followed, such as "if X then Y." "Or more likely, "if X, A, B, and C, then Y and Z." Human behavior is complex, and we usually do not have all the necessary relevant information. Many observations do not have a logical relationship to anything or do not have much importance. The sleuthing and logical analysis needs to focus on those observations that will potentially have a major impact on the program.

Belief in Cause and Effect

The evaluator ultimately must believe in cause and effect. The evaluator must consider the world to be ordered. What we mean is that time and money spent on a program were intended for a particular outcome. If the purpose was not obtained, was it because (a) of a poor implementation of the program, (b) staff were not hired in a timely fashion, (c) implementation was thwarted in any number of ways, or (d) the program was poorly conceived in the first place? Even if the desired outcome was achieved, the evaluator must consider whether the outcome could have been achieved sooner or better with an alternative program. Finally, the evaluator must consider whether something else besides the program caused the outcome.

Some social science researchers and evaluators have taken the stance that cause and effect is a concept that should no longer be entertained in the social sciences. If there can be no presumed effect from investing in these social service activities, should we throw away all these activities, including education? Certainly discarding cause and effect is not tenable.

Having meaningful comparison groups is a positive step in ascertaining cause and effect. When a good comparison group cannot be obtained, then qualitative information should be relied upon to guide decisions. Indeed, there will always be threats to internal validity (Wilkinson & McNeil, 1996) in the best of all possible qualitative worlds. Therefore, evaluators need to be careful concluding that the new program is the only cause or even one of the causes. Several years of implementation (and in several locations) would be a minimum requirement to even consider concluding that the program is the primary cause.

Puzzle Solver

The evaluator must determine what is happening, why it is happening, and if there is any good resulting. If there is not, why not? If there is, could there be a better approach with the same cost, or a similar approach with less cost? Most developers of new programs are convinced that their approach is the "best way." Whether that approach is the best way is a question that must be answered empirically in the evaluation.

A problem solver is one who does not avoid a problem situation. The problem solver attacks the problem with energy, with the desire to solve the problem as quickly and as elegantly as possible. Evaluators in their spare time play word games or cards or attack mechanical puzzles. If you walk away from board games or whodunits, you may not be a prime candidate for being an evaluator. The evaluator needs to (a) be attracted to problems, (b) be able to posit solutions to problems, (c) know how to test them, and (d) know when the problem has been solved.

Open Mind

During this problem-solving process, the evaluator must keep an open mind regarding the information to be collected and the interpretation of that information. Premature closure in this area can be as detrimental as not collecting information or ignoring information. In many cases, some of the information may be contradictory. Such contradictory information is another reason for needing to keep an open mind. The contradictory information might be explained through the puzzling process, or it may be a real contradiction that the evaluator needs to analyze logically. In most cases, the needs of the primary stakeholders must be considered. That is, if the only discordant piece of information is from a relatively unimportant stakeholder, then it can be discarded.

Healthy Skepticism

We hope this heading attracted your attention, because it is an important trait for evaluators. Every piece of information obtained by an evaluator needs to be analyzed for the reason it was provided. These analyses are especially critical if the information was unsolicited. Why did Mr. X tell you that Miss Y parked her car in Mr. Z's driveway 3 nights last week? How does this information affect the program? If that information does not affect the program, why do you even need to know it?

Much information in the social sciences comes from self-report surveys, attitudes, or data recorded by program staff and then turned over to the evaluator. The person providing the data can easily infect all such information. Social scientists long ago coined the term "social desirability." Another term, "demand characteristics" (Rosenthal & Rosnow, 1969) has alerted social science researchers and evaluators to realize that the people who provide information are thinking (and sometimes conniving) individuals. Sometimes they try to "help" the person collecting the data, and sometimes they try to "not help" the person. In order to accomplish this best, they need to figure out the purpose of the program. In some instances, the purpose can be hidden from the participants, but usually it is not. Most often when an evaluator is on the scene, all participants in the program have at least minimum knowledge of the program and its purposes. If the staff want the program to succeed, then their information may well be tainted by that desire. If they become disenchanted with the program, they might overtly or covertly sabotage the program either through actions in their position in the program or by the nature of the information provided to the evaluator. In the two previous sentences, we have identified two ends of the continuum. In our experience, most information providers are positive about the program but make every effort to provide unbiased information. However, let us remember that most golfers try not to slice, and most baseball hitters try not to strike out.

Many variables might affect the veracity of evaluation information, and some are listed below.

1. Age: Young children and young staff are more likely to provide unbiased information.
2. Centrality to the program: Those who are more central to the program are more likely to provide positively biased information. Those who are on the periphery are either not concerned about the program or do not know enough about the program to provide biased information.
3. Degree to which the informant's job depends on the program: Those whose next 3 years' employment is tied to the program are likely to give positively biased information. Those who have nothing to lose are likely to give unbiased information.
4. Big honcho's idea: Clearly if the informant is the person who dreamed up and got funding for the program, you are likely to get

positively biased information. Likewise, if the informant has a superior position and feels threatened by the success or existence of the program that was neither conceived of nor implemented by the informant, then negatively biased information is likely.

5. Length of the program: Programs, especially federally funded and state-funded programs mean extra dollars to the organization. An extremely negative evaluation may mean pulling of the funding. Positively biased information is more likely to be given when there is this fear that extra funding will disappear. The evaluator is also suspect in this situation, for if an evaluator thinks that 1 year of evaluation is worth doing, then surely 4 more years are also worth doing. A lot of time and effort of the evaluator goes into obtaining an evaluation contract. Getting a 5-year contract, rather than just a 1-year contract, is a big accomplishment.

6. Potential for the organization to pick up the funding: If there is no potential for the organization to pick up the program after outside funding is over, then there is little reason to bias the evaluation. However, if the local organization is likely to pick up the program when there is a positive evaluation, then the information obtained is more likely to be positively biased. Jobs will be kept, and the program will continue even if it does not produce the desired results.

7. Political strength of program director, program staff, or other staff: Often some stakeholder has enormous political pull. In this case, no matter how effective or ineffective the program, the political reality is that evaluations do not have an impact. The resources going into the evaluation could better be used elsewhere. If an evaluator senses that this is the case, it may be best to avoid that evaluation. For instance, when Keith McNeil was an inside evaluator for a public school district, he was assigned to evaluate all aspects of several new schools. After the implementation report was disseminated identifying a weak component, he was called to the superintendent's office and was told that this component was the most effective component that the superintendent had ever been associated with. An outside contractor who knew how to pull political weight was running the component for approximately $1 million a year. The evaluator and the superintendent met that first

and last time. Both are now gone from the public school district, but the political pull contractor was still in business there 15 years later.

Trust Data

Once the evaluator has determined that the information has not been overly inflated or deflated, then the evaluator has to trust that data. The evaluator has to base decisions on that information, not on unsubstantiated comments from one or two individuals. Evaluation decisions should not be made based on the evaluator's impression or what the evaluator would do, but on data from all of the involved participants—all of the stakeholders. The more familiar an evaluator is with an organization and the goals of similar organizations, the more likely the evaluator's recommendations are to be based partly on the evaluator's experiences with those other organizations. Since the goal of evaluation is to assess the value of a program for that organization, using information from other organizations or the evaluator's frame of reference is not appropriate.

Have Inclusive Social Skills

Since the evaluator must interact with various stakeholders from different interest groups, a high degree of social skills is necessary. The evaluator must be sensitive to these stakeholders while at the same time being sensitive to the goals of the program. The evaluator must be able to incorporate these diverse viewpoints into the evaluation design and then must be able to communicate the results of the evaluation to the various stakeholders. The acceptance of the evaluation reports may rely more on the social skills of the evaluator than on the content of the reports. The continuation of the evaluator's contract is often more a function of social skills than of the quality or results of the evaluation.

INSIDE VERSUS OUTSIDE HIRES

The evaluator's role depends somewhat on whether the evaluator is contracted to perform the evaluation (outside hire) or the evaluator is a regular employee of the organization (inside hire). This section further defines the two options and presents the positive and negative aspects of each. The section concludes with a discussion of how an outside evaluator is obtained and what should be included in that person's contract.

Definition of Inside Hire and Outside Hire

The inside hire is a person who is permanently employed by the organization. The outside hire is a person who is external to the organization and has been hired solely to evaluate a specific program. Some evaluators concurrently fill both roles, although one is usually the primary employment. We, for instance, have performed evaluations in both roles. The next four sections discuss the positive and negative aspects of these two identities.

Positive Aspects of an Inside Hire

The inside hire can begin the evaluation as soon as he or she is assigned the task. Such a person may have some knowledge of the program or at least of the organization. The inside hire is usually known to the organization and thus is likely to have the requisite skills to conduct the evaluation. Since the individual is employed by the organization, it is unlikely that the evaluator will do or say anything that is life-threatening to the organization. Finally, the inside hire is usually available during the day, every day, and has an office in the organization.

Love (1983) stated that "in contrast to external evaluators, those responsible for internal evaluation are often charged with remedying problems, not only with diagnosing them and developing recommendations" (p. 1). Love identified the following three reasons for increased use of internal evaluators. They included (a) disillusionment with the use of external evaluators, (b) reductions in funding for large-scale evaluative research programs, and (c) mounting concern for the management of human service organizations.

Negative Aspects of an Inside Hire

The inside hire may not have the requisite set of credentials or experience. The inside hire may have other priority assignments that can be used as excuses for not getting the evaluation tasks completed on time. The inside hire may feel compelled to "tone down" reports to keep his or her job. The inside hire may be privy to too much contextual information or to too much historical information and feel constrained in certain ways because of that information.

Positive Aspects of an Outside Hire

Hiring someone from outside the organization has many positive aspects. First, the outside hire can be chosen from a number of candidates and hopefully has the desired traits for the specific evaluation.

Second, the outside hire is not constrained by the organization's politics. In particular, the evaluator's job may be lost if the political winds do not blow the right way. Most outside hires have other evaluation contracts or have a full-time job. Thus, losing one evaluation contract is not usually a major blow to an outside hire.

Third, the outside hire is more flexible with respect to attending evening and Saturday advisory board meetings or conferences. Inside hires often either demand compensatory time or do not make themselves available outside the normal workweek schedule.

Fourth, the outside hire usually lends professional credibility to the role, especially if the evaluator lives more than 50 miles from the organization. The various stakeholders act as though the "outsider" is evaluating the program "objectively."

Negative Aspects of an Outside Hire

First, the outside hire is not likely to be physically available on a daily basis. Second, the outside hire may not be aware of the specific policies and procedures of the organization, such as vacation days, reporting hierarchy, purchasing, and invoicing. Third, the outside hire may provide more fluff (appearance of quality) than real substance. Fourth, the outside hire may not be able to communicate to all stakeholders. Fifth, some outside hires may insist on implementing the evaluation in a certain way, irrespective of the desires of the program director and the program staff. Ciarlo and Windle (1988) argued for conducting both an internal as well as an external evaluation. External evaluations can provide greater objectivity in choosing which program characteristics to address, and can offer a more critical and challenging perspective on a program. Internal evaluations, however, address more specific issues of immediate relevance to managers and the decisions they face. The two types also reinforce each other, in that external evaluations often require data from internal studies, may spur programs' use of findings, and may stimulate internal evaluations. (p. 116)

When any of these problems occur, the program director may not be in a powerful enough position to rectify the problem. However, if the evaluation has been conceived of, and initially implemented as, a team effort, then it is less likely that these problems will occur.

How Is an Outside Hire Obtained?

Whenever an outsider has been hired, there should be a contract specifying the processes and outcomes expected, timelines, and payment schedule, including penalties for nonresponsive performance. An example of such a contract is in "Example of an Evaluation Contract" in appendix G. Unless there are economic penalties for nonperformance, the program director must live with whatever the evaluator does on whatever schedule. Most contracts are renewable on an annual basis, contingent upon the agreement of both parties.

There are four primary ways to obtain an outside hire. First, word of mouth is often used to identify a successful evaluator. Second, the outside hire may have conducted evaluations on programs for the same organization. Third, the evaluator may have conducted an evaluation for similar programs in other organizations. Fourth, the outside hire may have been on the vendor list, responded to the RFP (request for proposal), and obtained the contract on a strictly competitive basis. Appendix H details how Keith McNeil obtained evaluation contracts from 1989 through 2000. It should be noted that in the summer of 1989 he moved from a position where he was a full-time inside hire, limited in his time to conduct any outside evaluations, to a university position where he had a more flexible time schedule and was encouraged to spend some of his time in service to the community. Notice that all four ways to obtain an outside hire were used. Once an evaluator has been hired, additional years of evaluation are almost automatic. Since the funded life of a program may be 3, 5, or more years, obtaining the evaluation contract for the initial year is crucial. Reflection on appendix H indicates that most of the evaluations were for multiple years.

The current trend is for an RFP to be advertised and a committee to rate the proposals. Such a process may appear to be objective, but experience and trust level between the program director and the potential evaluator often outweigh other factors. One such RFP (with the identifying particulars changed to protect the innocent) can be found in "Request for Proposal for Evaluation Services by Outside Evaluator" in appendix D.

The due date is a crucial component, as any submission after that due date will not be considered. If you are a prospective bidder, you should feel free to call the contact person, even if you do not have a specific question. There is value in letting the organization know that you are intending to submit a proposal, as there may be additional clarifying information that will be of value to you.

The "scope" identifies general activities that must occur. Your responses will provide additional substance to those activities. Particular attention should be paid to deadlines for reports.

Many RFPs require multiple copies; the one in appendix D requires 5 copies (see III A). The proposal should follow the same outline as the RFP. If you follow the same outline, it is important that you include all of the information sought by the organization (otherwise your proposal will not be acceptable for award; see IV A). Following the same outline also makes the review process easier for the reviewers.

Most RFPs indicate how the various factors are weighed. Those factors that have higher points should receive more attention in the response. The factors (and their points) in the RFP in appendix D were identified as:

1. Respondent's qualifications and experience (15 points)
2. Respondent's performance history as provided by references (5 points)
3. Respondent's level of service as determined by the proposed approach to the evaluation and follow-up (40 points)
4. Cost of the evaluation (40 points)

An evaluation may have already been budgeted when the program was originally funded, and this is likely public information. If that is the case, the program director will want to spend all that money on the evaluation, and we suggest that you budget the same amount in the proposal. Any evaluation can be expanded, and this expansion can be described in the level of service section. Hence, this section, containing the proposed approach, in our opinion, is extremely important. Each respondent has certain qualifications, experience, and performance history. These areas cannot be "beefed-up." (They can be presented well, but what is included must be the "truth.") How the respondents plan the evaluation in an innovative, systematic, and timely way is where points can be earned or lost.

Evaluators and consumers of evaluations should be cognizant of potential conflicts of interest and political influences on an evaluation. The organization funding the evaluation may have an overt or covert agenda. For instance, an evaluation of the value of teacher certification (Goldhaber & Brewer, 2000) was identified by Darling-Hammond, Berry, and Thoreson (2001) as having been funded by a foundation that advocates for the elimination of teacher certification requirements.

Another example of influence is the evaluations of the Perry preschool project operated by the High Scope Research Foundation (Epstein, Montie, & Weikart, n.d.; Oden, Schweinhart, & Weikart, 2000; Xiang & Schweinhart, 2001). All of these evaluations have been conducted by the employees (inside hires) of the High Scope Research Foundation. One wonders if the same magnitude of positive results would occur if an independent evaluator (outside hire) conducted the evaluation.

IMPACT OF MULTICULTURAL ASPECTS ON EVALUATION

Various multicultural aspects can have an extreme effect on all components of the evaluation. By multicultural we mean any distinct cultural group or variable. These may be gender based, ethnicity based, politically based, religion based, age based, or any of an infinite number of other variables. The evaluator must remember that he or she has a particular cultural background as well. The backgrounds of the evaluator, the program director, and the various stakeholders do not have to be the same, but they need to coexist, and all the people involved need to communicate. In addition, if the evaluator wants the evaluation to have an impact, then the evaluator must understand the cultural framework of the stakeholders. This understanding of the cultural framework must occur at all stages of the evaluation process. If there is misunderstanding at Stage 1—needs assessment—there will be difficulties at the subsequent stages. How reports are written and disseminated will also be impacted by cultural factors.

Evaluation of a program being implemented in a language (e.g., Spanish) that is not that of the evaluator (e.g., English) is a difficult task. Even if the ultimate goal is for students to understand English, many of the activities may be in a language other than English. Communication to stakeholders may be difficult if not impossible. Comprehending activities may be particularly difficult. We have evaluated several programs that contained language-based challenges and tried to respond to those challenges in several ways, as depicted next.

Challenge	Interviews of parents who spoke only Spanish.
Solution	Hire a bilingual professional who was familiar with the goals of the program. Interviews were translated into English for inclusion in the report.
Challenge	Classroom observation of bilingual teachers.
Solution	Hire four bilingual doctoral students and train them on the observation instrument and general evaluation principles and procedures.
Challenge	Evaluation of Title IV Bilingual Education Training Grant.
Solution	Collaborate with a bilingual colleague who was familiar with bilingual programs in particular and evaluation in general.
Challenge	Reporting results of Family Literacy Program to parents who were learning English in the program.
Solution	These parents were learning English, but had varying levels of command of the English language. All were fluent in Spanish. The evaluators decided that it was best to report in Spanish. The mono-English evaluator wrote the report in English, and the bilingual colleague translated

the report into Spanish. Two days before the report was to be delivered to the parents, the bilingual colleague had to leave town. Before leaving town, she put the report on tape for the mono-English evaluator to practice. However, when the time came to give the report, the mono-English evaluator felt insecure. He told the audience in his broken Spanish that the Spanish-speaking evaluator was going to report, but that she was out of town. Then he said, "Vamos, a lip sync" and flicked on the tape, lip-syncing the report with the female voice. At first, the audience looked surprised (astounded perhaps), but they finally overcame the discrepancy between the male mouth moving and female voice coming out. The crowd applauded at the end, and hopefully understood more of the evaluation report than if it had been presented in English.

EVALUATION CAPACITY BUILDING

Program directors should view evaluation as a valuable tool for their decision making. Evaluations should be conceived of as an integral part of the ongoing program. The planning, implementation, and utilization of evaluation should become a part of an administrator's framework.

CHAPTER 10

Evaluation Instruments

The major difference between evaluation, measurement, and research is that evaluation has a value judgment component. That is, research states a finding, and measurement states how much of a quantity one has (Newman, Frye, Blumenfeld, & Newman, 1974). Neither research nor measurement says whether something is good or bad. Evaluation includes a value judgment of whether the quantities measured are desirable (Newman et al., 1981).

An important part of the evaluation design is deciding what is to be measured. What are the behaviors, conditions, or effects to be looked at in deciding if something is desirable or undesirable? Then you must decide what instrument to use to obtain that measure. Very rarely is there one instrument that will effectively determine whether a program is good or bad or needs improvement. Usually, considerably more than one instrument is necessary. How many instruments should be used? The answer is simple: Use as many as necessary to fully answer the questions, given time and cost constraints. Chances are that not all relevant aspects will be considered, but an attempt should be made to get the best information available that reflects the concerns.

If there are 10 instruments available, all of equal cost and time, but there are only enough time and resources to implement 2 or 3, it would be wise to select the instruments that are

1. Most valid
2. Most reliable

3. Have the most documentation (that is, have been used most frequently, have been researched most thoroughly, and have been
cited most often).

4. Least subjective (that is, based less on personal feelings, but
rather on observable behavior). This is not to say that subjective
information is not important, but an attempt should be made to
get estimates of the accuracy of subjective measures, using one of
the available reliability techniques (Newman et al., 1981). Some
evaluations rely more on objective information than do others.
For instance, most federally funded programs require a substantial amount of objective information.

Many different ways can be used to collect evaluation information.
Some of the more structured include norm-referenced instruments and
existing records. Instruments can be specially constructed for the
unique needs of the evaluation of the program. Surveys are often used
to obtain perceptions and attitudes. Structured and unstructured interviews can also be used. Finally, unobtrusive measures could be used
more often. These separate discussions of the various classifications of
instruments are followed by a discussion of the advantages and disadvantages of the various classifications. The chapter concludes with a
discussion of instrumentation effect and resources for obtaining information on instruments.

NORM-REFERENCED INSTRUMENTS

A standardized instrument is one that has been administered and
scored in a standard way. Standardized instruments are usually
normed, that is, they are administered to a large group of specially selected people (the norming sample) who are selected because they represent some population. If standardized administration practices were
used in the norming sample, and if the norming sample represents the
stated population, then the scores from subsequent respondents can be
referenced to those norms. Some common norming variables are (a)
region of the country, (b) gender, (c) socioeconomic status, (d) ethnicity, and (e) the nature of the problem. There should be either specific

norms for the groups representing these variables or enough individuals included in the norms like the ones under consideration that valid inferences can be made. Examples of standardized instruments include achievement instruments, intelligence instruments, aptitude instruments, and perceptual motor instruments.

A nonstandardized instrument is one that does not meet the criteria for standardized instruments. There is no norming group, the administration is not standardized, or scoring is not done in a standardized fashion. When an evaluator wants to compare results or participants to a target population, a standardized instrument should be used. If the research question can be answered without making such comparisons, a nonstandardized instrument can be used. Nonstandardized instruments are also used when no adequate standardized measure exists, which forces the evaluator either to use an existing nonstandardized measure or to develop one. A third situation when nonstandardized instruments are called for is when a population is being investigated that is different from the population that the standardized instrument was standardized on.

CRITERION-REFERENCED INSTRUMENTS

Criterion-referenced tests (CRTs) are instruments that have specific criteria options for each question. The respondent either meets the expectation of the criteria or does not. CRTs are used when there is a desire to know what the respondent knows or can do, rather than the percentile standing of the respondent. For example, telling parents that their child can spell 85% of the expected words in their grade level conveys different information from telling them that their child can spell better than 85% of the children who are at the same grade level.

CRTs are used primarily at the state level for evaluation of student (and district) performance on state curricula. The trend in the late 1990s was that more states were adopting the statewide CRTs. CRTs are costly to develop, and hence few local school districts can afford to develop their own CRTs. The curriculum objectives are usually mandated at the state level, and hence all CRTs in that state should be assessing the same objectives. "Example of a Criterion-

Referenced Instrument" in appendix D was used to evaluate a Head Start program.

SPECIALLY CONSTRUCTED INSTRUMENTS

Often, an objective of the evaluation requires a more specific measure than those discussed above. When this is the case, library research can reveal whether or not a good instrument already exists. The best place to start is with the *Fifteenth Mental Measurements Yearbook* (Plake & Impara, 2003). Then the evaluator should investigate those resources that appear to be most relevant to the field and to the content area being assessed. These resources should be exhausted before an evaluator even considers constructing an instrument. Seldom can an evaluator develop an instrument that approaches the reliability and validity of those instruments in existence.

The specially constructed instrument should start with attention to the objectives that it is intended to measure. Only those objectives should be measured by that instrument. Many evaluations rely on specially constructed instruments because of the specificity of the objectives. Since evaluations are conducted primarily to inform the local stakeholders, there is no need to use or construct an instrument that measures objectives not relevant to the program.

One procedure used to develop an instrument is to begin with a table of specifications. The columns of the table indicate the content areas to be covered in the program. The rows specify the items that measure each content area. Once this information has been entered into the table, one can ask two questions. First, are the columns sufficient? If there are other content areas covered by the program, then those columns must be added. Second, how well do the items measure the content areas? It is unusual to find that any set of items measures 100% of the desired content, but an evaluator should aim to measure at least 80%.

Specially constructed instruments are used primarily in the needs assessment stage and the program implementation assessment stage. Specifically, most staff development, program implementation, participant satisfaction, and parent satisfaction objectives are measured with specially constructed instruments. As evaluators publish their evaluations and attend conferences such as the American Educational Research Association and the American Evaluation Association, ideas are shared and the format of specially constructed instruments begins to emerge. The actual items on each specially constructed instrument will still respond to the specific objectives of each evaluation. "A Specially Constructed Instrument" in appendix D is an example of a specially constructed instrument that has been used in an elementary school situation.

SURVEYS

Evaluation objectives often lead the evaluator to specific areas that existing instruments do not address. If the information needed to answer the evaluation objective can be obtained from participants without the evaluator personally being in their presence, the evaluator uses a questionnaire or survey. Another reason for using these tools is that they can preserve anonymity. However, in-person data gathering certainly reduces anonymity. Surveys can be administered by mail, phone, Internet, or in person to a large group, usually under some time limits. Since the evaluator does not have the luxury of explaining the instrument in detail and responding to questions, the survey needs to be carefully developed. The developer must anticipate any possible confusion as well as all possible responses. Appendix D contains an example of a survey that was developed to evaluate students' use of a new instructional compact disc.

INTERVIEWS

Interviews, conducted by the evaluator or trained observer, can provide in-depth information from different information providers. Interviews can be very structured, that is, they can follow a prescribed list of questions. Interviews that have no guidelines are called unstructured. Those interviews that gather the same basic information from each respondent and then probe for further clarification fall into the semistructured interview category.

The Structured Interview

The structured interview could be standardized on a large sample from a target population, which would allow for comparisons with that population. If an evaluator wants the same information from each respondent, a structured interview should be conducted. The advantage of a structured interview is that it provides comparable data from all those interviewed. See appendix D for an example of a structured interview.

The Unstructured Interview

The unstructured interview, on the other hand, allows the interviewer to probe interesting avenues that are identified during the interview. Such an interview would have a general purpose in mind, would be individually conducted, and would flow depending upon the responses provided by the interviewee. While such questioning may provide a deeper understanding of each individual, it usually does not provide data that are comparable across participants. In addition, unstructured interviews are susceptible to the interviewer's expectations. Appendix D contains an example of an unstructured interview, possible questions, reasons for branching to further questions, and instructions as to how far to go with the questioning.

The Semistructured Interview

Evaluators frequently use a semistructured interview, a combination of the structured and unstructured interview, to capitalize on the unique benefits of each. The semistructured interview provides the necessary general data on all respondents as well as amplified data on some aspects of some respondents. A final benefit of the semistructured interview is that an avenue can be explored for respondents that may not have been anticipated when the interview was designed. See "Example of a Semistructured Phone Interview" in appendix D for one such example.

UNOBTRUSIVE MEASURES

Unobtrusive measures are those obtained when participants are unaware that they are being measured. Such data can be collected during the study routinely, or they can be collected in a fabricated setting.

While ethical considerations often restrict the obtaining of data unob-
trusively, evaluators should consider this method as an option because
respondents often do not respond honestly. Some respondents try to
help the evaluator, while others try to counter the evaluation effort. If
respondents do not know they are being measured, they cannot do either one. The key to unobtrusive measures is inference. Most unobtrusive measures require more inference than do measures that directly
measure respondents' responses. Since the general goals of the program
drive the specific objectives, the "right data" on the specified population are not likely to already exist. Unobtrusive measures have not often been used because they require creative thought and often run
counter to ethical considerations. Nevertheless, using existing records
or unobtrusive measures should be considered before collecting new
data. Some examples of unobtrusive measures are:

- Enrollment figures for the different sections of the same course
- Long-range observation of compliance with handicapped parking
  restrictions
- Attendance at voluntary weekend activities
- Long-range monitoring of a new social area

Schneider and Buckley (2002) conducted an evaluation of school
choice by using an unobtrusive measure. They pointed out that the results from surveys asking parents if they would send their child to a
particular school were not consistent with actual behavior (Glazerman,
1997; Henig, 1990; Weiher & Tedin, 2002). Schneider and Buckley reported:

> In short, research based on surveys tends to find that parents of all races
> and social classes say they prefer schools that have good teachers and high
> test scores. In addition, very few admit to being concerned by the racial or
> class composition of the student body. However, these stated preferences
> are often not congruent with observed parental behavior, where researchers
> have found significant effects of race and class. (p. 136)

As an alternative to asking parents what they would do, or what they
actually did do, Schneider and Buckley decided to monitor:

the search behavior of parents as they access information from an Internet site that provides extensive data on all the public schools. . . . By observing the search behavior of parents, we transcend the bias in survey research toward socially acceptable response patterns, a bias that may account for the strong verbal endorsement of academic criteria compared to patterns evident in actual choice behavior. Because the search behavior we study is not as "costly" as actually moving a child to another school or school district nor is it constrained by the balancing rules inherent in many choice programs, we may get an even better idea of the place of demographics versus academics in parental preferences than by observing (expensive and constrained) actual choice. (p. 136)

The results of their unobtrusive data collection of parental search of the schools indicated that parents cared about the academics but also cared about the school demographics. Their conclusion is opposite from that obtained in socially desirable surveys but in line with actual choice behavior.

EXISTING RECORDS

Existing records are sources of data that have already been collected for reasons other than the evaluator's reasons. The advantage of such information is that it is readily available. Some disadvantages are that (a) such data have usually not been collected on all the participants, (b) the conditions under which the data were collected may have been unknown or less than desirable, and (c) certain additional pieces of information would have been desirable. Some examples of existing records are:

- Teacher's grades
- Student's attendance
- Decision to enroll in subsequent courses in same area, or with same instructor
- Minutes of meetings (for instance, to verify input decisions)
- Use of library, Internet, school health center
- Previous year's performance in student's cumulative folder or transcript

BEHAVIORAL OBSERVATIONS

Behavioral observations are recordings of behavior made by an observer. The real-time behavior is in some way captured, often by recording the entire behavior by scripting the event or by audiotaping or videotaping it. Often the evaluator or program director has not stated what specific behavior is being sought. Therefore, behavioral observations are probably the weakest kind of measurement, requiring much inference as well as providing data that could be contaminated by the evaluator's expectations. Whenever possible, an evaluator should provide additional information that goes beyond such an unstructured behavioral observation. On the other hand, if the desired specific behavior has been clearly identified, then behavioral observations can be a very valuable tool.

ADVANTAGES AND DISADVANTAGES
OF THE VARIOUS INSTRUMENTS

Perhaps the single greatest advantage of surveys is the amount of information that can be collected from many participants. In a somewhat quick and cost-effective manner, evaluators can learn a great deal about values, attitudes, socioeconomic factors, and demographic data from a large sample of respondents. A related advantage of surveys is the potential to sample respondents from extremely large arbitrary populations. Finally, surveys can be of great practical utility. Much of the remaining information in this section has been adapted from Newman and McNeil (1998). These issues are discussed in more detail in Newman and McNeil as well as Wilkinson and McNeil (1996).

As with all information collection methods, surveys have inherent limitations. One notable issue is the accuracy of survey data, since respondents may not see the importance of survey questions or, equally disturbing, may respond in biased ways. This latter concern is especially salient when survey questions cover sensitive topics, such as sexual patterns, drug habits, or AIDS awareness.

Another liability of surveys is return rates, especially when surveys are mailed. The result is not only a lower number of respondents, but also, more importantly, the respondents who did not return the surveys probably differ from those who did return the surveys.

Several recommendations are offered to improve the quality of surveys. First, evaluators must develop clear and detailed descriptions of the arbitrary population and the sampling procedures used to select members from this population. Sample representativeness is mostly a function of sampling procedure. Unfortunately, only some of the target population responds to most mailed surveys, so representativeness is usually an issue with surveys.

Some specific tips can be offered in terms of developing the survey. Often overlooked by evaluators is a rationale for why the survey contains the questions it does. One way evaluators can justify the content of their survey is via the needs assessment, which should provide the evaluator clues about what questions or sets of questions should be included.

In constructing survey items and selecting response formats, the evaluator must account for the literacy level of the respondents. Further, items on surveys must consist of clearly defined terms to reduce different interpretations of each item. For instance, the term *egalitarian* could be interpreted one way by some respondents, misinterpreted by other respondents, or simply unknown to many other respondents. The data derived from such a question would be useless.

A third recommendation, somewhat related to survey construction, is evaluating the degree to which respondents might answer questions dishonestly. Usually, the degree of dishonesty bias relates to the purpose of the evaluation as well as the type of attitude or behavior being surveyed. Consider the increased likelihood of a respondent giving false responses in a survey given to company employees when the purpose of obtaining the information is to fire those employees who have drug or alcohol problems. On the other hand, lying would be at a minimum in cases where an evaluator was using the survey as a needs assessment instrument.

When the accuracy of respondents' responses is likely to be highly questionable, evaluators have several tactics available. First, the evaluator should remove survey titles that directly state the survey purpose and substitute these titles with more socially acceptable terms. For instance, the Drug and Alcohol Survey could be changed to the Survey of Recreational Habits. This is common in the development of habit use surveys and some measures of personality (for example, *shyness* is titled *social reticence*). Other strategies to combat inaccurate responding are (a) using preexisting surveys that contain response bias scales, (b) including distractor items not relevant to the survey, which disrupt the development of response sets, and (c) alternating positive and negative statements, like "I like professors who stick to the facts," and "I find it annoying when professors tell anecdotes."

Finally, it is crucial that evaluators pilot the administration and practical utility of the survey before the full-fledged implementation. Evaluators should administer the instrument and request feedback from pilot participants after completing the survey. Feedback should be given about the clarity of directions, either oral or written, the clarity of the items, and if relevant, the degree of response bias. When direct administration is used, the evaluator should practice delivery of standardized instructions to respondents and develop a standardized proctoring procedure. In other words, the survey should be administered in the same way each time, much like any standardized test. Such standardized delivery of the survey will obtain better information.

INSTRUMENTATION EFFECT

One of the threats to internal validity that evaluators worry about is referred to as "instrumentation effect." Instrumentation effect occurs when the information resulting from two testing situations does not mean the same thing. Instrumentation effect can be a competing explainer when the same instrument is used at baseline and at posttest. The change in mean scores should be a function of the program being evaluated and not a change in the instrument itself. Some obvious examples of instrumentation effect are:

1. The copy quality of the instruments is very poor at one testing time.
2. The meaning of the instrument changes over time—words have different connotations or have different associations due to change in common usage.
3. If the instrument is a behavioral observation measure, the observer may become tired or may expect more at posttest. (One

way to avoid this problem is to videotape all observations and then have the videos randomly rated. Perceptive raters might still see time differences such as winter or summer clothing, different holidays displayed on the bulletin board, and the degree to which students understand classroom rules and procedures.)

CHAPTER 11

Reporting

Reporting occurs in various stages of the GEM. The function of reporting is crucial, as this is the major mechanism by which the evaluation is communicated to the various stakeholders. The evaluation reports must counteract the skepticism that often surrounds the utility of evaluations. Newman and Deitchman (1983) identified four reasons for such skepticism. The first reason is psychological, in that evaluations tend to be associated with personal accountability. Many people find it uncomfortable to have someone looking over their shoulder, judging them. This sensitivity can create an atmosphere of hostility and lack of cooperation. Staff often try to discredit the (negative) evaluation in order to protect themselves. The discrediting can be passive, such as shelving the evaluation. On the other hand, the discrediting can be active, such as focusing on only the positive outcomes, emphasizing limitations of procedures that obtained negative findings, or not rehiring the evaluator for the subsequent year.

The second reason for skepticism is political. Almost all funding for state and federal programs requires an evaluation. Without an evaluation component written into the grant proposal, funding is generally not considered. Therefore, often the evaluation component is a facade, written only to meet requirements, and everyone in the program knows it. Often not enough planning went into the evaluation component, the evaluator was not hired early in the life of the program, or staff are not committed to the evaluation. Since most federal and state programs are funded for just 1 to 3 years, many agencies have little interest in having the program evaluated because they do not foresee the program continuing or because they have little capability of continuing the funding at the local level. This is an unfortunate waste of taxpayers' money. We feel that all programs should have a high degree of replicability. By this we mean that any new program should have the potential of being replicated in future years and in other locations (Newman, McNeil, & Frass, 2004). If a proposed program has little probability of being in place next year, or 2 years from now, why implement it, let alone evaluate it? We would argue that too many educational and other social projects have been introduced and then disappeared because they had no "staying power." Some of the projects that disappeared might have been evaluated positively. However, we suggest that their eminent demise could have been determined before the program was implemented.

The third reason for skepticism is academic.

> In this case the evaluator may become so involved in the process of the evaluation sight is lost as to how it fits into the entire program. Evaluation then becomes almost autonomous; it becomes its own purpose. The evaluator is concerned about being very precise and becomes a stickler for detail at the cost of losing sight of the larger questions. The evaluation can then become an academic exercise in futility. (Newman & Deichtman, 1983, p. 294)

The fourth reason for skepticism is irrelevance. As Newman and Deitchman (1983) pointed out, "unfortunately, many evaluators look neither at their criteria nor at the objectives from a multidimensional point of view. Consequently, if the objectives or criteria are not perceived to be relevant to stakeholders with different interests, there is no way of achieving credibility" (p. 294). Hendricks (1994) discussed various aspects of improving the reporting of evaluation results. Carter (1994) focused on maximizing the use of evaluation results.

EXECUTIVE SUMMARY

The short and comprehensive executive summary overviews the entire evaluation report. This one- or two-page document suffices for many stakeholders. The executive summary contains the essence of the evaluation report and therefore is not bogged down by details. Several years later, the information in the executive summary may well be all that is remembered about the evaluation (and maybe even the program). Thus, it is crucial to write a quality executive summary. The executive summary must be comprehensive and unbiased. Most importantly, it must be understandable by the various stakeholders. Several versions of the executive summary aimed at different stakeholders may be called for. Even for those stakeholders who will read more of the report, the executive summary will be the first part of the report that is read. Appendix F contains an example of an executive summary.

TRADITIONAL REPORTING

The evaluation reports are written and disseminated for use by the stakeholders (not just for use by the program director or for the ego of the evaluator). The content and format must be appropriate to each stakeholder group, which may mean a different report for some stakeholders. The evaluator's responsibility should not end with the completion of the report but should extend to discussion and assistance in using the information for decision making. The evaluator's intimate knowledge of the evaluation process, including how each objective was measured and who provided the information, makes the evaluator a valuable resource (not decision maker) in the decision-making process.

Many evaluators make the mistake of writing an evaluation report that is too technical or includes jargon that is not commonly understood. Evaluators all too often write a report as if it were intended to be read by other evaluators rather than by teachers, administrators, and school board members. Jargon-loaded reports are usually rated as being difficult to read (Locatis, Smith, & Blake, 1979). One approach to checking on "understandability" is to "dry-run" the report on a small sample of stakeholders.

Evaluations are conducted for the purpose of providing information to decision makers. That information must be available at the time the decisions are to be made. Many evaluators come from an academic setting where research and articles emanating from that research are not time-bound. Whether the article is finished this month or next month or next year is often of little consequence. On the other hand, the evaluation will be of little value if it is not produced on schedule. Many programs operate on a recurring cycle (for example, annually as in school-based programs, semesters as in institutions of higher learning, and six or eight sessions as in many insurance-based counseling services). Evaluation information is needed at the time of planning for the next cycle. Planning for the next cycle should benefit from the evaluation of the previous cycle. When the program director is intimately involved with the evaluation, the process reports and draft final reports may well be sufficient for decision making. When a problem is identified early, attempts can be made to correct it. However, if the problem cannot be corrected, the stakeholders should not be surprised to discover in the final report that there remains a problem.

CHART ESSAY

The chart essay is a concise way to communicate the results of the evaluation. The chart essay describes (a) the evaluation question, (b) how the information was obtained—the data source, (c) the results, and (d) conclusions. The chart essay therefore links these four components on one page. Most evaluators and program directors could probably do the linking themselves, but other stakeholders may have difficulty. The chart essay has been enthusiastically accepted as a way to highlight evaluation activities and results. Appendix F contains an example of a chart essay. Notice the links between the four components.

DEBRIEFING WITH PROGRAM DIRECTOR

The program director is the one stakeholder who should have the most interest in the evaluation results. Although the evaluator keeps the program director informed throughout, a final meeting discussing the evaluation efforts and results is highly recommended. This meeting can also serve as a discussion for both program and evaluation modifications for the next cycle. This meeting may also serve as an opportunity for the program director to provide feedback on the draft report.

It is always a good idea to get input from the program director before the final report becomes final.

ALTERNATIVE METHODS OF REPORTING

The traditional paper report may not be the best method in certain circumstances. The reporting of process results may often require different methods. In addition, certain stakeholders may find methods other than the traditional written report to be of interest. We first present four alternative methods of reporting process results. Then we present one example of reporting to nontechnical stakeholders. The section concludes with a discussion of the value of "human-interest stories."

Four Alternative Methods of Reporting Process Results

Four alternative methods of reporting process results were discussed by McNeil (1991, 2002). The goal of methods other than written reports is to make the evaluation results useful to the stakeholders. If evaluators really want evaluation to improve the delivery of a program, then evaluators need to communicate the evaluation results to those implementing the program. Those who deliver the program often do not receive the evaluation reports, and if they do, they are often not inclined to wade through the usually sterile and often lengthy reports. Evaluators must find ways to communicate to these persons.

Table Excerpts

Table excerpts are one way to facilitate communication of evaluation results. Stakeholders have specific interests in the program, and thus the evaluator should report on those interests to them. Only selected tables may be of interest to them. Some tables might even be modified so that they will be of more interest to a particular stakeholder group.

In one reporting situation, table excerpts were presented to teachers. They were asked to interpret each table by discussing the positive and negative aspects of the information in each table. When teachers had trouble with the analysis, the evaluator facilitated discussion. Some teachers did ask about other aspects that were in the complete evaluation report, and they were given a copy. The vast majority of teachers, though, were satisfied with the information that was presented to them.

A Video

A video can be made if the same report is to be presented to a large audience or on several occasions to subgroups of similar stakeholders. For instance, when the evaluator had to report to five groups of teachers on five different occasions, a video was made. The video was a particularly good idea, as the evaluator subsequently was scheduled out of town on several of the dates. (Teachers who were absent could check out the video later.)

One immediately apparent advantage of a video is that it can be used in the absence of the evaluator. In addition, a consistent report is given to each of the stakeholders, with a record of just what was said that is available for later use. Another advantage is that the teachers identified with the background music and the short clips of students and teachers. The lead-in music attracted their attention, and when the talking head might begin to bore them, the video technicians cut to the children and the music. A commercial company provided the technical support in exchange for getting promotional recognition in the credits.

The Gong Show

The Gong Show was an unabashed attempt for the developer of many game shows, Chuck Barris, to have fun by doing his own thing on his own TV show. Chuck Barris was the host, and contestants were allowed to show their talents on national TV. A panel of celebrities judged the talent on a 1 to 10 scale. When the talent was judged bad enough, the contestant was gonged and not allowed to finish the act. The gonger had to defend the reason for gonging, which usually did not take much explanation and made for rich humor.

With the impetus of Keith McNeil, a team of three evaluators and three program directors planned a Gong Show presentation for reporting classroom observations of the implementation of several teaching strategies. The program directors had previously trained the teachers on the specific teaching techniques. The evaluators were responsible for determining if and how well the teachers were currently implementing the strategies in the classrooms. Essential to successful implementation was the correct order of components in each strategy, as well as the correct implementation of each component.

Each program director began to implement one strategy correctly and then purposefully either did something wrong, used components out of order, slowly self-destructed, or disintegrated. One other program director would gong the act and explain why the act was gonged. Then one evaluator shared whether these same problems were or were not observed in the classrooms.

Although this reporting method required extensive planning and cooperation between the evaluators and the program director, the teachers enthusiastically received it. In reality, the functions of staff development and evaluation had been blended. The teachers received a different dose of the strategies. The teachers became involved with the Gong Show reporting, watching closely for mistakes the program directors made even though they respected the program directors very much. Teachers began to hiss when mistakes occurred, and the hissing got louder when the program director was way off the accepted implementation process.

One of the program directors was somewhat hesitant to use this approach with the group for which she was responsible. However, when she saw the reaction of the teachers and realized the staff development benefits of this reporting method, she requested that her group also take part in the Gong Show.

While those who conducted the Gong Show were positive about the experience, such a reporting method would not always work. For instance, there was a lot of planning required between two units in an organization that often did not communicate well. In addition, such a presentation requires a certain personality of the presenters, and a certain camaraderie between the audience and the presenters. Finally, the impact of the Gong Show method would be seriously diminished if the content of the report was not appropriate or if the method had recently been used. For the right time and the right place, the program directors, the evaluators, and the teachers had some fun—and the teachers improved in their ability to implement the program.

Typical Teacher Caricature

Typical teacher caricature was used to report a set of classroom implementation results. The typical "nerd" or typical "valley girl" provided the inspiration for this technique, suggested by a colleague, Dr. Kate Jones. The typical "teacher" was constructed. Process information regarding classroom observations that the evaluators wanted to report to teachers was incorporated into the drawing of the teacher and surroundings. For instance, the teacher was wearing an "I Love A Priori" sweatshirt, showing that the teachers were very enthusiastic about the program called "A Priori." On the other hand, the trash basket had become the resting place for one poem that was supposed to be used during the observational period but was used by few teachers. The picture was crudely drawn, adding a further touch of informality to the method.

Each teacher was handed the drawing and asked to figure out what it depicted. Teachers enthusiastically tried to discover the hidden messages. Teachers easily grasped the notion that each was not being depicted, that the picture was a summary of all the teachers that the evaluators had seen. Although only a small part of the evaluation information was shared in this way, the teachers were provided with a visual image of the results that was easy to interpret. Since the goal of any reporting effort should be to maximize the amount of information that the stakeholders retain (rather than maximize the amount of information that the stakeholders receive), this reporting method seems to have face validity as a useful method.

Reporting to Nontechnical Stakeholders

There are four issues that an evaluator should consider when reporting to nontechnical stakeholders. First, the evaluator must always remember to communicate with each stakeholder group. Second, the format of the report will likely be very different from that of the report to the more technical stakeholders. Third, the content will be vastly different, as the interests of the nontechnical stakeholders are vastly different. Fourth, the language of the report will likely be constrained by the type of stakeholders. Each of these issues is discussed next.

Communicating With Each Stakeholder Group

Communicating with each stakeholder group is extremely important. A particular stakeholder group may be only tangentially interested in the intricacies of the program. Their primary concern may be that they or their children have benefited from the program. They are not as interested in small adjustments in the program that might improve the program in the future.

Nontechnical audiences also do not want a long evaluation report. Most nontechnical audiences appreciate a short report. They are not as understanding of the purpose of the evaluation and thus do not have much interest in the report. Many might prefer that evaluation resources be transferred to bolstering the program. The old and tried principle of KISS—Keep It Simple, Stupid—is quite appropriate in this instance.

Format of the Report

The format of the report is usually written but may be presented in some other way. The evaluator (in conjunction with the program director) should consider whether the report will be written or verbal. Some nontechnical audiences may feel challenged by a written report, whereas a verbal report may be more inviting. Verbal reports usually generate more audience participation than do written reports.

Whichever format is chosen, the report should not look expensive. Nontechnical stakeholders are more interested in the context of the report than they are in the packaging. The report must communicate with them, so you do not want the packaging to interfere with that communication.

Another way to facilitate communication with nontechnical stakeholders is to present the report in a consistent format. The consistency should be both within the report and from one report to another. You want to facilitate comprehension of the report as much as possible. Helping the reader of the report is one way to facilitate that comprehension. Some suggestions for making reports consistent are:

- Group objectives into categories.
- Discuss objectives one at a time.

- Put the objectives in bold type.
- Identify measurement instruments for each objective.
- Present all results the same way (pie charts or bar graphs communicate best to some audiences).

The final format consideration is to refrain from putting technical information into this report for the nontechnical audience. The technical reports can, and should, be referenced. If the technical report is referenced, the nontechnical audience will appreciate that they do not have to wade through the technical information. In addition, they will gain confidence that there is information in support of the statements in the nontechnical report. If someone does want to look up the more detailed information, they will know where to go to get the technical information.

Content of the Nontechnical Report

Content of the nontechnical report should be concise; the report should contain only the primary objectives and findings. Nontechnical audiences are usually interested in the general results of the program. If there are objectives that are of particular concern to a particular audience, those objectives, and only those objectives, should be discussed. Parents of School A are not particularly interested in the effects of the program in Schools B, C, and D. Likewise, parents of children in 3rd grade are not particularly interested in the success of the program in 1st and 2nd grades.

Reporting Human-Interest Stories

A human-interest story is a description of a single individual. This description may be short or rather long, but it depicts in human terms how a person has participated in and benefited from the program. Usually enough background characteristics (including a fictitious name) are provided so that the reader believes that a real person is being discussed.

These stories allow for in-depth description of the program and program effects. They also facilitate the illustration of how various facets of a program might affect one individual. All of this reminds the reader that the program was designed for and provided to real people.

Human-interest stories break up the monotony in most evaluation reports. Many readers are intrigued with these stories, as evidenced by the fact that newspaper reporters often use this strategy.

One problem with including human-interest stories is the difficulty in identifying a "typical" program participant. Often these "typical" participants have a combination of traits and experiences from many people that are attributed to one person.

The choice of the case can be guided by the expectations or biases of the evaluator or the program director. Most authors realize that they should use an alias; otherwise, they could put the participant at risk. Once an alias has been used, it becomes easy to invent convenient information for this case. If the information is consistent with the real information, there is no problem. On the other hand, there is an ethical violation if the invented information is a result of preconceived notions that are not supported by the evaluation information.

CHAPTER 12

Application of GEM to Evaluating Schools

Most of the GEM applications discussed in the previous chapters have been for "programs," identifiable components of larger systems. In this chapter we discuss how GEM can be used to evaluate an entire school. Each state has a system in place to monitor and rate schools. The federal government began monitoring schools, districts, and state educational systems in 2002 by enacting the No Child Left Behind Act (NCLB). With the new federal system of accountability, it may be possible for a state to rate a school as "meets expectations," yet the same school is rated as "needs improvement" by the adequate yearly progress (AYP) provision of NCLB. This chapter demonstrates how GEM can be applied to help campus administrators monitor student achievement in the state and federal system of accountability. One application of GEM is an organizational tool for writing campus action plans, also known as campus improvement plans (CIPs). GEM is more detailed than a CIP in that it documents how well, or how poorly, an action or improvement was implemented. The quality of implementation is additional information for school administrators when they are considering campus improvement. The final section of this chapter discusses GEM and how it can be applied to almost any definition of school improvement. We first discuss several of the crucial provisions of the No Child Left Behind Act (2002) that will have an enormous impact on how schools assess their effectiveness.

ACCOUNTABILITY

This section first describes NCLB and two of its crucial provisions— AYP and highly qualified teachers. State accountability systems for California, Florida, New York, and Texas are summarized with respect to AYP.

No Child Left Behind

The federal government increased its presence in educational accountability in January 2002. Nearly 40 years after the Elementary and Secondary Education Act (ESEA) of 1965, the No Child Left Behind Act (NCLB) was signed into law. NCLB focuses educators on four principles:

1. Increased accountability
2. More choices for students and parents of students attending Title I schools that fail to meet state standards
3. Expanding the "flexibility for accountability" bargain with states by using federal funds in exchange for stronger accountability
4. Reading First

In addition to these four principles, NCLB emphasizes (a) citing scientifically based research in preparing, training, and recruiting highly qualified teachers, (b) implementing programs that benefit all limited English proficient (LEP) students, and (c) ensuring that schools are safe (United States Department of Education, n.d.). The initial phase of NCLB has educators focusing on increased accountability by defining adequate yearly progress (AYP).

Adequate Yearly Progress

The definition of AYP is left to each state, with approval by the federal Department of Education. Every state plan must:

- Apply the same standards to all public school students
- Be statistically valid and reliable

- Demonstrate continuous and substantial improvements for all students
- Use high-quality yearly assessments in mathematics, reading or language arts, and science that are the primary measures of progress for public elementary schools, secondary schools, and the state
- Include science assessments by 2007
- Include additional measurable annual objectives for all public school students with subgroup reporting for economically disadvantaged students, major racial and ethnic groups, students with disabilities, and students with limited English proficiency
- Report graduation rates for high school students (No Child Left Behind Act of 2002)

Title I in No Child Left Behind stipulates that baseline data documenting student achievement begins in school year 2001–2002 with 100% of public school students meeting or exceeding the state's proficient level on selected assessments by 2014 (No Child Left Behind Act of 2002). State education agencies identify intermediate goals and design the process for achieving the 2014 goal identified in NCLB. The primary measure for student achievement in NCLB is standardized tests. At minimum, states are required to test in mathematics and reading or language arts once in grades 3–5, once in grades 6–9, and once in grades 10–12. Each student must be assessed in mathematics and reading or language arts in every grade 3–8 by school year 2005–2006. Each state plan measuring academic achievement must require schools to assess 95% of all students in each subpopulation (No Child Left Behind Act of 2002). The minimum percent assessed ensures that students from all major racial and ethnic groups, economically disadvantaged students, students with disabilities, and students who are limited English proficient are represented. The percent of students passing is also disaggregated by student groups and is set by the state. One requirement in NCLB is that the percentage of students passing the annual assessments increases in equal increments. A second requirement is that every school will have 100% of the students passing all assessments by 2014. Table 12.1 is an example of two states with different accountability systems and different assessments. Beginning in 2005–2006 states are required to assess all students in mathematics and language arts in grades 3–8 and at least once in grades 10–12. Beginning 2007–2008, science is required at least once in grades 3–5, grades 6–9, and grades 10–12. The example shows starting percentages and equal increments for the first state, State A, as compared to another state, State B.

In the example, the assessment plan for State A has different passing percentages for the three assessments with increases in equal increments until the goal of 100% passing is reached. The plan for State B has all assessments beginning at 33% with identical increases in equal increments until 100% passing is achieved. Educators in both states chose not to require an increase in percent passing from the 1st to the 2nd year. Two years of a stable baseline provides more flexibility for school administrators by increasing the margin for error while teachers adjust to a system of accountability heavily dependent on standardized tests. The plan for State B keeps passing rates constant for 3 years after 2003–2004 and requires a 17% percent increase of students passing all three tests every 3rd year. The plan for State A begins at a lower passing rate than State B and requires an increase of student passing rates less than 10% every year. In this example, failing to meet AYP is defined as any campus in the respective states not meeting the passing standards for any assessment by any subgroup of students. In addition, any campus that does not have 95% participation in any subgroup would be considered as failing to meet AYP.

Table 12.1. Sample AYP Intermediate Goals for Two States

| | Passing Rates | | | | | |
| | State A | | | State B | | |
School Year	Reading	Math	Science	Reading	Math	Science
2002–2003	35.0%	25.0%	30.0%	33.0%	33.0%	33.0%
2003–2004	35.0%	25.0%	30.0%	33.0%	33.0%	33.0%
2004–2005	41.5%	32.5%	37.0%	50.0%	50.0%	50.0%
2005–2006	48.0%	40.0%	44.0%	50.0%	50.0%	50.0%
2006–2007	54.5%	47.5%	51.0%	50.0%	50.0%	50.0%
2007–2008	61.0%	55.0%	58.0%	67.0%	67.0%	67.0%
2008–2009	67.5%	62.5%	65.0%	67.0%	67.0%	67.0%
2009–2010	74.0%	70.0%	72.0%	67.0%	67.0%	67.0%
2010–2011	80.5%	77.5%	79.0%	84.0%	84.0%	84.0%
2011–2012	87.0%	85.0%	86.0%	84.0%	84.0%	84.0%
2012–2013	93.5%	92.5%	93.0%	84.0%	84.0%	84.0%
2013–2014	100.0%	100.0%	100.0%	100.0%	100.0%	100.0%

Monitoring AYP and needed improvements should be organized with an evaluation model. Before describing how to apply GEM as an AYP monitoring instrument, we discuss another provision in NCLB that will impact schools almost as much as AYP. NCLB requires every classroom to have a highly qualified teacher.

Highly Qualified Teachers

The highly qualified teachers provision defines such a teacher as (a) having at least a bachelor's degree, (b) having completed full state certification or licensure, and (c) having demonstrated competence in subject areas taught (United States Department of Education, 2004). Districts receiving Title I funds are required to contact all parents of children attending Title I schools by letter, informing them of their rights to request information regarding the qualifications of the teachers in their child's classroom. In addition, schools are required to notify parents when a child is taught 4 consecutive weeks by a teacher who is not highly qualified (No Child Left Behind Act of 2002). Because of requirements in Title II, districts may need to change staff development procedures to comply with NCLB.

Title II is the set of guidelines in NCLB for preparing, training, and recruiting quality teachers and principals. As described in the law regarding local use of Title II funds, districts must develop initiatives that effectively retain highly qualified teachers and principals. A partial list of other professional development initiatives includes:

- Training teachers and principals to involve parents in education, especially parents of limited English proficient and immigrant children
- Providing training on how to teach students with special learning needs
- Developing and implementing innovative programs that train teachers to integrate technology into curricula and instruction
- Reforming tenure systems
- Improving the knowledge of teachers, principals, and paraprofessionals in core academic subjects, effective instructional strategies, academic content standards, student achievement, and state assessments

Administrators with experience in standardized assessments as a measure for accountability are very much aware of the percent of students passing the state tests on their campus. Standardized testing is part of the decision filter for campus administrators when it comes to creating class schedules. Past research shows that test scores increase as instructional time increases. In general, campus administrators (a) are the best systems thinkers in the organization, (b) understand how different programs interact with each other, and (c) know how to work within the constraints of a bureaucracy to maximize instructional time. The professional development provisions of NCLB are intended to increase the quality of instruction. In many instances, the connection between teacher in-service and student achievement is not obvious. Title II requires some documentation that implies the connection. Evaluation of staff development requires little time, especially if the administrator has experience in using an evaluation model. Results of the evaluation will increase the quality of professional development and, combined with student achievement results, give administrators more information to assess instructional strengths and weaknesses.

Selected State Accountability Systems for Educators

The primary measure of school and district adequate yearly progress is student performance on state assessments. Each state department of education is required to set academic standards and administer assessments to measure how well students learned the standards. States have the flexibility to set the starting percentages for passing rates and use alternative assessments for LEP students and students with disabilities. Schools are responsible for implementing the state plan for NCLB. Part of the state plan must include how schools will measure performance in reading, mathematics, and science.

Four state plans approved by the U.S. Department of Education were selected for a comparison of how schools are to meet AYP. Measures in reading performance, mathematics performance, and science performance for elementary, middle, and high schools are analyzed. In addition to test scores, AYP also requires an additional academic indicator for elementary, middle, and high schools chosen by state educators. Graduation rates are another key indicator in evaluating high schools. The comparison of AYP plans for California, Florida, New York, and Texas focuses on each state's definition of AYP based primarily on the academic assessments. Table 12.2 is a summary of the assessments for AYP in the selected states.

California students take the California Standards Test (CST) and the California High School Exit Exam (CAHSEE). The AYP indicators for California include the CST for grades 2–9 in reading and mathematics performance and the CAHSEE in reading and mathematics for grade 10. Science assessments exist for the grades required in NCLB. The additional indicator is the academic performance index (API) plus graduation rate (State of California, 2003). The API is a score achieved by schools and includes California Standards Tests, California Achievement Tests, and California High Schools Exit Examinations (California Department of Education, 2004). The battery of tests contains both criterion-referenced and norm-referenced examinations.

Florida educators use the Florida Comprehensive Assessment Test (FCAT) as one measure of school effectiveness. AYP indicators include the FCAT for reading and mathematics in grades 3–8 and 10 and FCAT science in grades 5, 8, and 10. The additional academic indicators for Florida students are the FCAT writing test in grades 4, 8, and 10, and graduation rate. Educational administrators in Florida manage schools with the guidance of a state accountability system. The Florida A+ School Grading System rates schools from A to F. Any school graded as a D or F in this system does not meet AYP (Florida Department of Education, 2003).

New York State uses a variety of exams in defining AYP. Elementary and middle schools report student scores in grades 4 and 8 on reading and mathematics assessments. Grades 3, 5, 6, and 7 will be added in school year 2005–2006. Additional academic indicators for elementary and middle schools include a science test in grades 4 and 8. By school year 2006–2007, attendance will replace the science test as the additional academic indicator in grades 4 and 8. Assessment scores for high school seniors are reported for English language arts and mathematics. Tests include Regents Comprehensive Examinations, Regents Competency Tests, or approved alternatives to either of the Regents tests. The approved alternatives generally include SAT II, Advanced Placement, or International Baccalaureate. The additional academic indicator for

Table 12.2. Assessments and Other Measures for AYP in Selected States

Performance Indicator/Grade(s)	California	Florida	New York	Texas
Reading	CST 2–9; CAHSEE 10	FCAT 3–8, 10	Reading 3–8, 12	TAKS 3–8, 10
Mathematics	CST 2–9; CAHSEE 10	FCAT 3–8, 10	Math 3–8, 12	TAKS 3–8, 10
Science	In development, grades 5, 8, 10	FCAT 5, 8, 10	Science 4, 8	TAKS 5, 10; in development, grade 8
Additional indicator: elementary and middle school	API	FCAT writing, grades 4 and 8	Science, grades 4 and 8 (attendance 2006)	Attendance
Additional indicator: high school	API; graduation rate	FCAT writing; graduation rate	Graduation rate	Graduation rate

Note: CST = California Standards Test, CAHSEE = California High School Exit Exam,
API = academic performance index, FCAT = Florida Comprehensive Assessment Test,
TAKS = Texas Assessment of Knowledge and Skills

high school is graduation rate (New York State Education Department, 2003).

Texas educators assess students in grades 3–11 with the Texas Assessment of Knowledge and Skills (TAKS). Scores on TAKS reading and mathematics are reported for AYP in grades 3–8 and 10. Science will be reported in the required grades in 2007–2008. An additional academic indicator for elementary and middle schools is attendance. High schools use graduation rate as the additional academic indicator (Texas Education Agency, 2003).

The Role of Standardized Tests

Standardized tests are the instruments required to measure adequate yearly progress in No Child Left Behind. Standardized tests serve two purposes. The first is to measure instructional quality. Students demonstrate learning by passing tests. Many argue correctly that there are other ways to measure learning, but standardized tests are the monitoring instrument of choice because they are easily produced and inexpensive to score. Districts are required to make accommodations for students with disabilities and limited English proficient students. Requiring schools to test at least 95% of all students and disaggregating scores by economically disadvantaged, major racial and ethnic groups, special education, and limited English proficiency is the process for monitoring the academic progress of all children. State educators used scores and graduation rates from 2001–2002 to set the baseline percentage of students passing and graduating high school.

It should be noted that nowhere in the No Child Left Behind Act of 2002 is it stated that retention or delayed graduation is a consequence for failing a test. The intent of the law is to make schools accountable for every child. In NCLB children do not fail to learn; schools fail to educate.

Some students require more resources to educate. Children with disabilities, economically disadvantaged students, and students at risk of dropping out of school are a few of the challenges students, parents, and educators must overcome in order to meet academic standards. Additional funding to help schools with these challenges is available through federal and state sources.

Funding for the initiatives in NCLB is channeled through customary means, such as Title I and Title II for qualifying schools. Schools do not lose federal funding for failing to meet AYP, but there are consequences for elementary or secondary schools failing to meet or exceed AYP for 2 or more consecutive years as defined by their respective state AYP plan. Schools identified as needing improvement for 2 consecutive years may be required to provide parents the option of sending their child to another school in the district at no expense to the family (No Child Left Behind Act of 2002). An effective school administrator operates a campus within the guidelines of some form of evaluation and takes corrective action before the school is identified as needing improvement. A typical campus evaluation document is a campus improvement plan, also known as a campus action plan.

CAMPUS IMPROVEMENT PLANS

Local educational agencies receiving Title I funds are required to prepare a local educational report card each year (No Child left Behind Act of 2002). Information in a campus improvement plan (CIP) includes (a) student achievement data, (b) percentage of students not tested, (c) graduation rates, and (d) professional qualifications of teachers. Campus administrators understand the value of an action plan. It serves to document the current status, or baseline data, of student achievement. The plan lists the goals and objectives for the current school year. Timelines are stated for each objective, and the person or persons responsible are listed for each initiative.

Every school program should be in a CIP. State and federal accountability systems emphasize reading, mathematics, and science. However, the arts, physical education, social sciences, and extracurricular programs are accountable also. Communities require quality educational programs in all disciplines, but some disciplines can be best evaluated with information other than standardized tests. This section introduces examples of educational programs that do not require standardized tests results for the CIP. An example requiring standardized tests results is introduced in the next section.

Current Status

Current status in NCLB is the same as baseline data in GEM. It is important to remember that *current* is a relative term in education. Current test results are the most recent standardized test results. In this case, current could mean a week to 11 months. Current status is important information in a CIP because it is what the subsequent results will be compared to. Consider three examples that do not include standardized test results.

The first example is a performing arts teacher who had 28 students participate in the spring dance recital last year. There were three performances, and 212 members of the community attended at least one show. The teacher received many compliments on the performances and plans to increase the number of student dancers for the show next spring. The second example is a school nurse who worked with physical education teachers and the school nutrition staff in a campaign designed to increase student awareness of healthy choices for lunch. She was mildly disappointed in survey results and has plans to improve the healthy choice campaign. The third example is an initiative by the computer teacher. The technology fair was a big success, but the organizer wished that more students in kindergarten through grade 3 participated. All three examples of students participating in school programs have much in common, but most important is a dedicated educator. In addition to teaching students new knowledge and skills, the staff takes the time to measure the impact their work has on the school and community. They know the current status of the program as measured by participation and questionnaires.

Goals and Objectives

A goal is a statement of intent and requires no measurable outcome. An objective must be measured and requires a rationale to exist. Generally, the rationale for an objective in a CIP is a documented need. The nurse, to continue the example from the previous section, witnesses many students eating snacks from the vending machines rather than purchasing lunch at the cafeteria. She compares daily lunch receipts provided by the cafeteria manager to the vending machine totals provided by the principal. Her objective is to increase the ratio of receipts in favor of the cafeteria. The goal is to help children choose a healthier lifestyle.

Timelines

Timelines are usually required for the current school year and are stated specifically. The performing arts teacher begins recruiting students in August. In addition to planning the show and supervising rehearsals, she must also find sponsors and recruit parent volunteers. Each sponsor and volunteer should have specific obligations or duties that will require a timeline stating when the specific obligations and duties are completed.

Person Responsible

Principals are responsible for supervising all of the staff in the school, but few entries in a CIP list the principal as the person responsible. For instance, the reading specialist's name may be listed in the CIP as the person responsible for implementing the new reading program. An assistant principal may be listed as the person responsible for improving the quality of student data reported to the school district's central office. Action items pertaining to special education may have a licensed professional in special education listed as the person responsible. Attaching a name to an objective assigns ownership for the objective listed in the CIP.

ADEQUATE YEARLY PROGRESS AND CAMPUS IMPROVEMENT PLANS

A campus improvement plan should contain a section on adequate yearly progress. The information collected through AYP is valuable information for assessing a program. Principals and program managers can communicate achievement results, by student group, about their campus on reading, mathematics, science, and other indicators required by the state. The information in AYP reports shows where schools need to improve in order to meet requirements under NCLB. This section examines a fictitious high school in Texas with sample AYP data. The focus of the analysis is on current status of the school by AYP standards, goals and objectives for AYP, and consequences for failing to meet AYP.

Current Status According to Adequate Yearly Progress

For AYP, baseline data is (a) the percentage of students who participated in statewide assessments, (b) the percentage of students who passed the assessments, (c) graduation rates for high schools, and (d) any other academic indicators included in the AYP plan developed by state educators. Current status is documented for all student groups required by the state AYP plan. Table 12.3 is an example of current status for a fictitious high school in Texas. The Texas AYP plan disaggregates student groups by three major ethnicities (African-American, Hispanic, and White). Economically disadvantaged, special education, and limited English proficient are other student groups for which data is reported in the Texas AYP accountability plan.

Students attending Texas high schools are assessed with TAKS in grades 9, 10, and 11. Adequate yearly progress in NCLB is measured with reading and mathematics assessments for grade 10 only. The assessments have a performance standard as well as a participation standard. The performance standard in reading for 2003 is 46.8% passing for each student group. The performance standard in mathematics for 2003 is a 33.4% passing rate for each student group. The participation standard is 95% for both assessments. A fifth measure, graduation rate, was set at 70%. The information in Table 12.3 shows the high school did not meet AYP in math participation. Less than 95% of the students in the economically disadvantaged group were present for the test. (There is an alternative calculation for meeting AYP, but the discussion is lengthy and adds little to the example.) Table 12.3 is the final AYP status for the high school, and it did not meet the AYP objectives as defined by the State of Texas. The current AYP status of the high school is "Needs Improvement: Mathematics."

Table 12.3. Example of AYP Data for a Fictitious High School in Texas

AYP Indicator	All	African-American	Hispanic	White	Economically Disadvantaged	Special Education	LEP
Reading participation	96.2	97.0	96.7	95.1	95.0	99.1	96.9
Reading performance	61.8	65.4	62.0	56.1	49.4	47.0	48.0
Math participation	96.1	95.9	98.1	96.2	94.8	98.8	97.3
Math performance	45.9	41.9	48.9	47.2	38.7	36.3	39.4
Graduation rate	78.0	72.6	76.2	83.0	71.1	81.9	73.4

Objectives According to Adequate Yearly Progress

In the previous section, the principal of the fictitious high school has two concerns with AYP. The first concern is the school is labeled as "Needs Improvement: Mathematics," and that must be addressed in the CIP. Getting 95% or more of the students in school to take the test is all that is needed to regain the acceptable rating the school once had. The principal and school staff should brainstorm strategies for increasing test participation. The second concern is to increase the number of students passing the tests. Even though the school was above AYP standards for each of the student groups, the number of students passing should be a concern. The objective, or passing rate, is documented in the state AYP plan. In Texas, the objective for reading is 46.8% passing in 2002–2003 and 2003–2004. The percentage increases to 53.5% in 2004–2005 and 2005–2006. Mathematics has a lower passing rate at 33.4% for 2002–2003 and 2003–2004 and increases to 41.7% for the next 2 school years. The scores represented in Table 12.3 are dangerously close to not meeting the state AYP targets. Student groups with less than 60% passing rate in reading or less than 50% passing rate in math are high priority in a CIP because of the annual automatic increases in performance standards. The long-term objective is to have all students passing reading and math tests by 2014. The immediate objective is to improve from the previous year. It would be valuable to revisit how teachers teach mathematics, and how students learn mathematics.

A CIP should have a table showing AYP targets to compare with baseline. Projecting scores for the next year based on historical passing rates is instinctive for a campus administrator who utilizes a school improvement model. A campus that does not improve will fail to make AYP and may be subject to consequences.

Failure to Meet Adequate Yearly Progress

The local educational agency must identify any elementary or secondary school that fails to make adequate yearly progress, as defined in the state AYP plan, for 2 consecutive years (No Child Left Behind Act of 2002). Failure to make AYP for 2 or more years begins a series of corrective actions to help the school improve. These actions may include:

- Transporting students to schools that do meet AYP
- Incorporating scientifically based strategies to strengthen the core academic subjects
- Assuring that the school will provide high-quality professional development
- Providing a teacher mentoring program
- Replacing the school staff relevant to the failure
- Implementing a new curriculum, with professional development, for all relevant staff
- Decreasing management authority at the school
- Extending the school year or school day
- Restructuring the school

Most schools will meet AYP and never need to worry about the consequences listed above. Schools that improve and document improvement are valuable institutions in the community. Schools that do not improve according to the AYP accountability system will be restructured until they do improve. The final section of this chapter details how the General Evaluation Model can be applied to evaluating a school.

APPLYING THE GENERAL EVALUATION MODEL TO EVALUATING A SCHOOL

The definition of school improvement in NCLB is narrow and minimal; therefore, defining school improvement beyond standardized test scores is a local responsibility. Passing reading tests, passing math tests, and graduating from high school in 4 years are very important, but educators know that schools are much more than standardized tests. Schools are also about writing well, debating ideas, and learning about past civilizations. They are about athletic competition, collaboration in the classroom, and individual responsibility for learning. Schools are defined by local priorities that go beyond AYP standards. Examples of local priorities are magnet schools emphasizing health science, or the arts, or technology. Another example of a local priority is restructuring the school in order to accommodate different instructional methods. Local educational priorities are important to stakeholders and deserve to be evaluated. This section concentrates on applying GEM to evaluate federal initiatives, such as adequate yearly progress, efficiently so school administrators and community leaders can concentrate more time and effort on evaluating local initiatives.

The first two stages of GEM, needs assessment and baseline, require few resources because the state does most of the work by collecting test data and reporting the results. The third and fourth stages, procedures to achieve objectives and program implementation assessment, require a plan for improving test scores and a process to measure how well the plan is working. The fifth stage, post assessment, is about the same amount of work as Stages 1 and 2 because the state sends the test scores to the school. Typically the principal will have content specialists and other curriculum experts analyze test results and discuss staff development needs for next year. It is important for the principal to understand these levels of responsibility in the context of program evaluation.

Levels of Responsibility

GEM emphasizes the roles and responsibilities of the evaluator and program director. A school may be defined as a program with many functions or as an institution with many programs. The principal who wants to consider a school as a program is the program director and works closely with the evaluator to improve the school through evaluation. The principal who wants to consider the department chairpersons directors of programs within the school may view herself or himself as the manager of directors and ask the evaluator to work closely with the chairpersons. In a large school district, for example, a math or reading specialist may act as program director during an evaluation of new instructional strategies.

One complication that happens quite often when the evaluator is not communicating regularly with the principal is that the summative report is too narrowly focused on the interest of the department chairperson. A principal's disappointment in the evaluation may be in the limited questions or inappropriate questions asked, rather than the results. Carefully analyzing the results and the questions that led to those results often generates more useful questions.

Needs Assessment for Adequate Yearly Progress

Chapter 3 is a description of the first stage in GEM, needs assessment. Needs assessment is defined as the process of collecting information, and the relevant information is the difference between "what should be" and "what is." In the case of AYP, "what should be" is the percentage of students who must pass the reading and mathematics tests. "What is" is the current passing rate. The test results must be disaggregated according to student subgroups listed in the state AYP plan. This is the baseline for AYP.

Baseline for Adequate Yearly Progress

Chapter 4 is a description of baseline in many different contexts. In the context of AYP, the baseline is the percentage of students passing the required tests in each subgroup. Schools must improve on the baseline to a percentage of students passing as listed in the state AYP guidelines. The percentage of students passing required by the state is the objective. The staff must use procedures to achieve objectives that are based on relevant, scientifically based research.

Procedures to Achieve Objectives for Adequate Yearly Progress

Chapter 5 discussed procedures to achieve objectives. The first suggestion in chapter 5 is to identify the planning team. It is very likely that the principal has already done this. Many planning teams include an LEP teacher, a special education specialist, a specialist in math education, a reading specialist, and a science specialist. Procedures to achieve objectives for AYP may include tutoring and testing students throughout the year. The planning team may recommend using a curriculum that is aligned more closely with the state's objectives. If the curriculum is not the problem, perhaps teachers need staff development on how to implement the curriculum or vary instructional strategies.

Whatever procedures are implemented, they should be assessed to determine how well they were implemented before the students are assessed at the end of the year.

Program Implementation Assessment for Adequate Yearly Progress

As discussed in chapter 6, the program implementation assessment stage of GEM is three of the four components in Stufflebeam's CIPP model of evaluation (1983, 2001). The first three components of the CIPP model are context, input, and process. The planning team needs to decide the context for evaluating the program to improve AYP. If staff is trained to implement a new curriculum, then evaluation questions should include: (a) Are the trainers knowledgeable? (b) Are the resources adequate? (c) Is the training received well by the teachers? and (d) Are the teachers implementing the training? If this stage of GEM is managed correctly, the results of the post assessment will, in general, be known before the students are tested.

Post Assessment for Adequate Yearly Progress

The description of post assessment is in chapter 7. For AYP purposes, the post assessment stage in the GEM is the standardized test results. The new test results replace the test scores from the previous year as the new baseline. The new school year will have higher AYP targets, and the entire process begins anew.

A middle school principal is at her desk analyzing student achievement data. It is early June; time to plan for next year. She looks at the data and reflects on her 4 years as principal. There has been improvement over the past 4 years, but this past year has been the most satisfying for her as a leader. There is a change in the school climate that she intentionally created. It is a fact that student achievement improved, which pleases stakeholders, but the principal is equally pleased with the progress the staff has made in planning school improvement. She sees the staff more confident in meetings. Teachers are using terms and phrases such as stakeholders, baseline, procedures to achieve objectives, formative evaluation, and summative evaluation with assurance. The planning team has learned to conduct a needs assessment.

The process of evaluating the reading and math instructional programs with respect to AYP has helped them to understand that test scores are part of school improvement. They have learned to interpret information better and use the results of the analysis to improve education. The school improvement committee has also become more confident in planning staff development.

The principal thinks about the teacher workshops this past year. Training teachers to evaluate school programs was a very positive experience. At first, the planning teams were timid and somewhat awkward in drawing conclusions from data. However, using an evaluation model through one complete cycle has taught them how to use baseline data in planning the procedures to achieve objectives very effectively. The members of the planning team are more confident in explaining campus objectives, and more importantly, they can articulate the procedures to achieve objectives much more confidently with stakeholders.

Community members are generally pleased with the progress of the school over the past 4 years, but the principal knows it can be much better. She is confident student achievement will increase because stakeholders see a need to improve, and teachers are acquiring the tools to evaluate educational programs. The principal's goal is to increase the school's role in the community by improving education, according not only to AYP standards but also to local priorities.

Appendix A: Acronyms

AEA	American Evaluation Association
AERA	American Educational Research Association
API	academic performance index
AYP	adequate yearly progress
CAHSEE	California High School Exit Exam
CIP	campus improvement plan
CIPP	context, implementation, process, and product model of evaluation
CRT	criterion-referenced test
CST	California Standards Test
DISD	Dallas Independent School District
ESEA	Elementary and Secondary Education Act
FCAT	Florida Comprehensive Assessment Test
GEM	General Evaluation Model
JDRP	Joint Dissemination and Review Panel
LEA	Local Education Agency
LEP	limited English proficient
NCE	normal curve equivalent
NCLB	No Child Left Behind Act
NRT	norm-referenced test
RFP	request for proposals
SEA	State Education Agency
SES	socioeconomic status

TAC	Technical Assistance Center
TAKS	Texas Assessment of Knowledge and Skills
TEA	Texas Educational Agency
TIERS	Title I Evaluation and Reporting System

Appendix B: Personal Evaluation History of the Authors

EVALUATION HISTORY OF KEITH MCNEIL

My first evaluation was conducted in 1968, the year after I received my PhD in Educational Psychology from the University of Texas. Educational evaluation was a relatively new endeavor, and there were few evaluation models at that time. Evaluators focused on measurable outcomes specified when the program was funded. These programs tended to be 1 or 2 years in length. Since I taught statistics at a university, I focused on objective measures and was willing to consider and use large databases, as I was computer savvy. Unfortunately, some of the programs were funded as innovative programs, and therefore could have benefited from having an evaluation model that was more broadly focused. When I left Southern Illinois University, I continued evaluating this innovative effort and tried to obtain other evaluations in my new home state of Michigan. I learned that evaluators are often obtained through word of mouth, not necessarily because of how useful their previous evaluations were. I did pick up a contract to evaluate community education in the five states surrounding Michigan. The evaluation relied on a mailed survey and included a barometric assessment of (a) where the ideal was, (b) where the respondent thought he or she currently was, and (c) where the respondent thought the program would be in 1 year.

I then worked for the State of Michigan in the Research and Evaluation office conducting the evaluation of the Title I Neglected or Delinquent Programs in the state as well as the Migrant Program. Most of these evaluation efforts were with mandated forms and were of little interest to anyone other than those wanting to survive in a bureaucratic environment. The visits to the prisons were of interest, though, especially when the door closed behind me. One creative effort involved attempting to evaluate the staff development received by the Neglected or Delinquent staff. Evaluation of staff development was defended based on "If it doesn't work, why do it? We are spending dollars on it; let's make sure we are getting our money's worth." I have continued to use that philosophy in explaining to anyone why we evaluate programs funded or implemented in the public domain.

At that time, the Title I Evaluation and Reporting System (TIERS) was being developed and implemented by the federal Title I office, with a Technical Assistance Center (TAC) being established in 10 companies throughout the country. I joined the TAC located in Durham, North Carolina. There we generated a lot of interest in Title I evaluation at the State Education Agency (SEA) level as well as at the Local Education Agency (LEA) level. We provided workshops at state and regional meetings and assisted SEA personnel in implementing TIERS. TIERS focused on test scores; it was an objective evaluation model. We did, though, expand TAC services to such related areas as (a) methods for selecting students into Title I, (b) communicating results to the public, and (c) using evaluation results for decision making. We pushed TAC services beyond the objectives-based evaluation model. I was involved in developing materials to encourage school people to look at the effectiveness of their programs for a period of time longer than the traditional 9 months (referred to as sustained effects, McNeil, Huff, Lamble, & Smith, 1983). We also developed a workshop to assist schools in getting their programs cited as exemplary by the Joint Dissemination and Review Panel (JDRP). I also took an active role in facilitating information entry into microcomputers. Both Pennsylvania and West Virginia benefited from statewide microcomputer information entry (McNeil, Mengel, & Moran, 1984).

My evaluation journey took me to the Dallas Independent School District (DISD). DISD had an extremely large Research and Evaluation Office, once the largest in the country. That office had adopted the CIPP model, which considers the components of context, input, process, and product. This model accepts the fact that what a project sets out to accomplish sometimes does not occur because of problems in the context, input, or process. I applied the CIPP model to (a) the State Compensatory Education program for seventh and eighth graders,

(b) the Neglected or Delinquent Chapter 1 (refunded Title I), (c) the nonpublic Chapter 1, (d) Dallas Learning Centers (refurbished inner city schools when bussing was discontinued), and (e) the Chapter 1 A Priori Program. The DISD Research and Evaluation staff conducted many classroom observations as part of the process evaluation. In addition, it was through these observations that I came to realize that the same scripted curriculum could be delivered very differently by various teachers. After 5 years with DISD, I had an opportunity to return to university teaching at New Mexico State University (NMSU).

Since joining NMSU in 1989, I have implemented the CIPP model in numerous evaluations. I have evaluated three bilingual programs, a family literacy project, a Fund for the Improvement of Post-Secondary Education (FIPSE)–funded project incorporating Spanish into several career courses at a community college, two National Science Foundation (NSF)-funded projects (one that developed CD instructional material teaching the concepts of vectors and electromagnetic circuits, the other reforming math, science, and technology courses at the university level). I evaluated three programs for the Las Cruces Public Schools: (a) Bilingual Education, (b) Safe and Drug-Free Schools, and (c) Even Start. And finally, I evaluated three projects for Region 19 Head Start: (a) Transition from Head Start to the Public Schools, (b) Early Start, serving children from birth to age 3, and (c) Texas State Initiative incorporating additional literacy into the pre-K curriculum.

Several trends seem to have occurred over these 32 years. The projects are now funded at a much higher level, and for longer periods (often 5 years). The data-gathering systems are more sophisticated and more expensive. Finally, there is more interest in evaluation on the part of the funding agency as well as on the part of the project directors.

EVALUATION HISTORY OF ISADORE NEWMAN

I received my BA in Psychology from the University of Miami, Florida, my MA in Psychology from the Graduate Faculty, New School for Social Research, New York, and my PhD in Educational Psychology with a specialty in Statistics and Measurement from Southern Illinois University at Carbondale in 1972. My first evaluation reports were written in 1978. These included a needs assessment survey of older adults and evaluations of various federally funded Title IVA, IVC, and XX programs. In addition, the Ohio National Guard funded my evaluation of *Company Commander's Advisory Manual*. Since then I have evaluated programs funded by the (a) U.S. Department of Agriculture, (b) National Institute for Mental Health, (c) Norlin Foundations, and (d) Institute for Life-Span Development and Gerontology.

I have also conducted evaluations of the following funded programs (with the total program funds in parentheses):

- GOALS 2000 (3 grants—total of $616,000) to implement innovative educational programs
- SUMMA Foundation ($75,000) for establishing the Cardiovascular and Wellness Research Institute
- Ohio Department of Mental Health ($330,000) to diagnose the dual problems of substance abuse and mental disorder
- United Nations to study the effects of modern technology on family communication and relations
- National Science Foundation TIES grant
- National Science Foundation ($5,000,000) New Mexico Collaborative for Excellence in Teacher Preparation
- Eisenhower Project for the sciences
- GAR Foundation ($50,000) to set up database for Family Friendly Cities
- Fund for the Improvement of Post-Secondary Education ($186,000) to the University of Cincinnati
- State of Ohio Supreme Court experimental program in divorce mediation
- Ohio Department of Mental Health Grant ($250,000) on home-based instruction.
- Ohio Department of Mental Health Grant ($44,0000) on Emotionally Disturbed Youth: An Exploration of Family Functioning Treatment Approaches and Changes
- Kennedy Foundation ($150,000)

I have continued to champion the notion that there should be a match between the purpose of the evaluation, the evaluation questions asked, and the methodology used to answer those questions. I have tried to make my reports meaningful to the stakeholders that were the intended audience. As such, I have written about various evaluation models, and I developed the initial thoughts for the General Evaluation Model. I have had the opportunity to apply my evaluation expertise in the content areas of education, mental health, aging, emotionally disturbed youth, in-service workshops, development of a military manual, divorce mediation, and wellness in the elderly.

EVALUATION HISTORY OF JIM STEINHAUSER

I received my PhD in 2000 from New Mexico State University. Before that, I was a secondary mathematics teacher for 10 years. In 1995, I began working with Keith McNeil on the evaluation of Head Start programs. When the Head Start administrators decided to establish a Research and Evaluation department, I was hired to direct that department. Since 2003 I have been an evaluator for the El Paso Independent School District (ISD), focusing on the evaluation of the State Compensatory Education program and the evaluation of the Mathematics/Science Partnership between El Paso ISD and the University of Texas at El Paso. I have taught both statistics and program evaluation at the graduate level. In addition, I have an administrative license and have served as a secondary school administrator.

As an outside evaluator, I have conducted evaluations of Even Start, Head Start, K–12 mathematics curricula, a district-wide mathematics assessment program, an elementary school service delivery project, and a bilingual education master's degree administrator-training program. I was invited to present on curricular auditing standards at the Texas Association for Supervision and Curriculum Development conference.

Appendix C: Summary of the Program Evaluation Standards

UTILITY STANDARDS

The utility standards are intended to ensure that an evaluation will serve the information needs of intended users.

U1 Stakeholder Identification—Persons involved in or affected by the evaluation should be identified so that their needs can be addressed.

U2 Evaluator Credibility—The persons conducting the evaluation should be both trustworthy and competent to perform the evaluation so that the evaluation findings achieve maximum credibility and acceptance.

U3 Information Scope and Selection—Information collected should be broadly selected to address pertinent questions about the program and be responsive to the needs and interests of clients and other specified stakeholders.

U4 Values Identification—The perspectives, procedures, and rationale used to interpret the findings should be carefully described so that the bases for value judgments are clear.

U5 Report Clarity—Evaluation reports should clearly describe the program being evaluated, including its context, and the purposes, procedures, and findings of the evaluation so that essential information is provided and easily understood.

U6 Report Timeliness and Dissemination—Significant interim findings and evaluation reports should be disseminated to intended users so that they can be used in a timely fashion.

U7 Evaluation Impact—Evaluations should be planned, conducted, and reported in ways that encourage follow-through by stakeholders so that the likelihood that the evaluation will be used is increased.

FEASIBILITY STANDARDS

The feasibility standards are intended to ensure that an evaluation will be realistic, prudent, diplomatic, and frugal.

F1 Practical Procedures—The evaluation procedures should be practical to keep disruption to a minimum while needed information is obtained.

F2 Political Viability—The evaluation should be planned and conducted with anticipation of the different positions of various interest groups so that their cooperation may be obtained and so that possible attempts by any of these groups to curtail evaluation operations or to bias or misapply the results can be averted or counteracted.

F3 Cost Effectiveness—The evaluation should be efficient and produce information of sufficient value so that the resources expended can be justified.

PROPRIETY STANDARDS

The propriety standards are intended to ensure that an evaluation will be conducted legally, ethically, and with due regard for the welfare of those involved in the evaluation, as well as those affected by its results.

P1 Service Orientation—Evaluations should be designed to assist organizations to address and effectively serve the needs of the full range of targeted participants.

P2 Formal Agreements—Obligations of the formal parties to an evaluation (what is to be done, how, by whom, when) should be agreed to in writing so that these parties are obligated to adhere to all conditions of the agreement or to renegotiate it formally.

P3 Rights of Human Subjects—Evaluations should be designed and conducted to respect and protect the rights and welfare of human subjects.

P4 Human Interactions—Evaluators should respect human dignity and worth in their interactions with other persons associated with an evaluation so that participants are not threatened or harmed.

P5 Complete and Fair Assessment—The evaluation should be complete and fair in its examination and recording of strengths and weaknesses of the program being evaluated so that strengths can be built upon and problem areas addressed.

P6 Disclosure of Findings—The formal parties to an evaluation should ensure that the full set of evaluation findings along with pertinent limitations are made accessible to the persons affected by the evaluation and any others with expressed legal rights to receive the results.

P7 Conflict of Interest—Conflict of interest should be dealt with openly and honestly so that it does not compromise the evaluation processes and results.

P8 Fiscal Responsibility—The evaluator's allocation and expenditure of resources should reflect sound accountability procedures and otherwise be prudent and ethically responsible so that expenditures are accounted for and appropriate.

ACCURACY STANDARDS

The accuracy standards are intended to ensure that an evaluation will reveal and convey technically adequate information about the features that determine the worth or merit of the program being evaluated.

A1 Program Documentation—The program being evaluated should be described and documented clearly and accurately so that the program is clearly identified.

A2 Context Analysis—The context in which the program exists should be examined in enough detail so that its likely influences on the program can be identified.

A3 Described Purposes and Procedures—The purposes and procedures of the evaluation should be monitored and described in enough detail so that they can be identified and assessed.

A4 Defensible Information Sources—The sources of information used in a program evaluation should be described in enough detail so that the adequacy of the information can be assessed.

A5 Valid Information—The information gathering procedures should be chosen or developed and then implemented so that they will assure that the interpretation arrived at is valid for the intended use.

A6 Reliable Information—The information gathering procedures should be chosen or developed and then implemented so that they will assure that the information obtained is sufficiently reliable for the intended use.

A7 Systematic Information—The information collected, processed, and reported in an evaluation should be systematically reviewed, and any errors found should be corrected.

A8 Analysis of Quantitative Information—Quantitative information in an evaluation should be appropriately and systematically analyzed so that evaluation questions are effectively answered.

A9 Analysis of Qualitative Information—Qualitative information in an evaluation should be appropriately and systematically analyzed so that evaluation questions are effectively answered.

A10 Justified Conclusions—The conclusions reached in an evaluation should be explicitly justified so that stakeholders can assess them.

A11 Impartial Reporting—Reporting procedures should guard against distortion caused by personal feelings and biases of any party to the evaluation so that evaluation reports fairly reflect the evaluation findings.

A12 Metaevaluation—The evaluation itself should be formatively and summatively evaluated against these and other pertinent standards so that its conduct is appropriately guided and, on completion, stakeholders can closely examine its strengths and weaknesses.

Source: Joint Committee on Standards for Educational Evaluation, 1981

Appendix D: Evaluation Forms and Instruments

COLLECTING DATA ON JOB DESCRIPTION, PRESENT FUNCTIONS, AND IDEAL FUNCTIONS

In an evaluation of community education in five midwestern states, the goal was to obtain the discrepancy between one's job description, one's present function, and what one considers the ideal functions. The following instrument was used.

This survey contains a number of potential functions of the person in the State Department of Education responsible for community education. Not all of these functions should necessarily be a part of that person's responsibility. This study is interested in what people think is happening (whether in the state plan or job description) and what you are really doing. Since few of us are really doing all that we think should be done, we would also appreciate your checking those functions that ideally should be occurring.

Since a formalized community education program is a relatively new concept in many states, your state may not have a state plan. You may, though, have a written job description that specifies certain functions.

EXAMPLE 1. A possible response to item 1 below—if

- Your state does not have a state plan and you have no written job description, but
- You think that this is really a function of the SEA, and
- You do assist communities in surveying their needs,

You would check the last two columns—those labeled "my present function" and "ideal function." You would leave blank the column headed "State plan or job description."

EXAMPLE 2. A possible response to item 2 below—if

- The state plan indicates that the SEA should help LEA compensatory education programs to develop evaluation plans, but
- Either you are too busy, or your staff is not large enough to accomplish this function, although
- You feel that ideally this is a meaningful function of the SEA,

Then you would check the first and last columns and leave blank the middle column ("my present function"), since you do not perform that function.

	State plan or job description	My present function	Ideal function
PLANNING 1. Involve citizens in the planning of the state community education program: 2. Help LEA plan and develop applications for assistance:			
NEEDS ASSESSMENT 3. Provide assistance in surveying the community education needs of the local community:			
PROGRAMMING 4. Carry out a statewide survey of existing and planned community education programs:			
COORDINATION OF SERVICES 5. Coordinate the state community education effort:			
EVALUATION 6. Help community education programs to develop evaluation plans:			

(continued)

DISSEMINATION
7. Disseminate information
    from federal government to
    the LEA:

An alternative to the above data collection procedure would be to ask respondents to place a D (for job description), a P (for present job function), and an I (for ideal job function) on a 5-point Likert scale, for example: Rate the degree of importance:

Disseminate information from federal government to the LEA:

1	2	3	4	5
Not at all	A little	Average	Somewhat	Very
___	___	___	___	___

A response pattern such as the following would indicate that the respondent felt that little was presently being done (P), and that the job description (D) called for more effort, but not as much as was called for ideally (I).

Disseminate information from federal government to the LEA:

Not at all	A little	Average	Somewhat	Very
1	2	3	4	5
___	P	___	D	I

ONE POSSIBLE MANAGEMENT PLAN
FOR A NEEDS ASSESSMENT

Activity	Person responsible	Assisted by	Start date	Completion date
1. Identify audiences and scope of NA:				
2. Define information needs:				
3. Identify potential information sources:				
4. Set information collection priorities:				
5. Select or develop instrument:				
6. Make arrangements for collecting:				
7. Collect information:				
8. Analyze information:				

(continued)

9. Determine high priority needs from discrepancies: _____

10. Prepare and submit findings: _____

11. Act upon findings: _____

DEVELOPMENT OF END-OF-TRAINING INSTRUMENT

Staff development topic:
1. _____
2. _____

Training objectives:
1. _____
2. _____
3. _____
4. _____

Attitude items:
1. _____
2. _____

Newly learned items:
1. _____
2. _____
3. _____

Willingness-to-implement items:
1. _____
2. _____

TRAINING EVALUATION FORM

Head Start Transition Activity Form
Continuity in Early Childhood Education

Date _____ Place _____

Primary topic _____

The meeting started on time. Yes _____ No _____

Meeting was about the right length. Yes _____ Too short _____ Too long _____

My students will benefit from this meeting. Yes _____ No _____

(continued)

1. Was this an important topic for early childhood education? _____

(On a scale of 5 = Agree, 1 = Disagree)

Would you recommend this presentation? Yes _____ No _____

The best thing about this meeting was . . .

_____

_____

_____

How could the presentation have been improved?

_____

_____

What will you take from this presentation?

1. _____

2. _____

3. _____

Other comments:

_____

_____

Thank you for your cooperation in filling out this survey.

A STRUCTURED INTERVIEW

Hello, how are you today?

I am the evaluator of the "High Expectations Program," Mr. _____.

I am visiting with each of the program staff to gain information about their experience with the organization, how they felt about last year's program, and what they see as the challenges of the new program.

1. How long have you been employed with _____?
2. In what capacity have you worked here?
3. How many years did you implement the program that was in effect last year?
4. How did you find out there was going to be a new program this year?

5. How much do you know about the new program?
6. Do you think that 4 staff development days will be adequate to prepare you to be able to implement the new program?
7. Do you think the new program will be better for the students than was last year's?

A SURVEY FOR COLLECTING CONTEXT INFORMATION

1. Independent school district: _____

2. Transition advisory committee representative: _____

3. Transition advisory committee representative phone number: _____

4. Approximate number of elementary students: _____

5. Approximate number of pre-K students: _____

6. Approximate number of K students: _____

7. Future plans for implementing pre-K in the district:

   _____

   _____

   _____

8. Approximate number of additional Head Start classrooms needed in the next 2 years: _____ classrooms

9. Please describe your pre-K or K curriculum (rough estimates will suffice):

   a. Percentage of time spent on reading and readiness: _____

   b. Percentage of time in learning centers: _____

   c. Name of commercial curriculum: _____

   d. Average number of computers in K classrooms: _____ or campus lab: _____

   e. Name of curriculum package in computers: _____

   g. Percent of bilingual classrooms: _____

EXAMPLE OF A STAFF DEVELOPMENT EVALUATION

Section A: Planned staff development for 2000–2001

July 14—Overview of the new program
July 21—Literacy in math activities
July 28—Literacy in social studies activities

(continued)

Aug. 11—Literacy in play*****TODAY'S SESSION****
Aug. 18—Record keeping
Sept. 15—Working with parents
Oct. 20—Incorporating literacy into holiday lessons

Section B: Demographics

Site: _____

Check one: Teacher _____   Aide _____   Other _____

Section C: Understanding of today's topics

How well do you understand today's topics?

| 5 = Very well | 4 = Fairly well | 3 = Not sure | 2 = Somewhat confused | 1 = Totally confused |

_____ 1. Description of curriculum

_____ 2. Numeracy awareness

_____ 3. Print awareness

_____ 4. Phonemic awareness

_____ 5. Use of language to communicate

Section D: Implementing today's topics

How likely will you implement today's topics?

| 5 = Very likely | 4 = Somewhat likely | 3 = Not sure | 2 = Somewhat unlikely | 1 = Very unlikely |

_____ 1. Description of curriculum

_____ 2. Numeracy awareness

_____ 3. Print awareness

_____ 4. Phonemic awareness

_____ 5. Use of language to communicate

Section E: Specific techniques

What are two specific techniques that you will take from this staff development and use in the next 2 weeks?

1. _____   2. _____

Section F: What topics do you feel should be reviewed, expanded upon, or introduced in the future?

_____

_____

ANOTHER EXAMPLE OF A CLASSROOM EVALUATION FORM

Language Development Checklist

Teacher: _____   Date observed: _____

Duration of observation: _____   Observer: _____

Activities observed: Circle time   Centers   Transition   Playground

Number of staff in room: ____

Oral language use with students	Rating
1. Spoke clearly	1 2 3 4 5
2. Used grammatically correct sentences	1 2 3 4 5
3. Rephrased children's sentences into more complete sentences	1 2 3 4 5
4. Used "rich" language (nouns, descriptors, action words)	1 2 3 4 5
5. Used "thinking" questions (open-ended, "who," "how")	1 2 3 4 5
6. Used simple directions (one or two steps)	1 2 3 4 5
7. Used "suggestive guidance" more than directives	1 2 3 4 5
8. Modeled use of words rather than actions for child's behavior	1 2 3 4 5
9. Integrated new (theme-related) vocabulary words	1 2 3 4 5
10. Related previously learned words/concepts to activity	1 2 3 4 5
11. Provided rationale for learning (letters, numbers, words, etc.)	1 2 3 4 5
12. Encouraged children's use of language in learning activities	1 2 3 4 5
13. Encouraged use of children's language in other times	1 2 3 4 5

Rating criteria: 1 = Almost never   2 = At times but not often   3 = About half the time
4 = More often than not   5 = Almost always

INTERVIEW OF PRINCIPALS

Purpose of Transition Evaluator Visit to Kindergarten (K) Classrooms

1. See if transition cards arrived and assess their usefulness to the K teachers.
2. Assess the value of transition services to principal and K teachers.
3. Obtain recommendations from principal and K teachers as to improved transition services.
4. Observe K students in classroom.

Principal:
   Meet and discuss purpose of the visit.

(continued)

Show:
1. Transition cards—where are they? Have they been of use to the teachers?
2. Newsletter—have you seen any of these?

Ask:
1. Assessment of the Head Start visits to the school.
2. Assessment of the K and 1 teachers' visits to the Head Start site.
3. Overall, what can be done to improve transition services?

Encourage sending their K and 1 teachers:
1. To the Head Start site this year.
2. To the Early Childhood Education fall and spring conferences.

Teacher:
Meet and discuss purpose of the visit.
Verify placement of cards in the cumulative folders.
What was the value of the cards?
Have you received any of the newsletters?
What was the value of the newsletters?
What can be done to improve transition?
Are Head Start students ready academically?
Are Head Start students ready socially?
Observe students:
Identify the 5 most sociable.
Identify the 5 least sociable.
Check with teacher to see which were in Head Start.

Record of transition information from visit on _____

Transition staff: Mike _____   Jim _____   Keith _____

School: _____

Principal: _____
Meet and discuss purpose of the visit.

1. Are the transition cards in cumulative folders?

_____ Yes _____ No   If No, where are they? _____

2. Have they been of use to the teachers?

_____ Yes _____ No

3. Newsletter—have you seen any of these?

_____ Yes _____ No

4. Assessment of the Head Start visitation to the school:

Extremely helpful	Very helpful	Unsure	Not very helpful	A bother
1	2	3	4	5

5. Assessment of the K and 1 teachers visit to the Head Start site:

Extremely helpful	Very helpful	Unsure	Not very helpful	A bother
1	2	3	4	5

(*continued*)

6. Overall, what can be done to improve transition services?

_____

_____

7. Did any of the current K or 1 teachers visit the Head Start site last year?

_____ Yes _____ No

8. Did any of the current K or 1 teachers attend the Early Childhood Education conference last year?

_____ Yes _____ No

Encourage sending their K and 1 teachers

1. To the Head Start site this year.

2. To the Early Childhood Education fall and spring conferences.

PARENT MEETING EVALUATION

Head Start Transition Activity Form

Preparing our children for kindergarten
Preparando nuestros niños para kindergarten

Date: _____   Place: _____

Fecha: _____   Localidad: _____

The meeting started on time. Yes _____ No _____

La junta empezó a tiempo. Sí _____   No _____

The meeting was about the right length. Yes _____ Too short _____ Too long _____

La duración de la junta estuvo bien. Sí _____ Muy corta_____ Muy larga_____

I learned something new that I can do with my child. Yes _____ No _____

Aprendí algo nuevo que podré compartir con mi hijo en casa. Sí _____ No _____

My child will benefit from this meeting. Yes _____ No _____

Mi hijo se beneficiará de esta junta. Sí _____ No _____

The best thing about this meeting was . . . *Lo más importante de esta junta fué. . .*

(continued)

The meeting would have been better if . . . *La junta hubiera sido mejor si. . .*

Thank you for your cooperation in filling out this survey.
Gracias por su cooperación por haber completado esta encuestra.

EVALUATION OF PARENTS VISITING SCHOOLS

District: _____   Date: _____

School: _____   *Español en el otro lado*

****

The kindergarten teacher:

Please put a check in the blanks that apply to the teacher.

I did not see _____

Told me about kindergarten _____

Talked with the children _____

Showed me around the kindergarten classroom _____

The kindergarten teacher seemed (circle one)

****

The principal:

Please put a check in the blanks that apply to the principal.

I did not see _____

Was a nice person _____

Seemed busy _____

Was very informative _____

Took us on a tour _____

(*continued*)

The principal seemed (circle one)

****

Yes _____ No _____ 1. Did you see the cafeteria?

Yes _____ No _____ 2. Did you see the library?

Yes _____ No _____ 3. Do you feel more comfortable with this school after the visit?

Yes _____ No _____ 4. Were you a parent volunteer in this elementary school?

Yes _____ No _____ 5. Would you like to be a parent volunteer in this elementary school?

Yes _____ No _____ 6. Did you receive any information on rules and regulations?

Comments: _____

_____

_____

_____

_____

_____

EVALUATION FORM FOR AN ADVISORY BOARD MEETING

**Head Start Transition Advisory Board
Meeting Survey Form**

Date: _____

Place: _____

The meeting started on time: Yes _____   No _____

The meeting was about the right length: Yes _____   Too long _____   Too short _____

The best thing about this meeting was

_____

_____

_____

_____

_____

_____

(continued)

The meeting would have been better if

_____
_____
_____
_____
_____
_____

What would you like to see on the agenda for the next meeting?

_____
_____
_____
_____
_____
_____

REQUEST FOR PROPOSAL FOR EVALUATION SERVICES BY OUTSIDE EVALUATOR

RFP NO.: XX
DUE DATE/TIME: February 1, 2001, 12:00 Noon

I. INTRODUCTION

    A. The School District is requesting proposals from reputable firms interested in providing evaluation services for the School District's XXX Program and annual performance report as described herein. Responses will be evaluated for obtaining required services from the respondent submitting the highest ranked proposal based on criteria stated herein.

    B. Proposal responses must be received by the above DUE DAY/TIME at the XXX.

    C. Inquiries regarding this solicitation may be obtained by contacting XXX at (XXX) XXX-XXXX.

    D. All prospective respondents are responsible for complying with the laws prohibiting bribes, gratuities, and kickbacks.

E. By responding to this request, the respondent warrants that it has no interest and will acquire no interest that would directly or indirectly conflict in any manner or degree with the performance of the proposed service.

II. SCOPE

A. The School District seeks continuation of a federal grant award for its existing XXX Program. To meet XXX priorities, the School District's existing program must assess progress toward its stated goals and objectives, use those results to refine, improve, and strengthen its programs, discontinue programs that are not demonstrating positive outcomes, and report progress toward program goals and objectives to the public.

B. The assessment services and activities being sought by the School District include, but are not limited to:

1. Assess and report on data collected from school sites that are implementing program activities;

2. Observation of program activities and strategies utilized to meet program goals and objectives;

3. Interview program staff and community XXX;

4. Review and assess program based data pertaining to XXX in the schools and community;

5. Presentation of the assessment results followed by discussion with program staff with focus on areas in need of improvement; and

6. Preparation of draft and completion of final report by May 1, 2001.

III. REQUIRED PROPOSAL SUBMITTALS

A. Responses will consist of five (5) copies of the following information and in the sequence presented:

1. A statement of qualification that includes:

a. Educational achievement of the individual(s) that will be performing the services;

b. Experience in providing the required services (e.g., number of years providing the type of service offered, number and/or type of evaluation reports completed, and scope of completed work);

   c. A client reference list and contact person of at least three other school districts that have obtained services from the respondent. These references must be able to provide information regarding the respondent's performance and level of service; and

   d. A sample of previous report done by the respondent that is similar in scope to the services being sought herein.

  2. A description of the respondent's approach to the services being proposed that includes, but is not limited to:

   a. A summary of services;

   b. Method in obtaining data;

   c. Documentation of the review;

   d. The type and/or amount, if any, of School District resources required by the respondent in conducting the evaluation (e.g., office space, staffing, and clerical support);

   e. A tentative schedule for conducting the evaluation that describes the pertinent activities and deadlines; and

   f. Any follow-up support services that are available after completion of the report.

  3. A proposal listing all costs to be incurred by the School District for the proposed services.

IV. EVALUATION FACTORS

 A. Only responses that include the required submittals as specified in section III above will be evaluated for award purposes. Incomplete responses will be determined as "nonresponsive" and will not be accepted for award consideration.

 B. All responsive qualification statements received shall be evaluated based on the following weighted factors:

FACTOR	WEIGHT
1. Respondent's qualifications and experience	15 points
2. Respondent's performance history as provided by references	5 points
3. Respondent's level of service as determined by the proposed approach to the evaluation and follow-up	40 points

4. Cost of the evaluation   40 points
TOTAL   100 points

V. AWARD
    A. Evaluations will be conducted by a review committee consid-
       ering the evaluation factors listed in section IV above. The
       committee will rank the responses according to their relative
       merits. Respondents submitting responsive proposals may be
       offered an opportunity for discussion before award for obtain-
       ing the respondent's best and final offer.
       1. Any substantial revision will be accepted in writing from the
          respondent.
       2. The process of discussion may extend up to the time
          of award and may require public presentation by the
          respondent.
       3. Respondents may request within their responses nondisclo-
          sure of confidential data. Such data will accompany the
          proposal and will be readily separable from the proposal in
          order to facilitate eventual public inspection of the noncon-
          fidential portion of the proposal.
    B. Final award will be based on the highest ranked proposal as de-
       termined by the committee. The resulting contract may be re-
       newed annually, pending mutual agreement between the School
       District and the contractor, for up to 4 years total.

EXAMPLE OF A CRITERION-REFERENCED INSTRUMENT

Area of development	Demonstrates skill	
	Yes	No
A. Social/emotional development		
1. Demonstrates a positive self-esteem	——	——
2. Exhibits personal responsibility, self-discipline	——	——
3. Interacts cooperatively with others	——	——
B. Physical development		
1. Demonstrates large muscle control and coordination	——	——

(continued)

2. Participates in such activities as running, skipping	____	____
C. Aesthetic development		
1. Participates in creative dramatic activities	____	____
2. Participates in rhythmic and creative movement activities	____	____
D. Intellectual development		
1. Sorts and classifies	____	____
2. Recognizes and identifies basic colors and shapes	____	____
3. Demonstrates and identifies spatial concepts	____	____
4. Draws conclusions and predicts outcomes	____	____
E. Communication skill	____	____
1. Listens without interrupting	____	____
2. Recalls details	____	____
3. Expresses feelings and individual thoughts	____	____

A SPECIALLY CONSTRUCTED INSTRUMENT

SURVEY OF EDUCATIONAL ASSISTANTS—MARCH 1999

Number of classes I assist: _____   Grade levels: _____

TYPE OF PROGRAM (check all that apply):

Pull out ____ Self-contained ____ Follow the student__

Percent of time I speak Spanish in class: ____

First, identify the ACTUAL % of time you spend on each activity. The % should add up to 100%. Then place a check ✓ in one of the three IDEAL blanks.

		Ideal		
	Actual	Less	Same	More
INSTRUCTION				
Whole-group instruction	____	____	____	____
One-on-one instruction	____	____	____	____
Small-group instruction	____	____	____	____
Computer assistance	____	____	____	____
Translation English/Spanish	____	____	____	____

(continued)

TESTING

Preparing tests	___	___	___	___
Administering tests	___	___	___	___
Checking or grading	___	___	___	___

NONINSTRUCTIONAL

Directions for assignments	___	___	___	___
Transitions	___	___	___	___
Administrative routines	___	___	___	___
Waiting time	___	___	___	___
Discipline	___	___	___	___
Clerical (including copying)	___	___	___	___
Grades and attendance	___	___	___	___

TOTAL   100%

In my current position, I could be more effective if

_____

_____

_____

_____

_____

EXAMPLE OF A SURVEY THAT WAS DEVELOPED TO EVALUATE STUDENT'S USE OF A NEW INSTRUCTIONAL COMPACT DISC

Student Evaluation of Instructional CD

Major: _____

How many engineering technology courses have you taken? _____

The CD discussing vectors was intended to supplement the material presented in the text and in the lecture.

1. What impressed you most about the CD?

2. What did you learn form the CD that you didn't learn from the class lecture?

3. What concepts were strengthened by the CD?

4. What concepts were clarified by the CD?

5. What concepts were newly taught by the CD?

(continued)

6. Overall, the CD added to my knowledge of vectors:

   Strongly agree   Agree   Disagree   Strongly disagree

7. The CD increased my interest in this course.

   Strongly agree   Agree   Disagree   Strongly disagree

8. I think a CD like the one on vectors should be a part of all courses.

   Strongly agree   Agree   Disagree   Strongly disagree

9. Approximately how long did you use the CD on vectors outside of class?
   _____ hours

EXAMPLE OF A STRUCTURED INTERVIEW

Evaluation of Internship

Name: _____   Date: _____   Interviewer: _____

1. I recently completed an internship at _____

2. The most memorable aspect of the internship was _____

   _____

   _____

3. My courses particularly prepared me for _____

   _____

   _____

4. I felt particularly deficient in _____

   _____

   _____

5. Use of Spanish was particularly helpful in _____

   _____

   _____

6. I would recommend to future students in this internship to _____

   _____

   _____

7. Any other comments? _____

   _____

   _____

EXAMPLE OF AN UNSTRUCTURED INTERVIEW, INCLUDING POSSIBLE QUESTIONS, REASONS FOR BRANCHING TO FURTHER QUESTIONS, AND INSTRUCTIONS AS TO HOW FAR TO GO WITH THE QUESTIONING

Unstructured Interview for the Evaluation of the Revised Remedial Math Experience (RRME)

Suggest that rapport be developed during the first 5 minutes of the interview by sharing your own frustration with mathematics. You might also ask what high school the student graduated from, and what courses were easy and which ones were difficult.

Possible questions:

1. Why did you choose the RRME option?
   a. If respondent states that he or she was told to, pursue who it was.
   b. Was the option presented as a real option?
2. Would you choose that option again?
   a. If no, explore why not.
   b. If yes, explore why.
3. What did you like least about the RRME?
   a. If instructor, ask what about the instructor.
   b. If type of instruction, ask which types experienced in previous math courses.
   c. If group work, ask if participated in group work previously.
   d. If fellow students, do not pursue the question.
   e. If personal issues, do not pursue the issues.
4. Would you recommend RRME to your younger friends?
   a. Ask why or why not.
   b. What other options would be recommended.

Cautions:

1. If respondent becomes defensive, move on to the next question.
2. If respondent begins to get into highly personal areas, redirect the questioning.

3. If respondent begins to share rumors, tell respondent to not share rumors.

4. If respondent becomes nervous, end the interview.

EXAMPLE OF A SEMISTRUCTURED PHONE INTERVIEW

Phone Survey of College of Education Graduates of Graduate Programs

COE graduate's name: _____   Phone #: _____

Dates of attempts: _____

Date of interview: _____ Interviewer: _____

1. When did you graduate from New Mexico State University?
   1 = Before Dec. 1987
   2 = Dec. 1987–Summer 1988
   3 = After Summer 1988
2. Which of the following categories best describes your current occupation?
   1 = University faculty or staff
   2 = Elementary or secondary teacher
   3 = Counselor
   4 = Manager or administrator
   5 = Graduate student
   6 = Not employed
   7 = Other (please specify)
3. Which of the following best describes your employment as it relates to your major?
   1 = Employed in field
   2 = Employed in related field
   3 = Employed in unrelated field
   4 = Involuntarily unemployed
   5 = Voluntarily unemployed
4. Which of the following best describes your satisfaction with your present position?
   1 = Very satisfied
   2 = Satisfied
   3 = Unsatisfied
   4 = Not applicable
5. How would you rate your NMSU education as compared to colleagues' education received from other institutions?
   1 = NMSU much better
   2 = NMSU better
   3 = About the same
   4 = NMSU not quite as good
   5 = NMSU substantially worse

(*continued*)

6. What were the strong and weak points in your graduate program?

	Strengths	Weaknesses
Mentoring		
Practical		
Theoretical		
Other		

Appendix E: Evaluation Plans

TIMELINE FOR EVALUATION ACTIVITIES

Year 1 (focus is on context, input, and baseline)	Months
1. Clarify evaluation questions with stakeholders.	1
2. Catalog existing data.	2
3. Finalize evaluation plan and get board approval.	1
4. Design procedures for new data collection.	1
5. Collect new data.	2
6. Analyze data.	1
7. Develop reports.	1
8. Deliver reports.	1
9. Clarify evaluation for Year 2.	.2

Year 2 (focus is on program implementation assessment)	Months
1. Finalize evaluation plan and get board approval.	.3
2. Catalog existing data.	.3
3. Design procedures for new data collection.	.5
4. Collect new data:	
Attend transition activities.	1
Interview LEA staff.	.5
Interview board.	.2
Interview educational specialist for transition.	.3
Survey parents.	1
Interview students.	1

Survey LEA.	1
Survey Head Start staff.	.5
Interview Head Start central office staff.	.2
5. Analyze all data.	3
6. Develop reports.	1
7. Deliver reports.	1
8. Clarify evaluation for Year 3.	1

Year 3 (focus is on program implementation assessment)   Months

1. Finalize evaluation plan and get board approval.	.3
2. Catalog existing data.	
3. Design procedures for new data collection.	.5
4. Collect new data:	
Attend transition activities.	1
Interview LEA staff.	.5
Interview board.	.2
Interview educational specialist for transition.	.3
Survey parents.	1
Interview students.	1
Survey LEA.	1
Survey Head Start staff.	.5
Interview Head Start central office staff.	.2
5. Analyze all data.	3
6. Develop reports.	1
7. Deliver reports.	1
8. Clarify evaluation for Year 4.	.2

Year 4 (focus is on post assessment)   Months

1. Catalog existing data.	2
2. Finalize evaluation plan and get board approval.	.1
3. Design procedures for new data collection.	.8
4. Collect new data:	
Attend transition activities.	.4
Interview board.	.2
Interview educational specialist for transition.	.1
Interview parents.	.3

Survey parents.	.5
Survey LEA staff.	.5
Collect LEA student-level data from records.	1
5. Analyze all data.	3
6. Develop Year 4 report.	2.5
7. Deliver reports.	.5

Year 5 (focus is on post assessment)	**Months**
1. Catalog existing data.	2
2. Finalize evaluation plan and get board approval.	.1
3. Design procedures for new data collection.	.8
4. Collect new data:	
Attend transition activities.	.4
Interview board.	.2
Interview educational specialist for transition.	.1
Interview parents.	.3
Survey parents.	.3
Survey LEA staff.	.2
Collect LEA student-level data from records.	1.5
5. Analyze all data.	3
6. Develop Year 5 report.	1
7. Develop final report.	1.5
8. Deliver reports.	1

PLAN FOR ADMINISTERING BASELINE: SURVEY OF STAFF

Parameters for this example:

a. Ten-minute group administered survey.
b. Locally developed.
c. All program staff surveyed during regular meeting.

1. Reread purpose in program plan and evaluation plan for purpose of the survey.
2. Obtain instruments — will be developed locally:
   a. Draft cover letter.
   b. Provide for anonymity.

  c. Make all items relevant to program.
  d. Make format easy to respond to.
  e. Provide for constructed responses.
  f. Evaluator and program director review draft survey.
3. Arrange for testers:
   Evaluator will attend meeting to distribute survey — no extra testers required.
4. Pilot instrument administration:
   a. Ask respondents about readability.
   b. Ask respondents about length.
   c. Did respondents understand the survey questions?
   d. Could respondents answer the questions?
   e. Did respondents believe that their anonymity was ensured?
5. Plan for instrument administration:
   a. Make multiple copies of revised survey.
   b. Arrange for administration at regular meeting.
   c. Administer as part of the agenda (preferably not at the end, as less importance is placed on it if it is at the end).
   d. Get program director to discuss the importance of the survey.
   e. Take plenty of pencils with you.
   f. Devise a plan to collect the completed surveys — perhaps put in a large manila envelope as respondents exit.
6. Collect information:
   a. Introduce the survey and discuss the importance of honest and forthright answers.
   b. Distribute efficiently, providing pencils to those in need.
   c. Remind respondents to look over their surveys to make sure all questions are answered.
   d. Ask respondents to return surveys in person as they leave the room.

ADMINISTERING PRETEST: CLASSROOM OBSERVATION FORM

Parameters for this example:

  a. Sites in one school district = 10.
  b. Teachers per site = 6.

   c. Observations will be for 60 minutes per teacher.

   d. Observation must be conducted in a 1-week period, with 30 hours of class time available per week.

1. Reread purpose in program plan and evaluation plan:
   a. Must all teachers be observed?
   b. Observers must know the relationship between this classroom observation and teacher annual evaluation (none!).
2. Obtain instruments:
   a. Will be modified from available forms.
   b. Review with program director.
3. Hire classroom observers:
   Determine number of observers needed.
   (Number of teachers * time per teacher)/ total time available [in this example (60 * 1) / 30 = 2 observers].
4. Pilot test administration:
   a. Pilot with several teachers from several schools.
   b. Do teachers agree that they should be doing what is on the form?
   c. Can observer fill out the form?
   d. Is 60 minutes long enough to observe everything on the form?
   e. Revise and pilot again with the two hired observers.
   f. Get interrater reliability to acceptable level.
   g. Get school calendar for unavailable days.
   h. Inform principals and teachers of the classroom observation form (COF), dates of observation, and names of the observers.
   i. Remind teachers and principals that the COF is not a part of teacher evaluation, but it is a crucial part of program evaluation.
   j. Become aware of protocol, such as sign-in sheet, appropriate dress, required debriefing with teacher or principal.
   k. Share protocol with observers.
5. Plan for test administration:
   a. Provide maps, telephone numbers, and schedule of visits to each observer.
   b. Provide telephone numbers of program director and evaluator.
6. Collect test data:
   a. Collect COF every day until it is clear that each observer understands the COF and is able to complete it.

b. Are forms complete?

c. Was the observation schedule observed?

ADMINISTERING PRETEST: ADMINISTERING ACHIEVEMENT TESTS INDIVIDUALLY

Parameters for this example:

a. Number of children = 600.

b. Ages 3 and 4.

c. Individually tested in either Spanish or English.

d. Approximate testing time for each child = 2 hours.

e. Testing must start September 20 and be completed in 4 weeks.

f. About half the children will be tested in Spanish and half in English.

1. Reread purpose in program plan and evaluation plan.
2. Obtain instruments — standardized tests:
   a. Determine publisher.
   b. Determine kind of scoring sheet needed — hand or machine.
   c. Get purchase order (may require single source agreement).
   d. Allow for 2 weeks shipping.
   e. Inventory materials received.
3. Hire testers:
   a. Make sure half of testers can test in both Spanish and English.
   b. Require evidence of necessary public school forms, such as tuberculosis check and background criminal record check.
4. Train test administrators:
   a. Hire test trainer.
   b. Hire testers.
   c. Arrange for training day (half lecture and half live practice).
   d. Provide for trainer to be available first few days, and telephone support subsequently.
   e. Emphasize that tests and children's results are to be kept secure.
5. Plan for test administration:
   a. Provide schedule to testers.
   b. Provide map and names of students to be tested.

    c. Make sure sites know dates children are to be tested.

    d. Make sure there is a facility for testing.

6. Collect test data:

    a. Every Friday afternoon testers bring completed protocols to central location.

    b. Protocols checked for missing information or inaccurate information recorded.

    c. Testers turn in week's time sheets and get paid for previous week's testing (some testers may not work full-time).

    d. Testers pick up additional blank protocols.

    e. Testers share experiences and advice.

PROGRAM IMPLEMENTATION PLAN

Date	Event	Collector	Instrument	N	Census or Sampling
8/20	Overview of program	PD	In-service #1	60	Census
9/1	Baseline student performance	E	NRT, CRT	450	Census
9/15	In-service on new techniques	E	In-service #2	50	Census
9/20	Classroom observation begins	E	COF	50	Sampling
9/22	In-service on new policies	E	In-service #3	50	Census
9/29	Staff development on revised curriculum	E	In-service #4	50	Census
10/20	Parent meeting	PD	Parent form	25	Census
3/16	Presentation at state meeting	PD	Session eval	20	Sampling

Note. All teachers will be observed, but not at all times. PD = program director, E = evaluator, NRT = norm-referenced test, CRT = criterion-referenced test, and COF = classroom observation form.

Appendix F: Evaluation Reports

EXAMPLE OF A STAFF DEVELOPMENT EVALUATION REPORT

Report on Training for Teachers Conducted April 2000

On April 1, 2000, the Head Start Transition Program sponsored a training session for Head Start teachers, pre-K teachers, and 1st, 2nd, and 3rd grade teachers from throughout all of the service area. The workshop was held in the Multipurpose Center. The presenter was Dr. A, whose topic was "Emerging Literacy in Young Children." She first discussed the antecedents to literacy development. Then she presented numerous strategies for developing emerging literacy. The audience of 92 teachers was totally engaged in the workshop. It appeared that the teachers were very connected with the presenter.

The evaluation results indicate that of the 92 participants, 91 would recommend the presentation in the future. The vast majority of the teachers agreed that this was "an important topic for early childhood." The following pages provide detailed comments by the teachers from the various districts.

Some of the themes that appeared in these comments include the following:

1. Word wall and morning message were two strategies that were of particular interest.
2. Most teachers did identify several strategies that they were going to implement.

3. Many participants indicated that they would have liked a full-day workshop.
4. Several individuals indicated that principals and other administrators should be exposed to a similar workshop.
5. Several indicated that they would have benefited from more hands-on activities, copies of instructions for some of the strategies, and copies of the overheads.

District X (number of participants = 19)

1. Was this an important topic for early childhood education?
   Mean = 4.68 (on a scale of 5 = Agree, 1 = Disagree)
2. Would you recommend this presentation? Yes _19_ No _0_
3. The best thing about this meeting was:
   Exposure to many valuable strategies (6)
   Strategies were easy to follow (5)
   Strategies appear easy to implement (3)
4. How could the presentation have been improved?
   Need more time! (8); more handouts (2)
5. What will you take from this presentation?
   Word wall (4); morning messages (3); that children can increase in literacy (2)
5. Other comments:
   I am exhausted, but I am glad that I came—what a wealth of valuable, helpful, and wonderful information.

DIARY OF A PROGRAM DIRECTOR

August 15, 2002. It was my first day of work on the program, and I had a debriefing with my supervisor regarding the status of the program. Three of the four assistant program directors have been hired, but the fourth qualified person has not yet been identified. The organization used overhead funds to purchase the materials and supplies that will be used by program staff. Since the evaluator has yet to be hired, no baseline instruments have been identified and purchased.

All other program staff have been identified and informed of the program. Four days have been built into the program for staff development, and we agreed today to conduct them during the next four weeks so that staff could be trained as soon as possible. During the meeting with staff representatives, they indicated that more than once per week would not only be an overload but that it would interfere with direct service.

Immediate tasks are to (a) hire an evaluator from the pool of names my supervisor provided, (b) call the staff development office of the Regional Center to make arrangements with the trainer they think could best meet our needs, and (c) form an advisory board that will include community members. I also need to set up a meeting with the community liaison to obtain her input on possible members for the advisory board.

ONE WAY TO DOCUMENT INPUT INFORMATION

Resource	Planned Date	Actual Date
Staff salaries—$90,000	9/1	10/1[a]
Assistant program director (APD)—$60,000	9/1	1/1[b]
Teacher salaries—$99,000	8/15	8/15
Materials—$120,000	9/1	9/1[b]
Staff development—$9,000	10/1	10/5[c]

Note: a. Organization made sufficient funds available until funding agency check cleared. b. Hiring of APD delayed for 4 months—$20,000 was transferred to additional materials. c. Organization modified organization-wide staff development to meet the needs of the new program, thus saving $3,000.

TABLE OF CONTENTS OF A CONTEXT REPORT

Program Description
Purpose and Scope of Evaluation
Context of the Program
    Eligible Students Waiting and Number Served
    Ethnic Background
    Planned Staff Development
Program Management
    Organizational Structure
    How Various Departments Interface
    How Decisions Are Made
    Communication Networks

Mechanisms Program Director Plans to Use to Verify That Program Was Implemented as Designed

TABLE OF CONTENTS FOR A CONTEXT REPORT FOR A STAND-ALONE EDUCATIONAL PROGRAM

Participants
  Number
  Socioeconomic Status
  Language Spoken at Home
  Special Needs
Sites
  Number
  Structure
Delivery Staff
  Types of Staff
  Experience
  Training Needs
Support Staff
  Types
  Number
  Experience

EXAMPLE OF A TABLE OF CONTENTS OF AN INPUT REPORT

Award of Grant
  Date of Award
  Total Allocation
  Line Item Allocations
  Challenges in Spending Allocation
Hiring of Staff
  Program Director
  Program Staff
  Support Staff
  Evaluator
Stakeholders
  Students

Parents
Current Teaching Staff
Community Partner Organizations
Advisory Board
Challenges
Current
Anticipated

SUMMARY TABLE OF PERCENT OF OBJECTIVES MET

Report Card for Status of Benefits of Transition Program (July 1998 listed first, then July 1999, and then July 2000)

Percent of Objectives Met (** indicates to be evaluated in later years)

July 1998	July 1999	July 2000	
I. For administrators:			
0%	10%	20%	1. Alignment of educational program
50%	70%	80%	2. Continuity for children
40%	70%	80%	3. Increased collaboration with Head Start or kindergarten staff
30%	50%	70%	4. Linkages with children, their families, and the community
II. For teachers:			
**	**	30%	1. Awareness of child and family needs
**	**	10%	2. Parental support and involvement
60%	60%	60%	3. Network of professional staff
30%	50%	60%	4. Familiarity and understanding of educational programs
**	**	**	5. Renewed sense of professionalism and pride in reaching out to children and their families
III. For parents:			
95%	95%	95%	1. Confidence in their child's ability to achieve in a new setting
95%	95%	95%	2. Self-confidence in the ability to communicate with school personnel

95%	95%	95%	3. Pride and commitment in their involvement with their child's education
90%	90%	99%	4. Continuity of support services to address individual family needs

IV. For children:

**	20%	80%	1. Continuity of educational programs and experiences
**	**	**	2. Increased motivation and self-confidence
50%	50%	70%	3. Familiarity with kindergarten setting

EXAMPLE OF REPORTING ONLY MAJOR DIFFERENCES BETWEEN GROUPS

Table F.2.   Percentage of Teachers Receiving "Often" or "All of the Time" Teacher Ratings on Selected Implementation and Outcome Variables

Variable	New $n = 12$	Experienced $n = 39$	Total $n = 51$
Instruction appropriately paced			0
Smooth transition between instructional activities			74
Curriculum flows smoothly	64	79	76
Kids understand the stories			71
Kids understand the warm-ups			82
Physical arrangement is appropriate for new program	58	77	3
Kids are enjoying books	64	79	76
Kids are having fun	92	77	80
In-service needed in new program philosophy			19
In-service needed in new program curriculum			24
Learning appears to be going on			88

Note: Disaggregated information omitted when difference between experienced and new teachers was 10% or less.

EXAMPLE OF AN EXECUTIVE SUMMARY

Executive Summary
Public School Head Start Transition
Region 19, El Paso, TX
Keith McNeil and Jim Steinhauser
July 1998

This evaluation covers the academic year from September 1, 1997, through June of 1998. The evaluators attended all of the Transition Advisory Board meetings as well as most of the major activities conducted by the Transition project. The Transition Project has been positively received and supported by all those who have been involved, as well as those who have benefited from the project. Head Start staff now knows more about the public schools that their graduates are going into, and public school personnel are now more familiar about the Head Start graduates that are coming into their schools. Teachers indicated that visiting each other's facilities was a valuable activity. Parent information nights and the conference were well attended. The brochure to inform public school staff of the Head Start Transition project was impressive. As with any project there is room for improvement. More public school staff needs to be encouraged to visit the Head Start sites. The Transition staff needs to increase the use of the Head Start records in the public schools. Finally, a better mechanism needs to be developed to get the Head Start newsletter, Connection, in the hands of the public school staff.

Sources: McNeil & Steinhauser, 1998

EXAMPLE OF A CHART ESSAY

Objective 6. Transition Evaluators Visit Selected Schools

I. Purpose

1. To see how well the Head Start and public schools are communicating through the Head Start Graduate Student Record, Head Start Connection Newsletters, and teacher visitations.

2. To observe Kinder children in a public school setting to see if there are differences between children who attended Head Start the previous year and those children who did not.

3. To talk with Kinder teachers about the social and academic readiness of the children they receive from Head Start.

4. To see if there are relevant questions about Transition that have not been asked.

II. Evaluation effort

The evaluation form ["Interview of Principals" in appendix D in this text] was recorded by the evaluators on 34 teachers in 14 schools in 8 districts. The principal of the school was first interviewed and asked the questions at the top of the form. Then several teachers in each school visited were interviewed (ones that could be conveniently interviewed).

III. Summary of evaluation effort

Placement cards were in 10 of the 14 schools visited. Principals were split on the value of the cards. Principals did respond favorably to the Head Start visitation to the school, but were a little less enthusiastic about the public school teachers' visit to the Head Start site. Only a little over half of the teachers indicated receiving the Newsletters (a Newsletter was shown to each of the teachers, and one was left with them). When asked if they received the Newsletter, 8 of the 34 responded "Unsure" when asked if they were of value. Almost 3/4 of the responding teachers felt that Head Start students were ready academically, and all but 1 indicated that the Head Start students were ready socially. Approximately 2/3 of the teachers indicated that they had not visited a Head Start site in the last two years. Appendix D contains this detailed information, as well as the data broken down by public school.

IV. Recommendations

This report was discussed at the 12/15 TAC meeting. It was recommended at that time that training be held on the "Head Start Graduate Student Record" as there is a lot of effort put into this card and a lot of valuable information in the card.

Source: McNeil & Steinhauser, 1999

EXAMPLE OF A CHART ESSAY WITH TABLED INFORMATION

Focus: Bilingual Teachers—Quality of Classroom Activities

Evaluator: Mariela Rodriguez, Rachel Ortiz, and Dolores Gross-Delgado

Question: What was the Quality of Classroom Activties?

Data Source: Classroom Observation Form (checklist)

	Not Adequate	Less Than Adequate	Adequate	Does Not Exist
Teacher Feedback	—	5%	95%	—
Students Appeared on Task	3%	6%	91%	—
One-on-One Instruction	—	9%	65%	26%
Classroom Management	2%	9%	87%	2%
Teacher's Interaction with Students	2%	2%	94%	2%
Engaging Students in Classroom Activities	2%	8%	88%	2%
Transition Time Between Activities	—	2%	96%	2%

Conclusions:

The activities most frequently observed in the adequate range were (a) teacher feedback, (b) students on task, (c) teacher's interactions with students, and (d) transition time between activities. Classroom management and engagement of students in classroom activities were often observed in the adequate range as well. The use of one-on-one instruction was rated as adequate, but about one fourth of the time one-on-one instruction was not evident during the observation periods.

Overall, the classroom activities were rated as adequate for the majority of the observations conducted.

Source: McNeil, Arellano, Gross-Delgado, Ortiz, & Rodriguez, 1999

STATUS OF THE EVALUATION QUESTIONS

A total of 38 evaluation questions were identified in the evaluation plan to be answered over the 5 years of the Transition evaluation. Each of the questions is identified below with an estimate of the percentage that is believed to be known about the answers to that question. The first percentage is that estimated for the 1997–1998 year, and the second is for the 1998–1999 year.

Question 1. What were the various Head Start and LEA organizations doing about Transition? 80% 90%

The 12 LEAs have been quite cooperative in the various Transition efforts during the 1998–1999 year. Observations by the evaluators documented that there was a professional respect of each organization for the other.

Question 2. How could the curriculum be classified in each of the Head Start–LEA transitions? 55% 75%

Observation indicated that every Head Start classroom looked very similar. The curriculum was child-centered, with a high ratio of adults to Head Start children. The Head Start teachers always adhered to the published curriculum. The school visits by the evaluators indicated that the LEA curriculum was quite different. The curriculum was more focused on content and development of cognitive skills. Initially the desire of the Transition team was that there be a match between the two curricula, but it seems now to be more appropriate to know what the LEA curriculum is, and prepare the child and the child's parents for the "transition" to that curriculum.

Question 3. What was the attitude toward the Head Start curriculum by the LEA staff? 50% 80%

During the visitations by the LEA staff to the Head Start classrooms, LEA personnel were impressed with the curriculum plans, the number of adult volunteers in the room, and the demeanor of the children.

Question 4. What was the attitude toward the LEA curriculum by the Head Start staff? 80% 80%

During the visits by the Head Start staff to the LEA classrooms, Head Start staff indicated concerns about the curriculum and the expectations of the LEA staff. Perhaps more effort should be made to inform the Head Start staff about the LEA curriculum.

Question 5. What was the utility of any of the records sent to the LEA? 10% 80%

Records were often not incorporated into the LEA system. Since this is one of the major Transition activities, it needs to become more integrated into the LEA processes.

Question 6. What are the unmet opportunities for Transition? 90% 100%

The Transition staff is busy and productive. Transition seems to be attended to from many different activities. The region-wide conference for the teachers was not held in 1998–1999. It is recommended that the conference be held on an annual basis, and consideration be given for an additional conference. These conferences bring together Head Start and LEA teachers and highlight the local expertise of these teachers. The conference in 1997–1998 was a big plus for the Head Start Transition effort.

Source: McNeil & Steinhauser, 1999

EXAMPLE OF A TABLE OF INFORMATION THAT IS TURNED INTO A FIGURE

Example of a Table of Information

Table F.4. Comparison of National, Texas, and A Priori NCE Gains Over the Past 3 Years

1984–1985			1985–1986			1986–1987		
National	Texas	A Priori	National	Texas	A Priori	National	Texas	A Priori
1.50	1.40	3.30	1.10	0.30	7.00	—	—	6.00

Note: National and Texas data unavailable in 1986–1987.
Source: Mathews, Ramirez, Seibert, & McNeil, 1988.

Information Turned Into a Figure

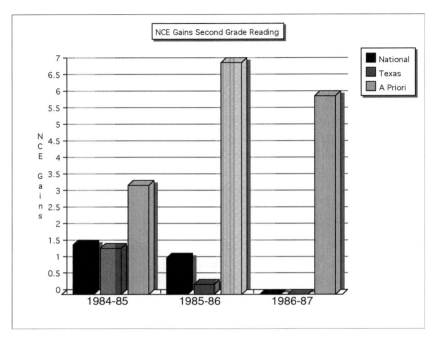

EXAMPLE OF AN EXECUTIVE SUMMARY

The Title IV Safe and Drug-Free Schools (SDFS) program has been in place since 1985. This past year a new management team was put in place. In addition, during the past year one of the key counselors missed many days of work because of major health problems. In spite of these events, the overall project seems to be meeting its goals.

The evaluation effort consisted of (a) a review of all the program documents, state guidelines, and recent reports, (b) interviews of the Title IV administrative staff on several occasions, (c) interviews conducted with the Title IV counselors and the school-based facilitators, and (d) a mailed survey distributed to the facilitators.

The recommendations for program improvement are:

1. Staff feels that prevention activities should be expanded in the elementary schools, and we agree. We further recommend that

services can be focused on those schools where interest and co-operation is highest.

2. There is a need to replace some of the physical elements on the Challenge Course.
3. Schools should be informed of how other schools have specifically implemented the program's Prom/Graduation component.
4. Staff from other school sites should be exposed to the successful Peer Helper/Peer Education component, and SDFS staff should facilitate the implementation of this component at other school sites.

The recommendations for interventions-support are:

5. Staff should review alternatives for the curriculum used in the Care Program.
6. Services will be expanded to special education first and second offenders next year, and we support those extended services.
7. We support the intent of SDFS staff in getting the Yellow Ribbon week on the calendars before school starts in the fall of 2001.

The recommendations for the substance abuse groups called Insight Groups are:

8. School administrators must be more diligent in sending students to the Insight Groups.
9. A room should be dedicated to the delivery of these groups.
10. Staff should be more supportive of students attending these group sessions, even when on a voluntary basis.

The recommendations for counseling at the academy are:

11. Develop outside parenting and counseling groups for families.
12. Teachers should be trained in basic counseling skills.
13. Clinical supervision should be obtained for the two Title IV counselors.
14. A third counselor should be hired to initiate a preventive substance abuse program at the elementary school level.

EXAMPLE OF A CHART ESSAY

Focus: Bilingual educational assistants

Evaluators: Keith McNeil and Mariela Rodriguez

Evaluation question: What are the actual and ideal percentages of time in which elementary bilingual educational assistants performed whole-group instruction?

Data Source: Survey of Bilingual Educational Assistants

Results:

% of Time Whole-Group Instruction	Actual	
	Frequency	Educational Assistants
0	5	31
1	1	6
3	1	6
4	1	6
5	2	13
10	1	6
11	1	6
14	1	6
15	1	6
25	1	6
40	1	6
% of Time Whole-Group Instruction	Ideal	
	Frequency	Educational Assistants
Same	13	100

Conclusions:

Five elementary educational assistants did not perform whole-group instruction. One fourth of the educational assistants reported using whole-group instruction more than 11% of the time.

Appendix G: Evaluation Resources

SOURCES FOR INSTRUMENTS

Chun, K., Cobb, S., & French, J. R. P., Jr. (1974). *Measures for psychological assessment: A guide to 3000 original sources and their application.* Ann Arbor: Institute for Social Research, University of Michigan.

Fink, A. (1995). *The survey handbook.* Thousand Oaks, CA: Sage Publishers.

Goldman, B. A., & Mitchell, D. F. (1995). *Directory of unpublished experimental mental measurements* (Vol. 6). Washington, DC: American Psychological Association.

Johnson, O. G. (1970). *Tests and measures in child development: Handbook II, Vol. 1.* San Francisco: Jossey-Bass Publishers.

Keyser, D. J., & Sweetland, R. C. (Eds.). (1994). *Tests critiques (Volume 10).* Austin: Pro-Ed.

Murphy, L. L., Conoley, J. C., & Impara, J. C. (1994). *Tests in print IV.* Lincoln: The University of Nebraska Press.

Murphy, L. L., Plake, B. S., & Impara, J. C. (2002). *Tests in print VI.* The Buros Institute of Mental Measurement, The University of Nebraska-Lincoln: University of Nebraska Press.

Plake, B. S., Impara, J. C., & Spies, R. A. (Eds.). (1995). *The fifteenth mental measurements yearbook.* Lincoln: The University of Nebraska Press.

Robinson, J. P., Shaver, P. R., & Wrightsman, L. S. (1991). *Measures of personality and social psychological attitudes.* New York: Academic Press.

Touliatos, J., Perlmutter, B. F., & Straus, M. A. (2001). *Handbook of family measurement techniques.* Thousand Oaks, CA: Sage Publishers.

INTERNET SITES THAT FOCUS ON INSTRUMENTS

One good place to go first is http://gsociology.icaap.org/methods/
links.htm where you will find these links:

1. http://www.policy-evaluation.org/
   Provides access to a variety of international web resources in the
   area of social policy. Very comprehensive.
2. http://npres.org/resources.htm
   A fairly comprehensive list of links to evaluation guides and
   checklists.
3. http://www.eval.org/EvaluationLinks/links.htm
   Provides a comprehensive list of links to evaluation resources
   identified by the American Evaluation Association.
4. http://www.slais.ubc.ca/resources/research_methods/index.htm
   Provides a comprehensive list of research methods resources.
   Links to commercial products.
5. http://www.ojp.usdoj.gov/BJA/evaluation/index.html
   Provides links to evaluation resources of the Bureau of Justice
   Assistance Evaluation.
6. http://www.social-marketing.com/RschLinks.html
   Provides links to general evaluation topics in social marketing.
7. http://www.qualitativeresearch.uga.edu/QualPage/
   Provides links to other qualitative pages.
8. http://www.nova.edu/ssss/QR/web.html
   The Qualitative Report, an online journal dedicated to qualitative
   research and critical inquiry since 1990, contains articles about
   how to do qualitative research.
9. http://pareonline.net/
   Practical Assessment, Research and Evaluation (PARE),
   an online journal supported, in part, by the Department of Measurement, Statistics, and Evaluation at the University of
   Maryland, College Park. Purpose is to provide education
   professionals access to refereed articles that can have a positive impact on assessment, research, evaluation, and teaching

practice, especially at the local education agency (LEA) level.

10. http://www.library.miami.edu/netguides/psymeth.html
    Provides links to many different resources.
11. http://buros.unl.edu/buros/jsp/search.jsp
    Provides access to nearly 4,000 tests exactly as information appears in the Mental Measurements Yearbook (can search by category or alphabetically; cost is $15 per review).

DESCRIPTIVE STATISTICS AND WHEN MOST APPROPRIATELY USED

Name	How Computed	When Used
Mode	Most frequently occurring value	When have categorical information or one value is predominant
Median	Half the scores below, half above	When information is not normal
Mean	Sum of all scores divided by the the number of scores	When data is close to normal. When want to do inferential analyses
Range	High score–low score + 1	To report total spread of scores
Standard deviation	Each deviation squared, then summed, then divided by the total number of scores, and then the square root taken	To report average amount of deviation from mean when want to do inferential analyses
Variance	Square of the standard deviation	Used also for inferential analyses
Frequency distribution	Number of scores at each value	Used also for descriptive analyses

POSSIBLE OBJECTIVES AND STATISTICAL TOOLS APPROPRIATE TO TEST THOSE OBJECTIVES

Objective	Design	Hypothesis	Statistical Tool
Posttest mean for program above some specified value, a	X_p O	$\mu > a$	t-test for single population mean
Pretest to posttest gain for program greater than some value, a	O_1 X_p O_2	$\mu_{02-01} > a$	t-test for the difference between two dependent means
Post mean for program greater than post mean for comparison	X_p O_p X_c O_c	$\mu_{0p} > \mu_{0c}$	t-test for the difference between two independent means
Gain for program greater than gain for comparison	O_{1p} X_p O_{2p} O_1 X_c O_{2c}	$\mu_{02p} - \mu_{01p} > \mu_{02c} - \mu_{01c}$	t-test for the difference between two independent gains
The post mean of the program is greater than the post mean of the comparison, taking into consideration variables of C_1, C_2, and pretest O_1	O_1 C_1 C_2 X_p O_{2p} O_1 C_1 C_2 X_c O_{2c}	$\mu_{02p} > \mu_{02c}$	Analysis of covariance covarying out the pretest O_{1p} and the C_1 and C_2 variables. μ is the adjusted mean, adjusted for the three existing variables.

NEWMAN AND BROWN'S ETHICAL DECISION MAKING PROCESS

Level 1: Intuition questions:
- Do I respond to my intuitive concerns?
- Do I have time for further analysis?

Decision 1: Stop if there are major concerns.
Otherwise, pursue concern analysis in level 2.

Level 2: Rules question:
- What rule, standard, or code applies?

Decision 2: If a rule, standard, or code does not apply, stop.
Otherwise, go to level 3.

Level 3: Principles and theory questions:
- What is the relevance of each principle (autonomy, nonmalefi-cence, beneficence, justice, and fidelity)?
- How do the criteria (consequences, duty, rights, social justice, and ethics of care apply?

Decision 3: If there are major concerns about principles or criteria, stop.

Otherwise, consider personal values in level 4.

Level 4: Personal values questions:
- How do my personal values, visions, and beliefs affect my thinking?
- What kind of a person do I want to be?

Decision 4: Stop if there are major concerns about personal values.

Otherwise, consider actions in level 5.

Level 5: Action questions:
- How much stress is involved?
- What are the risks to me?
- What are the risks to others?
- What is my plan of action?
- How will the organization react to this plan?
- What cultural perspectives are important to consider?

Decision 5: Stop if there are major concerns with action questions.

Otherwise, implement action plan.

Source: Adapted from Newman & Brown, 1996

EXAMPLE OF AN EVALUATION CONTRACT

Note: Underlined parts are specific to the contract.

Business Name
Address
City, State Zip
PERSONAL SERVICES CONTRACT

Contract Number: 42
Division: First
Account Number: 123456

1. This contract is entered into by and between Business Name, hereinafter designated "Center" and Dr. Keith McNeil, Social Security or Employer Identification Number 123-45-6789, hereinafter designated "Contractor" (W9 form must be completed).

(continued)

2. During the period <u>January 1, 2001</u> and ending <u>August 31, 2001</u> Contractor, as an independent contractor, who is not an employee or agent of Center, shall provide to the Center, the following services for the use and benefit of public education in the state of STATE:

<u>Will provide an evaluation of the ABC Program, which includes the following: Collect pretest and posttest information. He will evaluate each in-service: Relate teacher performance to class performance; survey teacher's perceptions regarding the curriculum; survey parents regarding increased performance; survey LEA teachers regarding their reactions to the ABC program; provide the Center data on all program children; compare intervention and comparison teachers and student growth; and document the intervention (e.g., hiring of staff, hiring of facilitators, training content curriculum implemented, in-service, parent training, and role of teacher facilitator.) Contract will be paid in three equal installments in March 2001, May 2001, and August 2001.</u>

3. For the performance, satisfactory to Center, of the services described above, Center shall pay to Contractor a fee not to exceed <u>$XX,XXX.00</u>. All payments due to Contractor shall be made by a Center check upon completion of work, and submission of an itemized invoice with necessary receipts.

4. Where the Contractor is called upon to design, develop, or study and report on information, materials, and products which are or form part of the work of Center, and/or involve the Center's clients or staff, for use by the Center to enhance, modify, or abandon its management approach or delivery system, or any component part thereof, the Contractor shall not assert any claim in law or equity, or assert any claim to statuary copyright and/or patent in such information, materials, and products without the prior written permission of Center. However, where a Contractor can demonstrate that the approach it used, the methodology implemented, or the form of the presentation originated with the Contractor or some third party preceding the work under this Contract and was merely being adapted to the work under this Contract, no prior written permission shall be necessary.

5. This contract in all its particulars is subject to all State of STATE and Federal Laws, rules, and regulations including, but not limited to Title VI of the Civil Rights Act of 1964, as amended. This contract shall be interpreted according to the laws of the state of STATE. This contract is valid upon signature by all legal parties (subject to approvals required under STATE statutes).

6. Contractor [   ] is [X] is not incorporated. If incorporated, Contractor must attach a current franchise tax Certificate of Good Standing, available from the STATE Comptroller to this contract when signed and returned to Center.

7. Contractor affirms that this contract does not create a conflict of interest with his/her present employer.

8. This contract may not be reassigned by the Contractor without the written consent of the Center.

9. This contract may be terminated by either party on 10 days written notice. This contract may also be terminated by the Center for cause. Specifically, although not exclusively, cause shall include the Center having to cancel an event related to the Contractor's performance for reasons beyond its control, or for the Contractor's failure to perform as contemplated by the Center. In the case of the cause described herein, should a dispute arise over whether cause exists the judgment of the Center will control. On termination, the Contractor shall be due only compensation earned, and

(*continued*)

reimbursement for approved costs. No fee will be due when termination was on ten (10) days notice.

10. The Contractor information on the reverse side must be completed, and/or an appropriate resume, if applicable.

Agreed and accepted on behalf of Contractor to be effective on the earliest date written above by a person authorized to bind Contractor.

_____
Authorized Signature

_____
Executive Director or Designee

Contractor must sign and return three (3) originals of this contract to:

_____

Address _____

Agreed on behalf of Center this _____ day of _____, by a person authorized to bind Center.   (Month and Year)

(Reverse of contract)
CONTRACTOR INFORMATION

Name, Address, & Phone: _____

Degrees Held: _____

_____

_____

Qualifications Relative
to Topic for Which
Employed (Include Certification,
Licensure, Registration, etc.):   _____

_____

Present Position
and Organization: _____

_____

How Contractor Will
Be Evaluated: _____

_____

Appendix H: Evaluation Contracts Obtained Over a 12-Year Period, Identified by Number of Years, How Obtained, Funding Agency, and Brief Name

Years	How Obtained	Funding Agency	Brief Name
1989–1992	Word of mouth	Head Start	Family Literacy
1990–1995	Similar to Family Literacy	Title 4	Roswell
1991–1992	Similar to Family Literacy	Title 4	Eastern New Mexico State University
1996–2000	Word of mouth	NSF	Astronomy
1996–2000	Word of mouth	NSF	Engineering #1
1997–1998	Word of mouth	NSF	Engineering #2
1997–2001	Similar to Family Literacy	Head Start	Transition
1999–2001	Similar to Family Literacy	Head Start	Early Start
1998–1999	Word of mouth	State of NM	Bilingual Education
2000–2002	Similar to Family Literacy	TX Head Start	State Initiative
2000–2001	Competitive bid	NM Title II	Even Start
2000–2001	Competitive bid	NM Title II	Safe and Drug Free Schools

Glossary

analysis of covariance. A procedure used to statistically adjust the posttest means by taking into consideration one or more variables existing before implementation of the program—thereby leveling the playing field.

anecdotal. A way of knowing that is unscientific that includes observations made without controlled, systematic methods.

annual yearly progress. A state's requirement for annually meeting increased performance.

anonymity. Evaluator action to ensure that the identity of participants cannot be ascertained during the course of the evaluation, in reports, or in any other way.

attribute. Characteristic or trait that is either present to some degree or absent in a thing or person being observed.

baseline. Behavior that has not been affected by the program in that cycle, collected at the beginning of the cycle.

campus improvement plan. A plan that details how a particular school will improve the performance of the students in that school.

categorical variable. A variable that has values that are discrete and not ordered when measured.

central tendency. A point in a set of scores around which the scores tend to center.

chart essay. A visual presentation that focuses the audience's attention on particular findings.

coding. Translating a given set of data or items into machine-readable categories.

comparison group. A group similar to (ideally identical to) the one participating in the program, except that they do not participate in the program. The comparison group may get the program at a later date, get some other program, or get the generally accepted best currently available program.

competing explainers. Competing explainers are those extraneous aspects that might have been the cause of the results, rather than the program that was implemented.

correlation. Indicates the relationship between two variables—how the scores on one variable are related to the scores on another variable. The index of correlation is r and ranges from high positive r of 1.00 to high negative r of –1.00. Lack of correlation is an r of .00.

criterion-referenced test. A test designed to provide specific knowledge or skills. Such instruments usually cover relatively small units of content and are closely related to objectives. These scores have meaning in terms of what the respondent knows or can do, rather than in relation to the scores made by some external reference group.

current status. An NCLB term that is synonymous with baseline in GEM.

demographic information. These are variables that describe the sample, such as the proportion of males and females, or the proportion of those in a particular year in school.

descriptive statistics. Statistics that describe empirical observations.

dissemination. The process of communicating information to specific stakeholders for the purpose of extending knowledge and, in some cases, with a view to modifying policies and practices.

ESEA. Elementary and Secondary Education Act—provided federal funding for many compensatory programs and ushered in the requirement of evaluation of educational programs.

evaluation. The continuous inspection of all available information concerning the program to ascertain the degree of change in the participants and form valid judgments about the participants and the effectiveness of the program.

executive summary. A nontechnical summary designed to provide a quick overview of the full-length report on which it is based.

existing records. Sources of information that are already available.

face validity. The extent to which a casual, subjective inspection of a measure's items indicates that they cover the content that the measure is supposed to measure.

focus group. A data-gathering tool in which an evaluator interviews a small group of people to obtain different perspectives on a particular issue.

formative evaluation. A type of evaluation that is carried out while a program is being implemented, in order to improve its effectiveness or to make a decision about further refinements.

frequency. The number of individuals who had a particular a score.

goal. A statement of intent that requires no measurable outcome.

high-inference measure. A measure that requires much judgment on the part of the evaluator to determine its presence or level.

high-stakes testing. Testing, usually at the state level, that results in a major decision for an individual or group (such as putting a school on probation).

highly qualified. A teacher who has (a) at least a bachelor's degree, (b) completed full state certification or licensure, and (c) demonstrated competence in the subject areas.

inferential statistics. Statistics that assess the probability of an unknown event.

input–output. One way to look at the effectiveness of a program, by comparing the results of the program with the effort (usually dollars) that went into the program.

inside hire. A person who is employed by the same organization, even if in a separate department from the one being evaluated.

instrument. An assessment device (test, questionnaire, survey, protocol, etc.) adopted, adapted, or constructed for the purpose of the evaluation.

instrumentation effect. Occurs when the information resulting from two testing situations does not mean the same thing.

interview. The collection of information through verbal interaction between the evaluator and the participants.

level of significance. Called alpha, the largest probability of error acceptable for rejection of the null hypothesis (statistical hypothesis). Often alpha = .05 or alpha = .01.

Likert scale. A type of scale on which respondents express degrees of agreement or disagreement with a statement.

line graph. The line graph has a line for each category and facilitates understanding of how that category has changed over time.

mean. A measure of central tendency corresponding to the average of a set of scores.

measurement. The process that assigns by rule a numerical description to observation of some attribute of an object, person, or event.

median. A measure of central tendency corresponding to the middle point in a distribution of scores.

mode. A measure of central tendency corresponding to the most frequently occurring score.

mortality. Attrition of participants. An internal validity problem if attrition is not the same for the program and comparison groups.

needs assessment. A set of procedures for identifying and prioritizing discrepancies between desired and existing conditions (i.e., needs).

nonstandardized instrument. An instrument that does not meet all of the criteria for standardized instruments. There is no norming group, the administration is not standardized, or scoring is not done in a standardized fashion.

norm. A value or set of values reflecting performance of a defined group on a measure. Used as an aid to interpretation of scores on standardized measures.

norm-referenced instrument. A test that measures the relative performance of the individual or group by comparison with the performance of other individuals or groups taking the same test.

norming sample. A large sample that represents a defined population and whose scores on a measure provide a set of standards to which the scores of individuals who subsequently take the measure can be referenced.

objective. An objective must be measured and requires a rationale to exist.

observation. The process of collecting information that will be used as a basis for evaluation. Also, any fact that is used as a basis for evaluation. Thus, observation (the process) generates observations (the results of the process).

open-ended question. A question that does not have fixed response alternatives but allows the respondent to respond as he or she chooses.

outside hire. A person from outside the organization contracted to perform work in an agency.

parallel forms. Two or more forms of a test that are equivalent in terms of the content.

percentile. One of 99 points that divide an ordered distribution into 100 equal parts. Each percentile shows the place in the distribution where a designated proportion of the total distribution falls below. For example, a percentile score of 70 is a score where 70% of the scores are less than that value.

performance test. A test that requires examinees to demonstrate their capabilities by creating some product or engage in some activity.

pie chart. The pie chart facilitates understanding of the relative contribution of each part to the whole and is usually displayed as a circle with slices radiating from the center, similar to a pie.

portfolio. A collection of the products of an individual, illustrating what the individual has produced.

post assessment (posttest). A measure that is administered after the program is over or after a predetermined interval, such as 1 year, in order to ascertain the effects of the program.

pre assessment (pretest). A measure that is administered at the beginning of the program in order to provide a basis for comparison with the posttest. Referred to as baseline in this text.

program evaluation. The determination of the objectives of the program in measurable ways and then the assessment of whether the objectives were reached.

program implementation assessment. The evaluation of the treatment or intervention. It focuses entirely on the activities between baseline and post assessment.

quantitative inquiry. Inquiry that is grounded in the assumption that features of reality constitute an objective reality that is relatively constant over time and settings; the dominant methodology for studying these features is to collect numerical information on the observable behavior of people.

questionnaire. A set of written questions that typically measure many variables.

rank. The position of a score or individual in relation to others in the group. The highest score is usually given a rank of one, the next a rank of two, and so on.

raw score. An individual score on a measure as determined by the scoring rubric, without any further manipulation (such as into a standard score of percentile).

reliability. Consistency of observation. The consistency with which a data-collection device measures whatever it is that the device measures. The degree of reliability may be reported as a correlation coefficient.

replication. The process of repeating a program implementation with different participants under similar conditions to increase confidence in the utility of the program.

representative sample. A sample that corresponds to or matches the population of which it is a sample with respect to characteristics important for the purposes under investigation.

sample. Any subset of persons or items selected to represent a larger group or population.

scale. A continuum, usually having quantitative units, that measures the extent to which individuals exhibit certain traits or characteristics.

scale scores. Scores that "mean the same thing" over time.

score. A number assigned to a test taker to provide a quantitative description of performance on the test.

semistructured interview. A combination of the structured and unstructured interview that capitalizes on the unique benefits of each.

SES. The socioeconomic status of an individual or community. Usually considered a function of education and income.

significance. In inferential statistics, an obtained probability that meets some predetermined criterion.

socially desirable responses. Responses respondents think they should be giving.

sociogram. A technique that identifies the degree of interaction among members of a group. The interaction may be behavioral, desired, anticipated, or fantasized.

stacked histogram. The stacked histogram has more than one category in each bar of the histogram thus facilitating the understanding of the composition of the groups in each category.

stakeholder. Any individual who is involved or concerned about the program.

standard deviation. An index of how much a set of scores deviates from the mean.

standardized measure. A commercially printed measure for which content has been selected and checked empirically. The measure is standardized so that administration and scoring procedures are the same for all individuals. Score interpretation is based on averages of performances of groups of people who have already taken the measure.

statistic. A number that describes a characteristic of the sample of participants.

statistical significance. An inference, based on a statistical test, that the results obtained for the sample (say, this year's cohort) that can be generalized to the population (say, next year's cohort).

structured interview. A conversation between an evaluator and respondent(s) that is guided by a set of specific predetermined questions.

summative evaluation. A type of evaluation that is conducted to determine the worth of a program at the end of the cycle.

survey. Collecting information about participants' beliefs, attitudes, interests, or behavior through a questionnaire, interview, or paper-and-pencil measure.

treatment. The program that is implemented and the focus of the evaluation.

unobtrusive measures. Measurements that are obtained without interfering with the normal routine of the person or entity being measured. These measures usually require a high level of inference.

unstructured interview. A purposeful conversation between an evaluator and respondent(s) in which the evaluator permits the direction of the conversation to evolve during the course of the conversation.

validity. The appropriateness, meaningfulness, and usefulness of specific inferences made from a measure.

variable. A quantitative expression of a construct.

References

Altschuld, J. W., & Witken, B. R. (1999). *From needs assessment to action: Transforming needs into solution strategies.* Thousand Oaks, CA: Sage.

American Psychological Association (APA). (2001). *Publication manual of the American Psychological Association* (5th ed.). Washington, DC: Author.

Bell, J. B. (1994). Managing evaluation projects step by step. In J. S. Wholey, H. P. Hatry, & K. E. Newcomer (Eds.), *Handbook of practical program evaluation* (pp. 549–575). San Francisco: Jossey-Bass.

Block, J. H., Everson, S. T., & Guskey, T. R. (Eds.) (1995). *School improvement programs: A handbook for educational leaders.* New York: Scholastic.

Bricker, D., & Squires, J. (2001). *Ages and Stages Questionnaires (ASQ)™: A Parent-Completed, Child-Monitoring System* (2nd ed.). Baltimore, MD: Paul H. Brookes.

California Department of Education (2004). *API description: Overview of the Academic Performance Index (API).* Retrieved June 1, 2004, from http://www.cde.ca.gov/ta/ac/ap/apidescription.asp.

Carter, R. (1994). Maximizing the use of evaluation results. In J. S. Wholey, H. P. Hatry, & K. E. Newcomer (Eds.), *Handbook of practical program evaluation* (pp. 549–575). San Francisco: Jossey-Bass.

Ciarlo, J. A., & Windle, C. (1988). Mental health program evaluation and needs assessment. In H. S. Bloom, D. S. Cordray, & R. J. Light (Eds.), *Lessons from selected programs and policy areas.* New Directions for Evaluation #37. San Francisco: Jossey-Bass.

Conyers, L. M., Reynolds, A. J., & Ou, S. (2003). The effect of early childhood intervention on subsequent special education services: Findings from the Chicago Child-Parent Centers. *Educational Evaluation and Policy Analysis, 25,* 59–74.

Darling-Hammond, L., Berry, B., & Thoreson, A. (2001). Does teacher certification matter? Evaluating the evidence. *Educational Evaluation and Policy Analysis, 23,* 57–77.

Desimone, L., Porter, A. C., Garet, M. S., Yoon, K. S., & Birman, B. F. (2002). Effects of professional development on teachers' instruction: Results from a three-year longitudinal study. *Educational Evaluation and Policy Analysis, 24,* 81–112.

Epstein, A. S., Montie, J., & Weikart, D. P. (n.d.). *Supporting families with young children: The High/Scope parent-to-parent dissemination project.* Ypsilanti, MI: High Scope Educational Research Foundation.

Florida Department of Education. (2003). State of Florida consolidated state application accountability workbook. Tallahassee, FL: Author. Retrieved June 1, 2004, from www.fldoe.org/NCLB/FINALNCLB-AYP-Workbook_4-25-031.pdf.

Floyd, J., & Fowler, F. J. (1993). *Survey research methods* (2nd ed.). Thousand Oaks, CA: Sage.

Fuller, B., & Liang, X. (1997). Market failure? Estimating inequality in preschool availability. *Educational Evaluation and Policy Analysis, 18,* 31–49.

Fuller, B., & Strath, A. (2001). The child-care and preschool workforce: Demographics, earnings, and unequal distribution. *Educational Evaluation and Policy Analysis, 23,* 37–55.

Gilovich, T. (1991). *How we know what isn't so.* New York: The Free Press.

Glazerman, S. (1997). *A conditional logit model of elementary school choice: What do parents value?* Chicago: University of Chicago, Harris School of Public Policy.

Goddard, R. D. (2003). Relational networks, social trust, and norms: A social capital perspective on students' chances of academic success. *Educational Evaluation and Policy Analysis, 25,* 59–74.

Goldhaber, D., & Brewer, D. J. (2000). Does teacher certification matter? High school teacher certification status and student achievement. *Educational Evaluation and Policy Analysis, 22,* 129–145.

Gordon, R., & Chase-Landsdale, P. L. (1999). *Women's participation in market work and the availability of child care in the United States.* Chicago: Sloan Working Families Center, University of Chicago (working paper 99-05).

Gredler, M. E. (1996). *Program evaluation.* Englewood Cliffs, NJ: Merrill.

Guskey, T. R. (2000). *Evaluating professional development.* Thousand Oaks, CA: Corwin.

Hatry, H. P. (1994). Collecting data from agency records. In J. S. Wholey, H. P. Hatry, & K. E. Newcomer (Eds.), *Handbook of practical program evaluation* (pp. 374–385). San Francisco: Jossey-Bass.

Heberlein, T. A., & Baumgartner, R. (1978). Factors affecting response rates to mailed questionnaires: A quantitative analysis of the published literature. *American Sociological Review, 43,* 447–462.

Heck, R. H., & Crislip, M. (2001). Direct and indirect writing assessments: Examining issues of equity and utility. *Educational Evaluation and Policy Analysis, 23,* 19–36.

Hendricks, M. (1994). Making a splash: Reporting evaluation results effectively. In J. S. Wholey, H. P. Hatry, & K. E. Newcomer (Eds.), *Handbook of practical program evaluation* (pp. 549–575). San Francisco: Jossey-Bass.

Henig, J. (1990). Choice in public schools: An analysis of transfer requests among magnet schools. *Social Science Quarterly, 71*(1), 76.

House, E. (1980). *Evaluating with validity.* Beverly Hills, CA: Sage.

Joint Committee on Standards for Educational Evaluation. (1981). *Standards for evaluations of educational programs, projects, and materials.* New York: McGraw-Hill.

Locatis, C. N., Smith, J. K., & Blake, V. L. (1979, April). *Effects of evaluation information on decisions.* Paper presented at the meeting of the American Educational Research Association, San Francisco.

Love, A. J. (1983). *Developing effective internal evaluations.* New Directions for Evaluation #93. San Francisco: Jossey-Bass Publishers.

Madaus, G. F., Scriven, M., & Stufflebeam, D. L. (Eds.). (1983) *Evaluation models: Viewpoints on educational and human services evaluation.* Boston: Kluwer.

Mathews, B., Ramirez, R., Seibert, J., & McNeil, K. (1988, February). *A Priori: A Chapter 1 program pre-teaching the regular curriculum.* Paper presented at the Large School Systems Conference, Atlanta.

McNeil, K. (1976). *A description and evaluation of 1974–75 ESEA, Title I Part B, projects in Michigan.* East Lansing, MI: State Department of Education.

McNeil, K. (1991, October). *Four alternate methods of reporting process evaluations.* Paper presented at the meeting of the Mid-Western Educational Research Association, Chicago.

McNeil, K. (2002, October). *What I've learned (so far) about program evaluation.* Invited presentation at the meeting of the Mid-Western Educational Research Association, Columbus, OH.

McNeil, K., Arellano, E., Gross-Delgado, D., Ortiz, R., Rodriguez, M. (1999, September). *1998–1999 Las Cruces Public Schools bilingual evaluation report.* Las Cruces Public Schools.

McNeil, K., Huff, J., Lamble, N., & Smith, R. (1983). *Sustained effects: Measuring the value of Title I over time.* Durham, NC: National Testing Service.

McNeil, K., Mengel, C. W., & Moran, E. (1984, April). *State-wide micro-computer software for fiscal and evaluation reporting.* Paper presented at the meeting of the American Educational Research Association, New Orleans (ED 244 967).

McNeil, K., Newman, I., & Kelly, F. J. (1996). *Testing research hypotheses with the general linear model.* Carbondale, IL: Southern Illinois University Press.

McNeil, K., & Steinhauser, J. (1998). *Public school Head Start Transition 1997–1998 final evaluation.* El Paso, TX: Region 19 Service Center, Head Start.

McNeil, K., & Steinhauser, J. (1999). *Public school Head Start Transition 1998–1999 final evaluation.* El Paso, TX: Region 19 Service Center, Head Start.

McNeil, K., & Steinhauser, J. (2001). *Final evaluation report: Region 19 Texas state literacy initiative.* El Paso, TX: Region 19 Service Center, Head Start.

Morgan, D. L. (1998). *The focus group guidebook.* Thousand Oaks, CA: Sage.

New York State Education Department (2003). *Accountability peer review.* Albany, NY: Author. Retrieved June 1, 2004, from www.emsc.nysed.gov/deputy/nclb/accountability/nclbaccountabilityplan.doc.

Newman, D. L., & Brown, R. D. (1996). *Applied ethics for program evaluation.* Thousand Oaks, CA: Sage.

Newman, I., & Deitchman, R. (1983). Evaluation/research: A suggested move toward scientific and community credibility. *Journal of Studies in Technical Careers, 5*(4), 289–298.

Newman, I., Frye, B., Blumenfeld, G., & Newman, C. (1974). *An introduction to the basic concepts of measurement and evaluation.* Akron, OH: University of Akron.

Newman, I., & McNeil, K. (1998). *Conducting survey research in the social sciences.* Lanham, MD: University Press of America.

Newman, I., McNeil, K., & Frass, J. (2004). Two methods of estimating a study's replicability. *Mid-Western Educational Researcher, 17,* 36–40.

Newman, I., & Newman, C. (1993). The need for outcome rather than process evaluations. *Ohio Journal of Science, 93*(3), 63–71.

Newman, I., Sugarman, M., & Newman, C. (1981). Making the most of evaluation and evaluators. *Journal of Studies in Technical Careers, 3*(2), 187–192.

Newman, I., Vukovich, D., & Newman, C. (1978). *Evaluate your jewels: A G. E. M. for the counselor.* Paper presented at the Ohio Association for Ethical Hypnosis.

Nielsen, V. G. (1975). Why evaluation does not improve program effectiveness. *Policy Studies Journal, 3*(4), 385–390.

Nightengale, D. S., & Rossman, S. B. (1994). *Managing field data collection from start to finish.* In J. S. Wholey, H. P. Hatry, & K. E. Newcomer (Eds.), *Handbook of practical program evaluation* (pp. 549–575). San Francisco: Jossey-Bass.

No Child Left Behind Act of 2002, Pub. L. No. 107–110, 115 Stat. 1425 (2002).

Oden, S., Schweinhart, L. J., & Weikart, D. J. (2000). *Into adulthood: A study of the effects of Head Start.* Ypsilanti, MI: High Scope Educational Research Foundation.

Plake, B. S., & Impara, J. C. (Eds.). (2003). *The fifteenth mental measurements yearbook.* Lincoln: The University of Nebraska Press.

Popham, W. J. (1975). *Educational evaluation.* Englewood Cliffs, NJ: Prentice Hall.

Rosenthal, R., & Rosnow, R. (1969). *Artifact in behavioral research.* New York: Academic Press.

Scheirer, M. A. (1994). Designing and using process evaluation. In J. S. Wholey, H. P. Hatry, & K. E. Newcomer (Eds.), *Handbook of practical program evaluation* (pp. 40–68). San Francisco: Jossey-Bass.

Schneider, M., & Buckley, J. (2002). What do parents want from schools? Evidence from the Internet. *Educational Evaluation and Policy Analysis, 24,* 133–144.

Sechrest, L. (Ed.). (1979). *Unobtrusive measures today.* San Francisco: Jossey-Bass.

Smith, M. L., & Glass, G. V. (1987*). Research and evaluation in education and the social sciences.* Englewood Cliffs, NJ: Prentice Hall.

State of California. (2003). *State of California consolidated state application accountability workbook.* Sacramento, CA: Author. Retrieved June 1, 2004, from www.cde.ca.gov/nclb/sr/sa/documents/yr03wb0131.pdf.

Stiggins, R. (2001). The unfulfilled promise of classroom assessment. *Educational Measurement: Issues and Practice, 20*(3), 5–15.

Stiggins, R. (2002). Assessment crisis: The absence of assessment FOR learning, *Phi Delta Kappan,* June, 758–765.

Stufflebeam, D. L. (1983). The CIPP model for program evaluation. In G. F. Madaus, M. Scriven, & D. L. Stufflebeam (Eds.), *Evaluation models: Viewpoints on educational and human services evaluation* (pp. 117–142). Boston: Kluwer-Nijhoff.

Stufflebeam, D. L. (2001). *Evaluation models.* San Francisco: Jossey-Bass.

Tallmadge, G. K., & Wood, C. T. (1976). *User's guide (ESEA Title I Evaluation and Reporting System).* Mountain View, CA: RMC Research Corporation.

Teitelbaum, P. (2003). The influence of high school graduation requirement policy in mathematics and science on student course-taking patterns and achievement. *Educational Evaluation and Policy Analysis, 25,* 31–57.

Texas Education Agency. (2003). 2003 *Adequate Yearly Progress (AYP).* Austin, TX: Author. Retrieved June 1, 2004, from http://www.tea.state .tx.us/ayp/2003/index.html.

United States Department of Education. (n.d.) *Executive summary.* Retrieved June 1, 2004, from http://www.ed.gov/nclb/overview/intro/execsumm.html.

United States Department of Education. (2004). *New, flexible policies help teachers become highly qualified.* Retrieved June 1, 2004, from http://www.ed.gov/news/pressreleases/2004/03/03152004.html.

Webb, E. J., Campbell, D. T., Schwartz, R. D., Sechrest, L., & Grove, J. B. (1981). *Nonreactive measures in the social sciences.* Boston: Houghton Mifflin.

Weiher, G. R., & Tedin, K. L. (2002). Does choice lead to racially distinctive schools? Charter schools and household preferences. *Journal of Policy Analysis and Management, 21*(1), 79–92.

Weiss, C. H. (Ed.). (1972). *Evaluating action programs: Readings in social action and education.* Boston: Allyn and Bacon.

Whicker, T. R. (2004). *Critical issues in Internet-based distance learning in community colleges: Perceptions of problems and strategies for solving those problems.* Unpublished doctoral dissertation, New Mexico State University, Las Cruces.

Wholey, J. S., Hatry, H. P., & Newcomer, K. E. (Eds.). (1994). *Handbook of practical program evaluation.* San Francisco: Jossey-Bass Publishers.

Wilkinson, W., & McNeil, K. (1996). *Research for the helping professions.* Pacific Grove, CA: Brooks/Cole.

Worthen, B. R., & Sanders, J. R. (Eds.). (1987). *Educational evaluation: Alternative approaches and practical guidelines.* White Plains, NY: Longman.

Xiang, Z., & Schweinhart, L. J. (2001). *Ready for success: Annual report of the Michigan School Readiness Program longitudinal evaluation.* Ypsilanti, MI: High Scope Educational Research Foundation.

Index

About the Authors

Keith McNeil has been professor at New Mexico State University since 1989. He teaches statistics, research design, and program evaluation courses. Previous to that he worked for 5 years as an evaluator in the Dallas Public Schools, worked 8 years on a federal contract providing evaluation assistance to state and local educational agencies, and worked in a state department of education for 1 year. He began his teaching career at Southern Illinois University at Carbondale in 1967 after receiving his PhD from the University of Texas. His previous texts include: *Conducting Survey Research in the Social Sciences* (1998, with I. Newman); *Theses and Dissertations: A Guide to Writing in the Social and Physical Sciences* (1997, with I. Newman, C. Benz, and D. Weis); *Testing Research Hypotheses with the General Linear Model* (1996, with I. Newman and F. J. Kelly); and *Research for the Helping Professions* (1996, with W. K. Wilkinson). He has conducted numerous program evaluations since 1969.

Isadore Newman is professor at the University of Akron, where he has been teaching statistics, research design, and program evaluation courses since 1971. During his professional career, he has served on over 300 dissertation committees and has presented hundreds of papers at state, national, and international meetings. His textbooks include the ones mentioned with McNeil above, as well *Qualitative-Quantitative Research Methodology: Exploring the Interactive Continuum* (1998, with C. Benz) and *Conceptual Statistics for Beginners* (1994, with C. Newman). Newman has been the editor of the

Ohio Journal of Science since 2001 and was the editor of *Multiple Linear Regression Viewpoints* from 1973 to 1992 and the editor of the *Mid-Western Educational Researcher* from 1985 to 1988. He received his PhD from Southern Illinois University in 1971 and has conducted numerous evaluations since then.

Jim Steinhauser is an evaluator for the El Paso Independent School District, focusing on the evaluation of the State Compensatory Education program and the evaluation of the Mathematics/Science Partnership between the El Paso school district and the University of Texas at El Paso. For 2 years he was the director of evaluation and research for the Region 19 Head Start program in El Paso, Texas. As an outside evaluator, Dr. Steinhauser has conducted evaluations of Even Start, Head Start, K–12 mathematics curricula, a district-wide mathematics assessment program, an elementary school service delivery project, and a bilingual education master's degree administrator-training program. He received his PhD in 2000 from New Mexico State University.